CLIO'S COSMETICS

Also available or forthcoming as IGNIBUS Paperbacks

The Authoress of the Odyssey, Samuel Butler
(Introduction by Tim Whitmarsh)
Euripides the Rationalist, A.W. Verrall (Introduction by P. Burian)
The Origins of Greek Religion, B.C. Dietrich

CLIO'S COSMETICS

Three Studies in
Greco-Roman Literature

T.P. Wiseman

An IGNIBUS Paperback
BRISTOL PHOENIX PRESS

Cover illustration: The Muse Clio, based on a 2nd- or 3rd-century CE mosaic from Trier

First published in 1979 by
Leicester University Press

Reprinted 2003 by
Bristol Phoenix Press
PO Box 2142
Bristol
BS99 7TS

A catalogue record for this book is available from the British Library.

ISBN 1-904675-00-X

Printed and bound by CPI Group (UK) Ltd, Croydon, CR0 4YY

COLLEGIS DISCIPULISQUE RATENSIBUS

ΧΑΡΙΣΤΗΡΙΟΝ

CONTENTS

PREFACE

Like its two predecessors, *Catullan Questions* (1969) and *Cinna the Poet and other Roman Essays* (1974), this book has grown out of an interest in the society and literature of the mid-first century B.C., and in particular the world of the poet Catullus and his mistress Clodia. In this case, however, the emphasis is on late-republican historiography: to find a satisfactory reason why Clodia's family was notorious for arrogance in the early history of Rome, and why Catullus should have dedicated his book of poems to an historian, it is necessary to understand how history was written in Rome in the age of Lucceius, Varro and Alexandros 'Polyhistor'.

—

Part I is an attempt to bring out the full consequences of two features of the ancient world which are well enough understood in themselves, but not sufficiently allowed for in their effects on historiography – and thus on our information about the ancient world itself. In the first place, the rhetorical nature of secondary education meant that all educated Greeks and Romans had been trained in the art of persuasion, where plausibility mattered much more than evidence; secondly, with the partial exception of Thucydides, the Greco-Roman historiographical tradition did not even approach the standards of investigation which have become normal since the coming together of history and antiquarianism in the eighteenth century. These facts become particularly important for Roman history when 'annals' in the proper sense begin to be written. I argue that Piso was the first to write history with an entry for every year, exploiting recently reconstructed consular and triumphal lists; this type of annalistic historiography carried with it the temptation of filling in the 'empty' years, for which nothing was recorded, with appropriate material which the historians' training in oratorical *narratio* amply qualified them to provide.

Part II discusses a particular example of the phenomenon: the invention, as part of the pseudo-history of the early Republic, of *superbia Claudiana* as a characteristic applying to every generation of patrician Claudii, and of a rival interpretation, less obvious but equally schematic, which portrayed them as responsible conservatives. The argument is that Valerius Antias was responsible for the first, and Aelius Tubero for the second. If it is cogent, then I hope that the *superbia* theme, along with the 'Sabine' *Leitmotiv* recently identified by Professor Musti, may make possible a better understanding of Valerius Antias and his work. That is something long overdue, in that Antias is not only the source of so much misinformation about Roman history, but also, in a sense, an important figure in the development of imaginative fiction.

Part III deals with another feature of the Greek and Roman view of the past which is not always given its full weight. Myth and history were not distinguished in any sense approximating to our own; the subject matter of history therefore had much more in common than is usually recognized with that of poetry. In the first century B.C., when Hellenistic literary culture was adjusting to the fact that Rome was now its main centre, and Roman traditions therefore had to be absorbed into its world-picture, Cornelius Nepos' *Chronica* represent most clearly the mythology, geography and aetiological ethnography which formed the common material of historians and 'learned poets' alike. Nepos had more than we think in common with Catullus, whose dedication of his collected poems is therefore neither paradoxical nor ironical. My last two chapters digress a little from the historiographical theme to argue about the dedication poem itself and the nature of the collection which it introduces; on this last point, the suggestions put forward in *Catullan Questions* are amended, and (I hope) improved.

—

Part II began life as a Graduate Seminar paper given at University College, Toronto, in 1971; chapters 9 and 10 were read to a Colloquium in Cambridge in 1976. I have benefited greatly from the comments and criticisms of those present on both occasions; also from those (particularly Duncan Cloud, John Pinsent and Elizabeth Rawson) who saw Part II in its earlier written form, and from Tony Woodman, who very kindly read the whole book in typescript and improved it in countless details. I am very grateful to all these helpers; the book's remaining shortcomings no doubt coincide with the places where I have not followed their suggestions.

Finally, a word about the Bibliography. It is no more than a list of the modern works referred to in the course of the argument: in only one minor area (work since 1950 on Catullus' first poem) have I made any attempt at completeness. In this, the bibliography reflects the book. *Clio's Cosmetics* is not the systematic account of Hellenistic and early Roman historiography which has long been needed (though I hope it may help a little towards the achievement of it); it is an enquiry rather than an exposition, and represents, as I am uncomfortably aware, one man's incomplete mastery of a ramifying succession of subjects.

Exeter, March 1978

PART I

Clio's Cosmetics

O reverend guardian of antique things,
you, golden Clio, taught well to report
Time's fugitive courses and the deeds of kings,
attend my thought.

You let no act that's great to fade away,
you save the notable thing from death and store
in books the monuments of a former day
fresh evermore.

You wipe all rouge of rhetoric from your pages,
and you alone. Whatever is truth's decision
you utter clear through all the coming ages
with plain precision. . . .

PHOCAS (*trans. Jack Lindsay*)

Chapter 1

'FUCATIO'

Phocas was a grammarian, who at some time in the fifth or early sixth century A.D. wrote a life of Virgil in hexameter verse. It is purely derivative, and in itself of much less interest than the Sapphic address to the Muse of History with which he introduced it, and of which I have used the first three stanzas as an epigraph.[1]

After hailing Clio as the guardian of the great deeds of the past, Phocas goes on in the third stanza to praise her for her simple language, reporting the bare truth with no artificial colour in her style:

sola fucatis variare dictis
paginas nescis, set aperta quicquid
veritas prodit, recinis per aevum
simplice lingua.

The idea of stylistic adornment as cosmetic colouring went back nearly a thousand years, and is, as I hope this book will show, of some importance for the understanding of ancient historiography. In reality, Clio was not always as free from rouge as Phocas' eulogy implies.

The invention of the 'colour' image may, perhaps, be attributed to the first theorists of Greek music. Their basic unit of analysis was the tetrachord, of which the upper and lower notes were fixed; three ways of classifying the 'movable' notes between them were identified, as the enharmonic, the diatonic, and the *chromatic*.[2] This idea of colour (*chroma*) in music was first applied, so far as we know, to Agathon and Philoxenus in the late fifth century B.C., and may even have been invented in order to describe the effects these innovators produced.[3] It was at that very time that Damon and his

1. *Anthologia Latina* (Riese) I 671, *Poetae Latini Minores* (Baehrens) V 49, p. 85; chosen by Garrod as the last piece in the *Oxford Book of Latin Verse* (no. 384). Translation: Jack Lindsay, *Song of a Falling World* (1948), 57, quoted with the author's permission.

2. See (e.g.) Henderson 1957, 344f.

3. Plut, *Mor*. 645E on Agathon as the first user of the chromatic *genus*; Antiphanes *ap*. Athen. XIV 643d on the *χρώματα* of Philoxenus' music.

successors were arguing the case later put forward by Plato and Aristotle, that different types of music imitated different characteristics in the soul, and could bring about corresponding virtues and vices in the hearer.[4] We happen to know from a late fifth- or early fourth-century opponent of this idea that the 'chromatic' *genus* was thought to make men cowardly – an attitude consistent with the way Aristophanes mocks the *effeminacy* both of Agathon's musical style and of his person.[5] Since the use of cosmetics was considered a sure sign of effeminacy and lack of the manly virtues,[6] 'colour' as used of music could easily be associated with 'colour' as used of make-up, two corresponding indications of the same characteristic in the musician.

It was precisely 'the *colours* of music' that Plato objected to in poetry, and the verb he uses of the poet employing his stylistic devices is *epichromatizein*.[7] Similarly Thucydides (in disapproval) and Isocrates (in envy) refer to the 'adornments' (*κόσμοι*) of poetry, an idea closely related to, if not identical with, that of cosmetics.[8] The metaphor was equally apt for artistic prose: Isocrates used the phrase *τῷ λόγῳ κοσμεῖν* also of prose eulogies (9.76), and by the first century B.C. *chroma* and *color* were standard terms for literary style in general.[9] In some cases, this was a result of applying to literature the terminology of painting, but the frequent use of *fucus* and *fucare* in similar contexts (with disapproval implied) makes it clear that the paint-pots of the boudoir were what the critic had in mind more often than the artist's palette.[10]

Two examples from the second century A.D. show the continuity of the idea. Aulus Gellius, following Cicero and Quintilian, says of the various styles in poetry and prose that each of them can be made more distinguished by chaste and modest adornment, but becomes

4. Damon: Athen. XIV 628c, Plato *Rep*. IV 424c6, Aristid. Quint. II 14. Cf. Plato *Rep*. III 398c–399d, Ar. *Pol*. VIII 1339a–1342b, esp. 1340a18ff; Anderson 1966, 38–42.

5. *Hibeh Papyri* 13.15–23, tentatively assigned by the editors to Hippias of Elis; cf. Anderson 1966, 147–52. Aristophanes *Thesm*. 130–72.

6. E.g. Plato *Phaedrus* 239c–d, who describes the unmanly lover as *ἀλλοτρίοις χρώμασι καὶ κόσμοις . . . κοσμούμενον*.

7. Plato *Rep*. X 601a–b (*γυμνωθέντα γε τῶν τῆς μουσικῆς χρωμάτων τά τῶν ποιητῶν*.

8. Thuc. I 21.1 (cf. p. 144 below), Isocr. 9.8–9. Isocrates uses *διαποικίλλειν* (cf. Plato *Laws* 812d on *ποικιλία* in music), which suggests that he had costume rather than make-up in mind; cf. Fantham 1972, 167 n.27, who observes that this analogy was never as popular in Greek as in Latin.

9. Philodemus *de mus*. 17.35 (Kemke p.84), Dion. Hal. *ad Amm*. II 2 (793); Cic. *de or*. III 96, 100, 217, *Brut*. 171 etc.

10. E.g. Cic. *de or*. II 188, III 199, *Brut*. 162, Quint. VIII 3.6 etc; Fantham 1972, 168 and 172.

mere mummery when 'made up and bedaubed'.[11] And Lucian, following Plato and Isocrates, compares the use of poetic ornament in history to dressing an athlete up like a harlot and painting his face.[12] Though Lucian preserves the traditional Greek contrast between cosmetics and manliness, his reference to the harlot shows that he has been influenced by the more characteristically Roman concept of the unpainted face as chaste and *feminine*. That is how it appears in Gellius, and in later Latin literature, where the image was very widely used for the contrast of truth and deception.[13] Phocas' Muse is an honest woman, not a seductive deceiver.

It was more than just stylistic adornment in general that the Greek or Roman reader understood by 'make-up' (*κομμωτική*, *fucatio*) in a literary context. From beginning to end of the metaphor's long history, it was applied particularly to the techniques of rhetoric.

In the course of arguing, against Polus in the *Gorgias*, that political oratory is merely a kind of flattery, Plato's Socrates observes that its relation to real statesmanship (which pursues not pleasure but the good) is like that of cooking to medicine, or of *cosmetics* to gymnastics: it is an illiberal art, deceiving men with shapes and colours and smooth texture and making them affect a spurious beauty instead of the real thing.[14] Six hundred years later Minucius Felix' Octavius, in a very different dialogue, defends the theological notions of the uneducated as being closer to the truth because they are not obscured by the make-up of attractive eloquence.[15] Midway between these two disapproving references to the deceptive superficiality of rhetoric, the master-orator himself applies the same cosmetic image to his own work, and only partly in self-deprecation. Cicero to Atticus, June 60 B.C.:[16]

11. Gell. *NA* VI 14.11: 'unumquodque . . . genus . . . cum caste pudiceque ornatur fit illustrius, cum fucatur atque praelinitur fit praestigiosum'.

12. Lucian *Hist.* 8 (*ad fin*): *ἐπεισάγοι τῇἱστσρίᾳ τὰ της ἑτέρας κομμώματα* (i.e. myth, encomium etc . . . *ὥσπερ ἄν εἴ τις ἀθλητὴν* . . . *περιβάλοι* . . . *κόσμῳ τῷ ἑταιρικῷ καὶ φυκίον ἐντρίβοι καὶ ψιμύθιον τῷ προσώπῳ*.

13. *TLL* VI 1460.43ff, 1462.24ff (*fucus*, *fucare*), cf. III 1721.32–46 (*color*). For Christian writers, Old Testament echoes may have helped: 2 *Kings* 9.30 (Jezebel), *Ezek*. 23.40 (harlot), *Wisdom* 13.14 (idolatry).

14. Plato *Gorg*. 465b: *ἡ κομμωτική, κακοῦργός τε καὶ ἀπατηλὴ καὶ ἀγεννὴς καὶ ἀνελεύθερος, σχήμασιν καὶ χρώμασιν καὶ λειότητι καὶ ἐσθῆσιν ἀπατῶσα, ὥστε ποιεῖν ἀλλότριον κάλλος ἐφελκομένους τοῦ οἰκείου τοῦ διά τῆς γυμναστικῆς ἀμελεῖν*. (Plato often uses *χρώματα καὶ σχήματα* to describe the world of sense perception as opposed to that of the ideal forms: e.g. *Rep*. II 373b6, X 601a2, *Laws* II 668e3, etc.)

15. Min. Felix *Octavius* 16.6: 'non fucatur pompa facundiae et gratiae'.

16. Cic. *Att*. II 1.1–2: Shackleton Bailey's translation.

> As I was on my way to Antium on the Kalends of June, eager to leave M. Metellus' gladiator show behind me, your boy met me with a letter from you and a sketch [*commentarius*] of my Consulship in Greek. I was glad when I got it that I had given L. Cossinius a piece on the same topic, likewise in Greek, to take to you some time before. Otherwise, if I had read yours first, you would be accusing me of plagiary. Actually though, your piece, which I have read with pleasure, struck me as a trifle rough and unkempt, but it was embellished by its very neglect of ornament and seemed fragrant because odourless, as with the ladies. Now *my* book has used up Isocrates' entire perfume-cabinet [*myrothecium*] along with all the little scent-boxes of his pupils, and some of Aristotle's rouge [*pigmenta*] as well. . . . Posidonius has already written to me from Rhodes that when he read this *ébauche* [*ὑπόμνημα*] of mine, which I had sent him with the idea that he might compose something more elaborate [*ornatius*] on the same theme, so far from being stimulated to composition he was effectively frightened away. The fact is, I have dumbfounded the whole Greek community, so that the folk who were pressing me on all sides to give them something to dress up [*quod ornarent*] are pestering me no longer.

Normally, a *commentarius* or *ὑπόμνημα* provided just the bare material for historical narrative, without any stylistic elaboration.[17] Atticus evidently stuck to this convention, and Posidonius was no doubt expecting Cicero to do so as well. But Cicero had provided his own ornamentation, from the Isocratean and Aristotelian theories of rhetoric. The bottles in 'Isocrates' perfume-cabinet' were the *λήκυθοι* Cicero used for elaborate set-piece speeches – perhaps the same *inanes rhetorum ampullae* to which young Virgil said farewell as he turned to philosophy, though there the dominant idea may be noise rather than colour.[18]

At any rate, the idea of stylistic and rhetorical effects as artificial colour, whether conceived of as justifiable beautification or meretricious deception, was clearly a commonplace in Cicero's day – so

17. See (e.g.) Cic. *Brut.* 262 and Hirt. *BG* VIII pref.4–5 on Caesar's *Commentarii*. Cf. Traub 1955, 229–31 on Pliny *ep.* VI 16.1 and 22, 20.20.
18. Cic. *Att.* I 14.3: 'totum hunc locum, quam ego varie meis orationibus . . . soleo pingere, de flamma, de ferro (nosti illas *ληκύθους*) . . .'. Virg. *Catalepton* 5.1, cf. Brink 1971, 180 on Hor. *AP* 97.

much so, indeed, that it gave rise in the next generation to a new technical term in rhetoric.

—

After the well-educated Roman boy graduated from the *grammaticus* to the *rhetor*, generally at about 14,[19] the exercise he found himself practising most often was the *controversia*. He had to argue one or other side of a case, just as a real orator would have to do in a real court; but the data of the imaginary case set by his tutor (the *thesis*) were deliberately paradoxical or melodramatic, in order to test to the utmost his ingenuity and persuasive powers. He was allowed to introduce whatever supplementary material he saw fit (provided that it was not inconsistent with that given in the *thesis*) so as to make the facts of the case appear in a light more favourable to his own interpretation, and this technique – putting, as we might say, a different 'complexion' on the facts – was known as *color*.

For example, two *theseis* on historical themes quoted by the elder Seneca: Lucius Flamininus, as proconsul in Gaul, was asked a favour by a courtesan at a dinner party, who said she'd never seen a man having his head cut off; so he sent for one of the condemned criminals and had him executed. Among the *colores* used in defence of Flamininus by the declaimers Seneca had heard were that he was drunk and didn't know what he was doing; that he considered it didn't matter where or when a man condemned to death died; that the party had been discussing his excessive leniency and he felt he had to show he could be severe; and that he gave the woman her wish in case she should ask for something worse, like the death of a free man. The second *thesis* supposed that a certain Popillius had been accused of parricide but successfully defended by Cicero; when Cicero was proscribed, he was sent to kill him, and did so, bringing back his head to Antony. The *colores* used on Popillius' behalf were that Antony forced him to do it against his will; that Antony chose him for the job *because* he was a client of Cicero, to increase the victim's humiliation; that he had pleaded with Antony for Cicero's life, and Antony punished him for it by making him the executioner; that he himself was willing to kill Cicero in case some client of Clodius should be sent to do it and insult and torture him first; and so on.[20]

'The *colores* are the Persian carpet of the declaimer; look at it from one angle and the colours are bright and clear, the pattern

19. Quint. II 2.3; Bonner 1977, 137.
20. Sen. *contr.* IX 2.20–21, VII 2.10–13.

simple, but observe it from another angle, and the shade deepens, the pattern changes, and the whole appears in a different light.'[21] In this striking image, the author of the standard work on Roman declamation is, I think, less true to the ancient than to the modern metaphor; we, who know the art of persuasion mainly through the media of journalism and advertising, find it more natural to speak of slants, angles and points of view. 'Angle' in this sense, both as a noun and as a verb, is now officially recognized in the 1972 Supplement to the *Oxford English Dictionary* (noun *s.v.* §1c, verb *s.v.* §4); 'slant', which the *OED* Supplement has not yet reached, so far only appears, as a noun, in Partridge's *Dictionary of Slang and Unconventional English* (*s.v.* §3) and in Mathews' *Dictionary of Americanisms* (*s.v.* §1). What the pupil of rhetoric did was to 'slant' the story in a way favourable to his own case; but what *he* saw himself doing was painting its face with convincing colours.[22]

It was a form of secondary education which left its mark on literature of every kind, and historiography – *pace* Phocas – in particular.

21. Bonner 1949, 56. His whole treatment of the *colores* technique (pp.55f) is important; cf. also Clarke 1953, 93f, Winterbottom 1974, xviii–xix, Bonner 1977, 293f.

22. Cf. Clarke 1953, 94: 'the colour was often make-up', which is how I think the Romans saw it; I am not convinced by Bonner (1949, 55) that the rhetorical sense of the word gives a 'quite different meaning' from the stylistic use of it in Cicero.

Chapter 2

ANNALS AND HISTORY

The first Roman historians were two senators who lived through the second Punic War, Q. Fabius Pictor and L. Cincius Alimentus. They wrote in Greek; their histories dealt with the legends of Rome's foundation, which they dated respectively to 747 and 729 B.C., but only 'summarily' with events after that, until they reached a period for which they had first-hand evidence to draw on.[1] The same was no doubt true of their successors, C. Acilius and A. Postumius Albinus (consul in 151); Acilius, at any rate, certainly dealt with the legendary story of Hercules and Evander but is not quoted on anything between Romulus and the battle of Cannae.[2] It was certainly true of M. Porcius Cato (consul 195, censor 184), whose *Origines* were the first historical work in Latin, though he disguised the gap between the foundation-legends and the recoverable history of recent generations by inserting those 'origins' of other Italian cities which gave his work its name.[3]

The reason is straightforward enough: Greek historians were interested in stories of the foundation of cities, in legends which linked foreign peoples to their own Hellenocentric world picture, and in law-givers to whom the customs of foreign peoples could be satisfactorily attributed. So Evander, Aeneas, Romulus and Numa had already attracted their attention, and the Roman historians could report, and build on, the material they had collected.[4] The Tarquins may have registered peripherally on Greek consciousness through the history of Cumae, but early-republican Rome could have provided nothing of interest. It took an event as devastating as the sack of the city by the Gauls to achieve even the most garbled notice.[5] For the first Roman historians, then, there was simply

1. Dion. Hal. I 6.2 (κεφαλαιωδῶς); cf. I 74.1, Pol. III 9.4 (foundation dates, senatorial rank). On Fabius, see Poucet 1976, esp. 209–15.
2. Frr. 1–3P; fr. 4 is of 212 B.C., fr. 5 of 193, fr. 6 of his own lifetime. Albinus' surviving fragments are on Aeneas and L. Brutus.
3. Badian 1966, 7 and 11: the evidence is the fragments themselves (1–83P).
4. κτίσεις etc: Pol. IX 1.4; cf. Bickerman 1952 *passim*, and p. 150f below. Romulus: Cornell 1975, esp. pp.16–27. Numa: Gabba 1967, 154–63.
5. Cumae: Gabba 1967, 144–7. Gauls: Plut. *Cam.* 22.3–4 (Heraclides Ponticus, Aristotle); Gabba 1967, 165f.

nothing to go on – except for a haphazard collection of traditional stories, only roughly dateable at the best – until they reached a period about which reliable information was available from their own elder contemporaries, remembering what their fathers had done and said.[6]

Most of the historians who treated Roman history from the beginnings evidently allowed this distribution of material to dictate the shape of their work.[7] The evidence is very unsatisfactory, book-numbers being only haphazardly reported and notoriously liable to corruption, but a rough idea may be obtained by seeing how many books it took each writer to reach the Hannibalic War. Cato did it in four, though two of those were devoted to Italian foundation-legends;[8] his contemporary L. Cassius Hemina, whose second book ran from Romulus and Remus to the Gallic sack, also reached the year of Cannae in book IV.[9] L. Piso Frugi (consul 133, censor 120) may have taken four or five, since his seventh book is cited for events in 158 and 146 B.C.[10] With Q. Claudius Quadrigarius a generation later, we find a more generous allocation: he only *began* with the Gallic sack, and was already in book VI for the Hannibalic War. The difference is not very great overall, his ninth book dealing with events some 10 or 20 years after those of Piso's seventh, but the significant thing may be precisely his deliberate avoidance of the regal period and the early Republic.[11] C. Licinius Macer (tribune of the *plebs* in 73) went back to the origins again: he reached at least 299 B.C., and wrote at least 16 books, but we have no information about the disposition of material within them.[12] Q. Aelius Tubero, writing in the 30s B.C., was half-way through the third century in book IX, which probably means about 12 books to the Hannibalic War – an allocation comparable with that of Fenestella in the age of Tiberius, who took 22 books to reach the middle of the first century B.C.[13]

From the origins to Hannibal in four books, rising to 12: though

6. Cf. Balsdon 1953, 161.
7. Gabba 1967, 135–8 (observing that the same applies to Ennius' *Annales*).
8. Fr. 84P (Nonius 142L): 'Cato in quarto originum', on 219 B.C.
9. Fr. 32P (Prisc. VII 294H), cf. Livy XXII 57.2. Second book: Diomedes *GLK* I 384, Macr. *Sat.* I 16.21 (frr. 11, 20P).
10. Frr. 36, 39P (Cens. *de die nat.* 17.11 and 13).
11. Frr. 57P (Gell. *NA* II 2.13, from book VI on 213 B.C.), 73–75P (from book IX, on the *foedus Numantinum*); Frier 1975, 92f (p. 19 below) on the reasons for his starting point.
12. Frr. 19P (299 B.C.), 22P (book XVI).
13. Tubero fr. 9P (Gell. *NA* VII 4.2, 250 B.C.), Fenestella fr. 21P (Nonius 615L, 57 B.C.). Cf. pp. 135–8 below on Tubero's identity and date.

the first-century writers spread themselves more than their predecessors in the second, the overall picture is roughly consistent. (Ennius, with a poet's greater opportunities for elaboration, had begun the Hannibalic War in book VIII.) It is very different from what we find in Livy, who deals with the Hannibalic War in books XXI-XXX, or in Dionysius, whose 20 books go down only as far as the beginning of the *first* Punic War.[14] The reason for the difference – and, no doubt, for the more generous treatment in Quadrigarius, Macer and Tubero – lies in the work of the two historians whom I have so far deliberately left out of the survey, in order to emphasize the magnitude, the enormity, of their achievement.

First, Cn. Gellius. He is quoted on the Secular Games of 146 B.C., in terms which do not suggest that he saw them himself,[15] but apart from that we have no reliable information on when he wrote.[16] There is a hint, however, that it was after Piso, whose work very probably post-dates his censorship in 120 B.C.:[17] according to Gellius, Numa Pompilius had no sons, but only the daughter whom Ancus Marcius married; that looks like a deliberate contradiction of the tradition reported by Piso, which derived several distinguished noble families, including the Calpurnii Pisones, from eponymous sons of Numa.[18] We shall probably not be far wrong in putting Gellius' career as a writer between, say, 110 and 90 B.C. Certainly we should allow a substantial period for the writing of his history, since one of the quotations from it is attributed to the 97th book. He treated in book XV an episode from 389 B.C. which had appeared in the second book of Cassius Hemina, and in book XXX or XXXIII one from 216 B.C. which even Livy was to record only in his 23rd.[19] In fact, the scale of Gellius' narrative is closer to Dionysius of Halicarnassus than to Livy – and he went on for over two centuries beyond where Dionysius stopped.

14. Dion. Hal. I 8.2.

15. Cens. *de die nat.* 17.11 (fr. 28P): 'At Piso censorius et Cn. Gellius sed et Cassius Hemina, qui illo tempore vivebat, . . . adfirmant . . .'. The distinction seems significant. (Piso, however, was already *tribunicius* at the time.)

16. The assertion that he was earlier than L. Coelius Antipater (a contemporary of C. Fannius *cos.* 122: Cic. *leg.* I 6) depends on the reading *proxume* at Cic. *div.* I 55. But *maxume* makes better sense: see Wiseman 1979a.

17. The sources insist that he is Piso Censorius (Dion. Hal. II 38.3, 39.1, XII 9.3, Pliny *NH* XIII 84, Cens. *de die nat.* 17.11), and his fragments betray an interest in censorial matters (Rawson 1976, 706 and 709).

18. Plut. *Numa* 21, Dion. Hal. II 76.5; Gabba 1967, 161. Calpus and the Calpurnii: Festus (Paulus) 41L, *Laus Pisonis* 5, 15, Hor. *AP* 292.

19. Frr. 29, 25, 26 (differently attributed by Charisius and Priscian).

A generation or two later,[20] Valerius Antias' history was evidently of similar size. There are insoluble problems about the dating of the fragments attributed to numbered books, and it is possible that not all the numbers are accurately reported, but since Priscian and Aulus Gellius independently cite his 74th and 75th books – the latter quotation plausibly assigned by Hermann Peter to an event of 118 B.C. – it is clear that Antias' work was not much shorter than Gellius'.[21]

—

Why is there such a difference in scale between the historians from Fabius to Tubero on the one hand and Gellius and Antias on the other? Though no answer can be more than speculative, we may perhaps make an intelligent guess if we remember the probability that Gellius wrote after Piso, and also to some degree in opposition to him.

We know one very important thing about Piso's work: he called it *Annales*. Citations of the early historians by authors of the second century A.D. or later tend to refer to *annales* and *historiae* indiscriminately, since by then the two words were practically interchangeable;[22] but in the case of Piso we have the excellent evidence of Cicero and Varro, who quote 'Piso *in annalibus*' four times between them, and of Dionysius of Halicarnassus, who normally cites just the author's name but in Piso's case three times specifies *ἐν ταῖς ἐνιαυσίοις πραγματείαις* (or *ἀναγραφαῖς*).[23] No previous historian is known to have used this title: Cato's work is never known as anything but *Origines*, while those who wrote in Greek, from Fabius Pictor to Postumius Albinus, probably called their books *Ῥωμαικά* or *Ῥωμαίων πράξεις* – *res Romanae* or *res gestae* in Latin.[24] Cassius Hemina and Fabius Servilianus are cited only by late authors, who alternate arbitrarily between *in annalibus* and *in*

20. See pp. 117–21 below: generally, but wrongly (I think), assigned to the Sullan period.
21. Frr. 57–62P. Livy treated 118 B.C. in book 62. Luce (1977, 174f, 177, 180) accepts the attribution of an event of 136 B.C. to book 22; but this makes nonsense of the other book-numbers recorded.
22. Gell. *NA* V 18.3, 'sed nos audire soliti sumus annales omnino id esse quod historiae sint'; see further below, p. 14.
23. Cic. *fam.* IX 22.2 (cf. also *Brut.* 106), Varro *LL* V 148, 165 and *ap.* Lact. *div. inst.* I 6.9, Dion. Hal. IV 7.5, 15.5, XII 9.3 (Piso frr. 6, 9, 14, 15, 25, 40, 41P); see Peter 1914, clxxxiii.
24. Dion. Hal. VII 7.1, Diod. Sic. VII 5.4; Gelzer 1933, 129=1964, 51. *Res gestae*: Nonius 835L (Fabius). *Res Romanae*: Gell. *NA* XI 8.2 (Postumius). Cf., however, Cic. *div.* I 43 ('in Fabi Pictoris Graecis annalibus'). Livy XXV 39.11 is no evidence for the title of C. Acilius' work.

historiis, but with Piso even the later citations are practically unanimous.[25] The contrast is striking.

Our casual habit of calling practically all the second- and first-century historians 'annalists' has obscured the true significance of the term. It ought, strictly, to mean a year-by-year account. When Cicero's friend Atticus compiled a chronological record of the magistrates of the Roman Republic, with notes on legislation, declarations of war and other notable events, he called it *liber annalis*[26] – with the singular used because it consisted only of one volume. If it had been longer, it would of course have been *annales*. A similar sort of book had been written two generations earlier, the *liber magistratuum* of C. Sempronius Tuditanus (consul 129 B.C.).[27] It was also known under the title *commentarii*, which is what the elder Pliny calls Piso's work.[28] Presumably Piso's *Annals* had something in common with those annotated lists of magistrates.

We call such lists 'fasti'; but that is another term which is often used with a misleading casualness. In the first place, its main reference is to the days of the year and their religious significance, *dies fasti et nefasti*.[29] The use of the word to indicate a list of the years themselves, with the magistrates who gave their names to the years, is essentially derivative; nor do we really know the reason for the derivation, since it is not at all self-evident that a calendar of the 'religious year' must necessarily develop – as the Roman *fasti* did – into a catalogue of eponymous consuls. In the second place, the assumption that an authoritative consular list was available as a public document is probably anachronistic for the second century B.C. – and indeed perhaps even for the first, until Augustus had the so-called 'Capitoline Fasti' inscribed for public view in the Forum.[30] We know that at Antium by about the 70s B.C. there existed a combined calendar and magistrate list painted on a wall

25. Hemina: the contrast between his *historiae* and Gellius' *annales* at Macr. *Sat.* I 16.21 is probably fortuitous. Piso: one late reference to *historiae* (fr. 17P), and one to *commentarii* (fr. 11P, see below); six, besides those cited in n.23 above, to *annales* (frr. 8, 13, 18, 19, 27, 36P).

26. Nep. *Att.* 18.1, 'in eo volumine . . . quo magistratus ordinavit. Nulla enim lex neque pax neque bellum neque res illustris est populi Romani quae non in eo *suo tempore* sit notata . . .'; Cic. *Att.* XII 23.2 (*in tuo annali*), Nep. *Hann.* 13, Asc. 13C.

27. Asc. 77C (like Atticus'), Macr. *Sat.* I 13.21 (title).

28. Messalla augur *ap.* Gell. *NA* XIII 15.4 ('in commentario tertio decimo C. Tuditani'), Pliny *NH* XIII 84 ('tradi Piso censorius primo commentariorum').

29. L. Cincius' work *de fastis* (Macr. *Sat.* I 12.12) is referred to in Greek by Lydus (*de mens.* IV 92) as *περὶ τῶν ἑορτῶν*.

30. This was already rightly emphasized by Pais (1906, 5–8, 277f.).

(presumably an inside wall), but we have no idea how accessible, or how authoritative, it was.[31] For Cicero, Horace and Livy, at any rate, consular *fasti* were books to be looked through, not an inscribed document to be consulted.[32]

When Livy considers what chance the Romans would have had against Alexander, he invites his readers to remember how many commanders the Republic had to call upon: 'just run through the pages of the *annales magistratuum* and the *fasti*'. For Seneca too, *fasti* and *annales publici* are evidently interchangeable as authorities for past events.[33] In Cicero's time, *annales* was the normal word for 'lists of magistrates'; he does use *fasti* as well, but much less often,[34] no doubt to avoid confusion with its primary meaning of 'calendar'. It was only later, when *annales* could be used to mean simply 'history', that *fasti* became the normal word for a consular list.[35]

Apart from the Alexander passage, Livy cites the *libri magistratuum* three times: once in book XXXIX (52.4), in opposition to Valerius Antias' fictitious date for the death of Scipio Africanus, and twice, more helpfully, in book IV. At IV 20.8 he specifies which books he means – the 'linen books' found by Licinius Macer in the temple of Moneta and used by him and by Tubero as sources for fifth-century history. At IV 7.10, however, the 'linen books' reported a consular pair (for the year 444) whose names were *not* found either in early histories or in the *libri magistratuum*; Dionysius, confronted with the same crux, observes that the Roman *chronographiae* do not agree, and chooses which ones to follow – i.e. presumably Macer and Tubero – on the strength of 'the testimony of the sacred and secret books'.[36]

31. Degrassi 1947, 159–66 and 1963, 1–28. The latest item it contains is of 84 B.C.; 67 and 55 are possible *termini ante quem* (Degrassi 1947, 159). The *lustrum* of 89 B.C. was recorded, *infelix* though it was: cf. Wiseman 1969b, 63f.
32. Cic. *Att.* IV 8b.2, 'in codicillorum fastis futurorum consulum paginulas'; Hor. *Sat.* I 3.112, 'tempora si fastosque velis evolvere mundi' (the same verb at Ovid *Fasti* I 657); Livy IX 18.12, 'paginas in annalibus magistratuum fastisque percurrere licet'.
33. Sen. *dial.* XII 14.2, 'ad fastus te et annales perducam publicos'. Cf. Porph. on Hor. *Odes* iv 14.4, glossing *memores fastus* as '*annales* qui ad commemorationem honorum vel rerum gestarum inventi sunt'.
34. Cic. *Sest.* 33, *Pis.* 30, *Att.* IV 8b.2 (n.32 above), *fam.* V 12.5 (p. 18 below). *Annales (publici*, etc): *dom.* 86, *prov. cons.* 20, *Sull.* 27, *Rab. perd.* 15, *Mur.* 16, *leg.* I 6, *rep.* I 25, II 28–9, *Brut.* 49, *de or.* II 52–3 (p. 18 below).
35. *TLL* VI (1912–26) 327–8: not many republican and Augustan examples. For *annales*, cf. n.22 above; in Livy, who never uses the word *historia*, the normal word for 'history' is *annales*, as in his formula 'in quibusdam annalibus invenio'.
36. Livy IV 7.10–12, 'neque in annalibus priscis neque in libris magistratuum';

A good cross-section of the second- and first-century chronographical authorities whom Dionysius may have consulted is provided in the first book of Macrobius' *Saturnalia*, where one of the interlocutors discourses on the origins of the Roman year and its months, explaining how Romulus' original system was modified by Numa and by the introduction of intercalation. The authorities he quotes are, in roughly chronological order:[37] Fulvius Nobilior, 'in the *fasti* which he placed in the temple of Hercules Musarum'; Cassius (Hemina);[38] Tuditanus, 'in the third book of his *Magistrates*'; Piso; Iunius (Gracchanus); Cincius, *de fastis*;[39] Licinius Macer; Varro; Verrius Flaccus; and Cornelius Labeo. (Nisus' *commentarii fastorum* are unfortunately undateable.[40]) The *fasti* of Tusculum, Aricia and Praeneste are also cited, of which the last-named, inscribed on marble in the 'forum' of the town, are known to have been the work of Verrius Flaccus in the time of Augustus.[41]

Whether painted, inscribed or written in books, the calendar *fasti* and the magistrate-lists with which they became associated were from the beginning works of antiquarian research rather than authoritative official documents. Even the earliest known example, the *fasti* placed in the Hercules Musarum temple by M. Fulvius Nobilior (consul 189 B.C.), is treated just as one source among many.[42] In some cases, we know where the authors found their information: Cincius in the dedications and other inscriptions he copied on the Capitol, Licinius Macer in the linen books he found in the Moneta temple,[43] and so on. 'Each historian or chronicler',

Dion. Hal. XI 62.3, *οὐκ ἐν ἁπάσαις ταῖς Ῥωμαικαῖς χρονογραφίαις ἀμφότεραι* [*ἀρχαὶ*] *φέρονται*.

37. Macr. *Sat.* I 12.12–20, 12.30, 13.20–1.

38. Cf. Rawson 1976, 700 on Cassius' interest in the calendar.

39. On the antiquarian L. Cincius (not to be confused with Cincius Alimentus the historian), see below, p. 45.

40. Macr. *Sat.* I 12.30; cf. Arnobius I 59, who mentions Nisus along with Cornelius Epicadus and Verrius Flaccus.

41. Macr. *Sat.* I 12.17 and 30. Verrius: Suet. *gramm.* 17, 'statuam habet Praeneste in inferiore fori parte circa hemicyclium, in quo fastos a se ordinatos et marmoreo parieti incisos publicarat'; Degrassi 1963, 107–45 and 1947, 260. The Fulvii were a Tusculan family (Cic. *Planc.* 20 etc): were the *fasti Tusculani* 'published' by M. Nobilior?

42. Macr. *Sat.* I 12.16, 13.21. Cf. Charisius 138K (on the spelling of *nobiliore*): 'comparativa Plinius e putat ablativo finiri; ⟨antiquo⟩s tamen ait per i locutos, quippe fastos omnes et *libros* "a Fulvio Nobiliori" scriptum rettulisse'. Similarly Varro (LL VI 33-4) classes Fulvius and Iunius Gracchanus together as *scriptores*. Presumably, Fulvius' *fasti* were a volume deposited in the temple, like the *libri lintei*, rather than inscribed or painted on the walls.

43. Cf. pp. 39f, 45 below.

wrote Dionysius, who had read them carefully, 'takes something out of old records kept on sacred tablets . . .'; as Gelzer realized, he was referring to temple inscriptions in general, not to one authoritative source.[44]

Tuditanus and Iunius Gracchanus, to judge by their titles,[45] may have restricted themselves to the Republic and its magistrates, but that was certainly not the regular procedure: the treatment of the calendar of Romulus and Numa in Macrobius' sources shows how far back these authors were prepared to go. Dionysius, in the passage quoted above, appeals to the historians' use of temple documents to justify an argument about the relationship of Romulus and Remus to Aeneas! They even provided a precise chronology: elsewhere, Dionysius cites 'the yearly records' to date an event to the 40th year of the reign of Servius Tullius.[46]

Dionysius' phrase translates '*annales*', and brings us back, at last, to Piso. Most of the authors quoted by Macrobius, whether they were writing recognizable narrative history or merely compiling chronological tables, could be called 'annalists' in the true sense: their works were, in Dionysius' word, *chronographiae*. Piso was one of them; and we may now, perhaps, see why he gave his work the title by which it was always known.

—

It is a reasonable assumption that by the 20s of the second century B.C. a complete list of yearly magistrates from the beginning of the Republic (or from what seemed to the second-century Romans to be the beginning of the Republic) was available in book form for anyone to consult – generally accurate, no doubt, as far back as the late fourth century, much less reliable before that.[47] Moreover, since *annales* also included notable military achievements,[48] we can also assume a list of triumphs, for which evidence could be found not only in honorary inscriptions and *elogia* but also in

44. Dion. Hal. I 73.1, *παλαιὸς μὲν οὖν οὔτε συγγραφεὺς οὔτε λογογράφος ἐστὶ Ῥωμαίων οὐδὲ εἷς. ἐκ παλαιῶν μέντοι λόγων ἐν ἱεραῖς δέλτοις σῳζομένων ἕκαστός τι παραλαβὼν ἀνέγραψεν*. Gelzer 1934, 54=1964, 101f.

45. Gracchanus *de potestatibus*? – cf. *Dig*. I 13.1.1 (Funaioli 1907, 120f), on the quaestors. In fact, he must have touched on the Romulean period: Varro *LL* V 55 cites him on Lucumo.

46. Dion. Hal. IV 30.3, *ἐν ταῖς ἐνιαυσίοις ἀναγραφαῖς*. Cf. IV 15.5, XII 9.3 (Piso's *Annals)*; and I 73.1 *ἀνέγραψεν* (n.44 above).

47. See Pinsent 1975, *passim* (esp. p. 66f) on variant *fasti* for the fifth and early fourth centuries, systematized by Procrustean chronographers to fit synchronisms and fixed points.

48. Cf. Nep. *Att*. 18.1 (n.26 above) on Atticus' *liber annalis*. Serv. *Aen*. I 373 ('domi militiaeque terra marique gesta') on the *annales maximi*.

the records of the palms and laurels dedicated to Jupiter Optimus Maximus.[49]

It was once generally assumed that the publication at about this time of the *annales maximi* (supposedly the annotated archives of the *pontifices*) provided an authoritative catalogue;[50] but since Elizabeth Rawson's epoch-making study we now know how little the Roman historians actually used the *annales maximi*, especially on the kind of chronological questions they might have been expected to answer, and the pontiffs' 80 books are convincingly identified as 'a great collection of aetiological explanations of Roman rites and institutions . . . a work of primarily religious antiquarianism'.[51] It is more likely that their publication *presupposes* the achievement of a list of eponymous magistrates by the second-century chronographers than that it provided an authentic independent document.[52]

The men who reconstructed the consular and triumphal *fasti* were consuls and *triumphatores* themselves: M. Fulvius Nobilior (if his *fasti* were indeed annual as well as calendar) was consul in 189, *triumphator* in 187, censor in 179; C. Sempronius Tuditanus was consul and *triumphator* in 129. As senior senators, they had privileged access to the documents that were their primary evidence.[53] They were followed in the writing of *annales* (or *commentarii*) by L. Piso Frugi, consul in 133 and censor in 120 – not a *triumphator*, though no doubt he would have been, if the enemy he fought as a proconsul had been more than just rebellious slaves. The work of reconstruction was done, and he could exploit it in his *Annals* for his own moralizing purposes.[54]

We must, I think, assume from his title that Piso recorded every year under the name of its consuls, military tribunes or dictator.[55]

49. Sil. It. *Pun*. XV 119f, Aug. *RG* 4.1, Degrassi 1947, 342–5.
50. E.g. most recently Badian 1966, 15; Frier 1975, 84f.
51. Rawson 1971, esp. 166–9 (quotations from p. 168, expressed in Miss Rawson's argument with the very proper reservation that all our quotations come from the earliest part of the work: 'there is, however, not enough evidence to show that the whole work . . . was of this character').
52. See Alföldi's comments *ap*. Gabba 1967, 172 (in the discussion).
53. It is quite possible that Cassius Hemina (cf. Rawson 1976, 700f, on fr. 28P) and C. Gracchus' friend Iunius 'Gracchanus' (Pliny *NH* XXXIII 36) were senators too.
54. On Piso as a moralist (esp. frr. 38 and 40P), see Rawson 1976, 705f. He was included by Philodemus among the Roman Stoics: cf. Peter 1914, clxxxv, Gentili 1975, 42f.
55. E.g. fr. 36P; Rawson 1976, 704f. Cf. Gentili 1975, 35: 'è chiaro che con il termine "annali" Cicerone [*fam*. V 12.5, n.60 below] intende referirsi all' annalistica letteraria, che narrava *anno per anno* le vicende di Roma dalla più remota antichità fino al tempo presente . . .'.

For many years, particularly in the early Republic, he would have nothing else to report; no wonder Cicero said that the *Annals* were 'thin', and lacking in literary elaboration.[56] He said the same of Piso's predecessors too,[57] but the strictly annalistic nature of the work must have made it particularly conspicuous in the case of Piso himself.

Certainly it provoked a reaction. Sempronius Asellio prefaced his *Res Gestae* with a famous polemic against writers of *annales*, who only show what was done and in what year it was done, as if they were compiling a diary: 'just to write down in whose consulship a war began or ended, and who held a triumph as a result of it . . . that is telling stories to children, not writing history'.[58] A generation later, Cicero echoed him with the comment that for Fabius Pictor, Cato and Piso, history was merely the compilation of annals, no more literary than the primitive notice-board of the *pontifex maximus* (which even Cato had dismissed with contempt) and recording simply dates, names, places and events.[59] Asellio's objection was to the historically jejune content of the annals; for Cicero, the trouble was their stylistic shortcomings. An annalistic account, he wrote to Lucceius, can hardly hold the reader's attention with a bare catalogue of *fasti*; how different the skilfully worked-up account of a great man's vicissitudes of fortune, as in the history he hoped Lucceius would write about himself![60] Perhaps he had Piso particularly in mind as an example to avoid, if we are right in supposing that Piso's incorporation of a consular and triumphal list had made him the 'annalist' *par excellence*.

Another distinguishing feature of *annales* was that they began at

56. Cic. *Brut.* 106, 'sane exiliter scriptos'; cf. *leg.* I 6, 'quid tam exile quam isti omnes?' (of Fabius, Cato, Piso, Fannius, Vennonius).

57. Cic. *leg.* I 6 (previous note), *de or.* II 51–3; on Fabius Pictor, cf. Poucet 1976, 209ff.

58. Gell. *NA* V 18.8–9 (frr. 1–2P), cf. Cic. *leg.* I 6 and Morelli 1975, 89–94 on Asellio's date – early first century? Cf. Gentili 1975, 31–3: there is no reason to suppose that by 'ei qui annales relinquere voluissent' (as opposed to 'ei qui res gestas a Romanis perscribere conati essent') he was referring to the editors of the pontifical *annales maximi*. For his own title, cf. Gell. *NA* II 13.2, IV 9.12, XIII 22.8; *Historiae* at XIII 3.6 and in the grammarians; *Res Romanae* at Charisius II 195K.

59. Cic. *de or.* II 51–3: 'erat historia nihil aliud nisi annalium confectio . . . hanc similitudinem scribendi [sc. the *annales maximi*] multi secuti sunt, qui sine ullis ornamentis monumenta solum temporum, hominum, locorum gestarumque rerum reliquerunt' (the same verb Asellio used, cf. previous note). Cato fr. 77P (Gell. *NA* II 28.6) on the pontiffs' *tabula*; cf. also Dion. Hal. I 74.3, Cic. *leg.* I 6; not to be confused with the published *annales maximi* (Rawson 1971, 168f).

60. Cic. *fam.* V 12.5, 'etenim ordo ipse annalium mediocriter nos retinet quasi enumeratione fastorum'; see below, p. 30.

the beginning. When Quintus and Atticus argue in the *de legibus* about whether Cicero should write a history of his own times or one 'on Romulus and Remus, as the saying is', Quintus urges the latter alternative on the grounds that existing accounts of the origins of Rome are written in such a way that no-one even reads them.[61] It must be the early historians, down to and including Piso, who are meant. Piso's successors largely avoided the regal period; even Claudius Quadrigarius, who called his own work *annales*,[62] began with the sack of Rome by the Gauls. The *Historiae* of Coelius Antipater evidently covered the Hannibalic War only, while those of Asellio and Sisenna were largely devoted to recent history.[63] A similar distinction is observable in epic poetry, with the *Annals* of Ennius and Accius in one category, Naevius' *Bellum Punicum* and Hostius' *Bellum Histricum* in the other; in that case, however, there seems to have been no marked change in fashion as there was in prose, no doubt because poetic *annales* could hardly be reduced to the level of dryness evidently reached by Piso.

The reactions to Piso's *Annals* and their systematically incorporated consular and triumphal lists seem to have been very varied. Asellio and those like him rejected the whole concept of annalistic history, but there were others for whom that *enumeratio fastorum* was a challenge. It has been persuasively argued that the 'Clodius' who wrote a critical work on chronology ἔλεγχος χρόνων) was Q. Claudius Quadrigarius, justifying the late starting-point of his own *Annals* by an attack on the reliability of any records ante-dating the sack of Rome by the Gauls.[64] If so, the main object of his polemic was probably Piso's work, incorporating the data amassed by Tuditanus and the other chronographers.[65]

But besides those who rejected Piso's method, and those who accepted his method but rejected his data, we can perhaps identify one man who accepted his data and used an entirely different technique to develop the same material into something Piso would

61. Cic. *leg.*I 8. 'illa sic scripta sunt ut ne legantur quidem'. Cf. Cic. *QF* II 13.4, *Att.* II 16.4 on Quintus' own *annales*.

62. Sen. *ben.* III 23.2, 17 citations in Gellius, 23 in Nonius, etc: consistently 'in annalibus' *vel sim.*

63. Titles: Gell. *NA* X 24.6, Festus 192L etc for Coelius (Nonius consistently calls his work *annales*, but all other sources have *historiae*); n.58 above for Asellio; Gell. *NA* IX 14.12, XI 15.7, XII 15.2 for Sisenna (confirmed by over 100 citations in Nonius). Sallust's *Historiae* are in the same tradition; he himself (fr. I 1M) called his subject *res populi Romani*, like Asellio.

64. Frier 1975, 92f on Plut. *Numa* 1.2.

65. Frier (1975, 93) assumes that the records he was attacking 'can only be the pontifical chronicle'. But see Rawson 1971 (p. 17 above).

never have dreamed of: Cn. Gellius, the earlier of the two historians whose works, so disproportionately huge in scale, were singled out in the first section of this chapter.

We know a certain amount about Gellius.[66] He had a great deal of material on the legendary history of the Italian peoples, including those allies of Rome whose dissatisfaction was soon to break out into open war.[67] His 'Italian sympathies' may be relevant to the date of his work (the later he wrote, the more intelligible they are),[68] and to his origin, if the legendary genealogy of his own family is correctly located in the Volscian territory of Minturnae and Formiae.[69] His fragments certainly betray an interest in that coastline – the Volturnus, Circeii, Ardea[70] – but his family had been active in Rome at least since his father's generation: a Cn. Gellius had been unlucky enough to encounter M. Cato as his opponent's advocate in a lawsuit, and another (perhaps son of the first, and possibly to be identified with the historian himself) held the position of *monetalis* in about 138 B.C.[71] As a *municipalis*, and no more than a junior senator (if that), Gellius may not have shared the consular historians' attitude to their subject-matter, or had the same access to documentary evidence. Certainly the work he produced was very different from theirs.

We know he was interested in chronology. Dionysius cites him for the dating of events to the fourth year of Romulus' reign, the first year of Ancus Marcius' reign, the eighteenth year after the expulsion of the kings, and the 363rd year from the foundation of the city.[72] It is possible that the detailed chronology of the regal period was his own work,[73] but for the Republic, as we have seen, a magistrate-list was already available, no doubt tied to an absolute chronology by means of dating *ab urbe condita*, *post reges exactos*

66. See Rawson 1976, 713–17.
67. Rawson 1976, 715f on frr. 7–9P, esp. fr. 7 (Solinus I 7) on the 'diplomatic contact' between Marsyas and Tarchon.
68. Cf. Rawson 1976, 716 ('was Gellius affected by the build-up to the Social War?'); quotation from p. 717. Cf. p. 11 n. 16 above.
69. Wiseman 1974b, 162f; based on *CIL* X 6017, Schol. Theocr. 15.40 and the Poseidon/Amphitrite relief on the so-called 'altar of Domitius Ahenobarbus'.
70. Frr. 7, 9, 16P.
71. Gell. *NA* XIV 2.21 and 26; Crawford 1974, 265. The Samnite Gellii (Rawson 1976, 715), and the fact that his family were in the tribe to which the survivors of neighbouring Fregellae were later allotted (Tromentina, *ILLRP* 515.4), are not enough to make Gellius a rebel sympathizer.
72. Dion. Hal. II 31.1, IV 6.4, VII 1.4–5 (frr. 11, 18, 20P).
73. Cf. p. 16 above; Piso's frr. 11 and 15P (Pliny *NH* XIII 84, Dion. Hal. IV 7.5) are not enough to show that he aspired to the level of precision which Gellius, followed by Licinius Macer and others, brought to the dating of events under the kings.

and *postquam Romam Galli ceperunt.*[74] It is what he did with it that sets him apart from his predecessors.

What Professor Badian has called 'the expansion of the past'[75] cannot be understood at first hand because of the loss of Gellius' history; no fragment survives as informative as that from Asellio's preface, and we do not know why he wrote as he did. There is, however, a revealing introductory passage in a surviving historian of quite a different period, which may give us some insight – if only by analogy – into the motivation of Cn. Gellius.

At the beginning of his *History of the Kings of Britain*, Geoffrey of Monmouth remarks how extraordinary it is that no history of the British kings before and after the Roman period has ever been written: 'yet the deeds of these men were such that they deserve to be praised for all time'.[76] Fortunately for Geoffrey and his readers, 'these deeds were handed joyfully down in oral tradition, just as if they had been committed to writing'; more fortunately still, Geoffrey – and he alone – has 'a certain very ancient book written in the British language', giving an account in chronological order of the deeds of every king from Brutus (grandson of Aeneas) to Cadwallader in the seventh century A.D., of which Geoffrey's own history purports to be a translation.[77]

Whatever genuine Celtic sources Geoffrey may have used, it is quite clear that most of his work is fictional: he was working 'not with historical material but with legends and with his own fertile imagination, in filling out the great unrecorded gaps in the British past'.[78] He had a king-list;[79] he had a chronological framework, even for dates before Christ;[80] he had literary sources – Gildas,

74. For the latter system (cf. *Gell. NA* V 4.3, from Fabius' Latin *annales*), see Pinsent 1975, esp. pp. 1–3, 10–12.

75. Badian 1966, 11f: 'there was simply not as much information to be had as Gellius produced'.

76. Galfridus Monemutensis *Historia regum Britanniae* I 1: 'Cum multa mecum et de multis saepius animo revolvens in historiam regum Britanniae inciderem, in mirum contuli quod intra mentionem quam de eis Gildas et Beda luculento tractatu fecerunt, nihil de regibus qui ante incarnationem Christi Britanniam inhabitaverant, nihil etiam de Arturo caeterisque compluribus qui post incarnationem successerunt, reperissem; cum et gesta eorum digna eternitatis laude constarent, et a multis populis quasi inscripta jucunde et memoriter praedicentur.' Translation by Thorpe 1966, 51.

77. *Ibid.*; also XII 20 (Thorpe 1966, 284 n.1), warning off his contemporaries, 'seeing that they do not have in their possession the book in the British language . . .'.

78. Hanning 1966, 124; cf. 136 on 'his independence of factual record'.

79. Piggott 1941, esp. 280ff.

80. Summarized in Thorpe 1966, 285–8.

Bede, the *historia Brittonum* – who told him something of Brutus and the origins story on the one hand, the Roman period and the English settlements on the other, but nothing in between; and he found it intolerable that so many kings should be just names and dates, instead of glorious or tragic history.

The parallel with the later annalists of the Roman Republic is close. Whether Gellius shared Geoffrey's patriotic motivation we have not enough evidence to say with any certainty, but the same *horror vacui* can surely be inferred from the sheer size of his work, and the likelihood that Piso and the chronographers had just produced the chronological framework that evidently provoked it. It was intolerable that so many consuls should be just names and dates – and so, no doubt, like Geoffrey he wrote their history himself.[81]

Most of our knowledge of Gellius' technique comes from the early books, where he used mythological accounts of the origins of civilized life, as well as the Italian-based legends noted above, to fill out the Aeneas/Romulus part of the story; but we should not therefore assume that it was applied only to the history of the kings.[82] After all, over 60 of his 97 books (if the number is correctly reported) dealt with the period from Hannibal to his own time.[83] The reason we have so little of his republican material is probably that his history – unlike Geoffrey's in this respect – was simply not very readable, and was superseded by later, livelier writers. Cicero mentions him once, or possibly twice, and Livy evidently did not use him at all. He might be cited on points of detail, but there is no evidence that his version of events had any larger influence.

The writers Livy *did* use are the ones who presumably rendered Gellius obsolete, at least for the Republic; Q. Claudius Quadrigarius, C. Licinius Macer, Valerius Antias, and Q. Aelius Tubero. Macer (in the 70s B.C.) and Tubero (in the 30s) were senators, who went against the grain of senatorial historiography in the first century B.C. by going back to the origins and writing *annales*.[84] In Macer's case it was because he had new evidence, the linen books,

81. 'It has all too often been the historian's assignment to assist his culture in remembering events that did not happen . . .' (Gay 1975, 206, rightly calling it a *cosmetic* activity). Cf. Luce 1977, 64f on *horror vacui* in Antias.

82. Rawson 1976, 714: 'one would suppose that the later books were largely filled out on the same principles of Greek rhetorical historiography' – i.e. εἰκός and ἀκριβεῖα, on which see below, pp. 49, 150.

83. Cf. p. 11 above: an event of 216 B.C. in book XXX (or XXXIII).

84. Unlike Coelius, Asellio, Sisenna and Sallust (n.63 above); but cf. Q. Cicero's *annales* (n.61).

to back up a new interpretation of the early history of the Republic.[85] Tubero used the linen books too, but it is possible that both these senatorial historians were provoked into writing annalistic history mainly by the necessity of refuting lower-class predecessors – Macer in answer to Quadrigarius, as Professor Frier has convincingly argued, and Tubero, as I shall try to show in Part II, in answer to Antias.

Antias, of course, is the other historian picked out at the beginning of this chapter as exceptionally voluminous. His history was nearly as long as Gellius', and very much more successful, exerting an extraordinarily powerful effect on contemporary and later writers, even when they refused to believe the material in it.[86] Like Gellius, he was evidently a *municipalis*, with a detectable bias towards his native town[87] – indeed, his *patria* was in the same Volscian country as Gellius' own. He was not a senator, but clearly needed neither experience of public affairs nor access to archives for his history of Rome; when he wanted documentary evidence, he invented it.[88] The expansion of the Roman past was probably Gellius' invention, but it was Antias who proved to be the master of the art.

The idea of creating history out of next to nothing was well known to the Greeks – Messenia, for instance, whose early history was as disappointingly blank as that of republican Rome, was equipped with a suitably heroic past by the third century B.C.[89] – and some of their techniques were borrowed by the Roman historians. One of them was the 'Homeric scene', which is found not only in the Battle of Lake Regillus, or the 'ten-year siege' of Veii,[90] but even in the details of such recent and un-legendary fighting as the Hannibalic War. (T. Quinctius Crispinus meets in battle a Campanian, Badius, who had once been his guest at Rome; unwilling to accept his insulting challenge, Crispinus vainly urges that they avoid each other in the fray, like Diomedes and Glaucus in *Iliad* VI.[91]) Herodotus and Thucydides could be similarly pressed into service, especially if there was a synchronism between the

85. Frier 1975, 94–6; cf. Ogilvie 1965, 7–12, Badian 1966, 15 and 22.
86. See below, pp. 33 (Livy and Antias), p. 46 (Varro and Antias).
87. Badian 1966, 36 n.110; Ogilvie 1965, 12 and 16.
88. Gelzer 1942, 223=1964, 272f, cf. 1935, 271f=1964, 222f, and Badian 1966, 21.
89. See below, p. 149.
90. Ogilvie 1965, 286, 670; also Münzer 1891, 21 (*Iliad* III 15).
91. Livy XXV 18.4–15, esp. 4.7 'Crispinus nec sibi nec illi ait hostes deesse in quibus virtutes ostendant' (*Iliad* VI 227–9).

events they described – Leonidas' Spartans at Thermopylae, the exile of Themistocles from Athens – and those of fifth-century Rome.[92] Famous or obscure, an episode from any foreign historical tradition might be fruitfully transplanted to early Rome.[93]

Native Roman material was available too: episodes of cultural history such as the origins of drama,[94] folk-tales and other fictional stories not previously tied down to a dateable occasion,[95] exemplary narratives invented to illustrate the origin or workings of particular aspects of Roman law,[96] and so on. All they needed was a plausible historical context and suitable names attributed to any previously anonymous characters.

The influence of contemporary politics on a historian's material can be detected from the very beginning of Roman historiography,[97] but it becomes all-pervading in the work of the later annalists, whose patricians and plebeians are given patently late-republican methods and motives; writers like Antias could draw on the history of their own time as profitably as on that of Homer and Herodotus. Moreover, politics in the Roman Republic were a matter of the *gloria* and *fama* of individual politicians and their families no less than of the ideological issues that divided *optimates* and *populares*. Here too there was a great opportunity for historians. The glorification of the writer's own family is demonstrable as early as Fabius Pictor,[98] and was brought to an extraordinary level of shamelessness by Antias.

That, however, is only the most obvious way in which the rivalry of the Roman aristocratic *gentes* could be exploited. The mere names in the consular and triumphal lists, that skeleton on which the later annalists fleshed out their narratives, could themselves provide ready-made historical material by the application of one simple principle.

92. Pais 1906, 176f, 221; Ogilvie 1965, 315, 359f. See further p. 31f below on Themistocles and Coriolanus, and cf. Münzer 1891, 44 n.5 on Dion. Hal. XIX 11=Hdt. VII 146.
93. E.g. Cornell 1974, 199–202 (on Livy X 38.2–12, from Campanian history), cf. 205 n.50 (Etruscan); Crawford 1976, 199 n.16 (Ser. Tullius and Hippias).
94. E.g. Livy VII 2.4–10, Val. Max. II 4.4; on which see the excellent discussion of Coffey 1976, 18–21.
95. Cf. Trenkner 1958, 9f and 169 on the anonymity of folktale characters; *ibid.* 23–30 and 180f on the debt of historiography to popular fiction; Mommsen 1870, 15–26=1879, 136–52 for a probable example (Coriolanus).
96. E.g. Livy II 5.10 (with Plut. *Popl.* 7.8), III 13.8, 44.5–12 etc; Ogilvie 1965, 241–3, 298, 417, 458, 477–8, 547.
97. See Pinsent 1964, 28f for a probable example in Cincius Alimentus.
98. Cf. (e.g.) Pinsent 1975, 16.

> It was universally accepted by the Romans as a literary (or psychological) technique that people act in character and that, therefore, you could assert things of people for which there was no actual evidence but which would have been characteristic of them to have done. Sp. Cassius . . . was said to have been a demagogue: very little is known of him, but, because he was a demagogue, he will have acted as historical demagogues, such as the Gracchi, did. So a historian was entitled to transfer the measures and policies of the Gracchi and attribute them to Sp. Cassius in order to give his life more verisimilitude.[99]

That principle could be applied to whole families as easily as to individuals.[100] A Decius once deliberately sacrificed his life to win victory for the Romans; a Manlius once had his own son executed for disobeying an order; a Valerius once gave the people the right of appeal. All those were genuinely ancient stories, whatever their historicity;[101] but in the later historical tradition, self-devotion can be attributed to any Decius,[102] over-strict discipline to any Manlius,[103] and care for the rights of the citizen to any Valerius.[104] In just the same way, a Fabian 'family character' was achieved by simply retrojecting the image of Q. Fabius Maximus 'Cunctator' back on to the earlier Fabii known from the consular and triumphal lists.[105] The type-casting of historical characters was an important part of the 'expansion of the past'.

—

I suggest, then, that it was through the *libri annales* of antiquarian writers that complete records of consulships and triumphs were made available by the last quarter of the second century B.C.; that Piso first incorporated them into a historical work, which he rightly called *Annals*; and that those records provided the raw material out of which the later annalists – in particular Cn. Gellius and Valerius

99. Ogilvie 1976, 20.
100. Cf. Klingner 1965, 82f – an innovation of Claudius Quadrigarius?
101. P. Decius Mus: Duris *FGrH* 76F56, cf. Diod. Sic. XXI 6.2. T. Manlius Torquatus: Cic. *Sull.* 32, cf. *fin.* I 23, 34–5, II 61. P. Valerius Publicola: Cic. *Flacc.* 1 and 25, cf. *rep.* III 53, *Acad.* II 13. (In his speeches, if not his theoretical works, Cicero is likely to have referred only to stories of Roman history that were well known to all his audience.)
102. Livy X 28.13 *familiare fatum*; Zonaras VIII 5, cf. VII 26, VIII 1.
103. Nisbet 1959, 73; cf. Pinsent 1975, 53 on Livy VII 4.2, 5.9.
104. Münzer 1891 *passim*, esp. 54–71. Cf., in general, Walsh 1961, 88–91.
105. See Pinsent 1977, 15 on Livy II 43.6, X 29.8, XXII 27.3.

Antias – constructed their voluminous, and largely imaginary, histories of Rome.

What they did with that raw material was what (for instance) the Greek dramatists did with the subject matter they inherited from Homer and the epic cycle: they had to keep to the basic outline of the story, but they considered themselves free to manipulate the traditional data to suit their own artistic purposes.[106] Essentially, the procedure was just the same as that of the rhetorician applying his *color* to the set of data provided by his *thesis*. The similarity is not fortuitous: the historians were trained in rhetoric, and applied their training to the art of history.

106. Arist. *Poetics* 1453b 22–6. Cf., for historians, Walbank 1960, 224; Poucet 1976, 208f.

Chapter 3

HISTORY AND RHETORIC

In the introduction to his *Roman Antiquities*, Dionysius of Halicarnassus announces his intention of combining three different types of historiography, which appeal respectively to connoisseurs of political debate, philosophical speculation, and simple enjoyment.[1]

The word he uses for the first type, *enagonios*, is the technical term for forensic and political oratory, as opposed to 'display' oratory where no element of real conflict was involved.[2] The *agones* of the lawcourts and the public assemblies were imagined as wrestling-matches, with the rival speakers as combatants[3] (an idea that survives in our use of phrases like 'the political arena'), and the metaphor extends also to the pleasure and knowledgeable involvement of the spectators. When Thucydides made Cleon attack his fellow-Athenians for treating political debate as a mere oratorical contest, which they could enjoy as if nothing important were at stake,[4] he was describing a state of affairs no different from that of late-republican Rome, where the audience in the Forum, at a prosecution which could be described with little exaggeration as a life-and-death struggle, enjoyed the performance 'as though Roscius were on the stage'.[5]

1. Dion Hal. I 8.3: *ἐξ ἁπάσης ἰδέας μικτὸν . . . μικτὸν ἐναγωνίου τε καὶ θεωητικῆς καὶ* ⟨. . .⟩, *ἵνα καὶ τοῖς περὶ τοὺς πολιτικοὺς διατρίβουσι λόγους καί τοῖς περὶ τὴν φιλόσοφον ἐσπουδακόσι θεωρίαν καί εἴ τισιν αὀχλήτου δεήσει διαγωγῆς ἐν ἱστορικοῖς ἀναγνώσμασιν ἀποχρώντως ἔχουσα φαίνηται*. (This tripartite distinction does not quite correspond to that drawn earlier in the sentence between narrations of wars, accounts of constitutions, and historical annals like the *Atthides*; for the third of these is explicitly described as monotonous and lacking in entertainment.) The political and philosophical readers reappear at XI 1.1, on which see p. 51 below.
2. So Dion. Hal. *Isaeus* 19, 20, *ad Amm*. I 3 (*ἀγών*). The term goes back at least to Aristotle (*Rhet*. III 1413b4, *ἀγωνιστική*).
3. Cf. Dion. Hal. *Dem*. 18, comparing Isocrates with the *ἐναγώνιος* orator: *καίτοι γε τοῖς ἀθληταῖς τῆς ἀληθινῆς λέξεως ἰσχυρὰς τὰς ἁψὰς προσεῖναι δεῖ καὶ ἀφύκτους τὰς λαβάς*. The courts and forum are an arena (Sen. *contr*. III pref. 13); the first stages of rhetorical education are *progymnasmata* (Bonner 1977, 250ff).
4. Thuc. III 38.2–7; cf. also 37.4–5 and 82.7 for the vocabulary (*ἀγωνισταί*, *ἀγώνισμα* etc).
5. Cic. *Brut*. 290, cf. 183–93 on the importance of popular approval to the orator: for the *corona*, see (e.g.) Cic. *fin*. IV 74, *ND* II 1, *TD* I 10, Catullus 53. *Vitae*

Where a policy debate or a political trial was part of his subject, then of course the historian had to report what was said. But from the very beginning this involved an ambiguity, stated in its classic form by Thucydides: since he and his informants found it difficult to recall the exact words used, 'my method has been, while keeping as closely as possible to the general sense of the words that were actually used, to make the speakers say what, in my opinion, was called for by each situation' (*ὡς δ' ἂν ἐδόκουν ἐμοί ἕκαστοι περί τῶν αἰεὶ παρόντων τὰ δέοντα μάλιστ' εἰπεῖν . . . οὕτως εἴρηται*).[6] Polybius as well, true to his Thucydidean standards, did his best to report what was actually said – 'the proper function of history', as he put it, in polemic against Timaeus[7] – but most historians simply took advantage of Thucydides' concession without attempting to fulfil his condition, and composed appropriate speeches for their characters *ad libitum*.

The language of conflict is still used, but on a different level: the historian is not only reporting the *agones* of his characters, he is fighting one of his own. As in a real wrestling-match, the man with the greater strength wins, but here *δύναμις* means *literary* force,[8] and the opponents are literary rivals. So Polybius' readers will expect him to take part in the 'contest' (*ἐν ἀγωνίσματι*) by providing set-piece speeches at each critical point in his narrative; and Diodorus Siculus, though protesting against the wanton insertion of speeches without regard for the proper demarcation between history and oratory, none the less insists that where the context requires it, the historian must steel himself to 'go down and enter the contest'.[9]

Timaeus, according to Polybius, wrote his speeches 'like one exercising on a set theme in the schools'.[10] and the pairs of speeches 'for and against' which Polybius' own readers evidently expected would have been no more than the two sides of a *controversia* on a historical theme, as produced by the pupils of a *rhetor*.[11] The Hellenistic historians had been brought up on that sort of competi-

---

dimicatio: Cic. *Planc.* 77, *Balb.* 23, *Arch.* 14 etc; *Cael.* 47, 'de salute aut de gloria dimicare'.

6. Thuc. I 22.1 (trans. Rex Warner); see Walbank 1965b, 3f and *passim.*

7. Pol. XII 25a.5–25b.4; Walbank 1965b, 7–18.

8. E.g. Pol. XII 25a.5, XXXVI 1.7, Diod. Sic. XX 1.2, Joseph. *contra Apionem* I 24.

9. Pol. XXXVI 1.1; Diod. Sic. XX 2.1, *τεθαρρηκότως συγκαταβαίνων πρὸς τοὺς ἐν τοῖς λόγοις ἀγῶνας.*

10. Pol. XII 25a.5, b.4, k.8, 26.9; Walbank 1967, 386.

11. Pol. XXXVI 1.1–2 and 5 (*κατὰ μέρος, εἰς ἀμφότερα τὰ μέρη, παράθεσις*). *Ibid.* 1.7 for historians 'practising [*sc.* oratory] on their readers'.

tive exercise, just as the Romans were, and they and their readers were connoisseurs of performance in it. The immense number of matching speeches in Dionysius of Halicarnassus' *Roman Antiquities*, so wearying for us, represents the element of his history which was specifically designed to appeal to the *enagonios* reader, and no doubt did so.

—

Dionysius, like Diodorus, defended the inclusion of speeches on the grounds that what was said, no less than what was done, is part of the material which the historian must preserve from oblivion.[12] Neither grasped that that admirable principle necessarily presupposed accurate first-hand knowledge of what *was* said, and therefore was only applicable to contemporary history of the kind Thucydides and Polybius wrote. The reason for their failure to understand the point is itself of some interest, and will occupy us in the next chapter; for the moment it is enough to point out that for both Diodorus and Dionysius this defence of speeches is essentially secondary, brought out for form's sake and perhaps because of an uneasy conscience. The real justification for the speeches was stylistic – to have the history 'adorned with varied colours',[13] for the pleasure of the reader.

We must not forget the 'commercial' necessity of providing the reader with what he wanted. Some historians wrote for a living,[14] and all were judged on their stylistic quality if (as was normally the case) they had no new material to justify their work.[15] Cicero's complaints about the style of the Roman annalists, and his enthusiasm for that of a writer familiar with Greek models, show what the historian had to provide if he hoped to be read.[16]

Rome in Cicero's time was a city of hellenized culture.[17] Cicero's own familiarity with the Greek historiographical tradition is best

12. Dion. Hal. VII 66.3 (see p. 52 below, on the significance of *διεξελθεῖν*); Diod. Sic. XX 2.2.

13. Diod. Sic. XX 2.1, *τῇ ποικιλίᾳ κεκοσμῆσθαι*: cf. p. 4 n. 8 above.

14. See Pol. XII 25e. 3, XVI 14.3 and 8 (*ὠφελείας χάριν*); cf. Juv. *Sat.* VII 1–7, 98–105 and p. 155 below, on patronage of historians. Cf. Cic. *fin.* V 52 on the *popularity* of history, even among readers of humble status. *Delectatio* was the aim, both of history (Cic. *de or.* II 59, Pliny *ep.* V 8.4, Lucian *Historia* 13) and of rhetoric (Sen. *contr.* 9 pref.1, Tac. *dial.* 6).

15. Livy *pref.*2; cf. Sall. *Cat.* 3.2, Livy VI 20.8, Pliny *ep.* VII 4.3 (on *facta dictis aequare*).

16. Cic. *de or.* II 51–64, *de leg.* I 5–6 (annalists); *fam.* V 12.1 (Lucceius). At *de or.* II 51 it is specifically the *non*-hellenized Roman who says of an historian 'satis est non esse mendacem'.

17. Griffin 1976, 89–96 for a review of its various aspects; cf. also p. 154f below.

illustrated by his correspondence with L. Lucceius, a senator and historian whose close friends included a Greek historian from Mytilene and a Greek philosopher from Alexandria.[18] The famous request of Cicero to Lucceius for a monograph on the years 63–57 B.C. is notable for the number of Greek *exempla* it cites: the models suggested are Callisthenes, Timaeus, Polybius and – by implication – Clitarchus,[19] and it is clear from Cicero's remarks on *ornatio* and the laws of history that Clitarchan rather than Polybian standards of historical rigour are what he has in mind. In particular, the subject is recommended as including 'changes of circumstance and vicissitudes of fortune' which will particularly delight the reader, giving rise as they do to 'surprise, suspense, joy, pain, hope and fear'.[20]

The reading public now wanted what Duris and Phylarchus had provided for their Greek audience 200 years before – dramatic presentation and the pleasure of stirred emotions.[21] It was in precisely such terms that Quintilian praised the affecting eloquence of Livy's *speeches*,[22] for the techniques of Phylarchan 'tragic history' were learnt in the schools of the rhetoricians.[23]

The influence of rhetoric on historiography was not confined, however, to the invention of agonistic speeches and purple passages designed to play on the reader's emotions. Cicero held that the right style for historiography was smooth, easy and flowing – which ruled out melodramatic scenes of the Phylarchus type – and would no doubt have agreed with Diodorus that the insertion of inappropriate speeches would break the flow;[24] yet he took it for granted that an *orator* was needed, to achieve both the flowing style itself

18. Cic. *fam.* V 12, cf. *Att.* IX 1.3, 11.3, Caes. *BC* III 18.3 (Theophanes), Cic. *Cael.* 54 (Dio).

19. Cic. *fam.* V 12.2, 3, 5, 7; cf. *Brut.* 43 for Clitarchus at 12.5.

20. Cic. *fam.* V 12.4–5 on *temporum varietates* etc: 'nihil est aptius ad delectationem lectoris' (n.14 above). Cf. Sall. *BJ* 5.1, and Tacitus' complaint at *Ann.* IV 33.

21. E.g. Duris *FGrH* 76F1 on Theopompus and Ephorus (*οὔτε γὰρ μιμήσεως μετέλαβον οὐδεμιᾶς οὔτε ἡδονῆς ἐν τῷ φράσαι*); Jacoby 1926, 117, 'dramatische anschaulichkeit und (daraus entspringende) ergötzung des lesers'; Pol. II 56.7–12 on Phylarchus; Walbank 1972, 34f and 38f. Cicero evidently approved of Duris (*Att.* VI 1.18, 'homo in historia diligens').

22. Quint. X 1.101: 'in contionibus supra quam enarrari potest eloquentem ... affectus quidem, praecipue eos qui sunt dulciores, ut parcissime dicam, nemo historicorum commendavit magis'.

23. Cf. Cic. *de inv.* I 27 on *varietas* and unexpected vicissitudes in the orator's narrative.

24. Cic. *de or.* II 64 ('genus orationis fusum atque tractum et cum lenitate quadam aequabiliter profluens, sine hac iudiciali asperitate et sine sententiarum forensibus

(*flumen orationis*) and also the 'variety of colours' necessary to adorn it, complaining that no instruction on this point was to be found in the manuals of the art of rhetoric.[25] Ephorus and Theopompus, criticized by Duris for not providing dramatic effects for the reader's enjoyment, are 'men of outstanding genius' for Cicero – precisely because they were the products of Isocrates' 'famous factory of rhetoricians' whose cosmetics Cicero himself made use of in his own historical work.[26] As Duris remarked, they paid attention only to style – no doubt in the manner of their master, 'the slave of smoothness'.[27] Since in Cicero's day elegance of prose style was to be found only in oratory, it was in that sense that he called the writing of history 'the one work most appropriate to the orator'.[28]

Even so, an effective prose style, whether smooth and flowing or vivid and dramatic, was only one of the habits the potential historian picked up from his oratorical education. Much more important, and more dangerous for the proper practice of history, was the cavalier attitude to historical fact which his training encouraged him to adopt.

—

In a famous passage of the *Brutus*, Cicero (as a character in the dialogue) dwells on the similar fates of Themistocles and of his Roman contemporary Coriolanus: both great patriots, both exiled by an ungrateful people, both deserting to their countries' enemies, both dying by suicide. 'For although you, Atticus, have a different version about Coriolanus, yet allow me to prefer this manner of his death.' At this Atticus laughs, and says: 'It's your choice – for orators *are* allowed to tell lies in history, in order to give more point to what they say'.[29] Clitarchus and Stratocles, he goes on, had invented a suicide for Themistocles just as Cicero had for Coriolanus, adding to Thucydides' account a dramatic swallowing

aculeis'), cf. 54 and 58 for *lenitas*; Diod. Sic. XX 1.1. Cf. Fantham 1972, 174f on the *flumen* image.

25. Cic. *de or*. II 62, cf. 51 (need for orator), 54 (*colores*), 64 (*artes rhetorum*); *ibid*. 53f on *ornatio* as the necessary ingredient. As Wardman rightly points out (1976, 75), the only available theoretical rules were rhetorical ones.

26. Cic. *de or*. II 57, cf. Duris *FGrH* 76F1 (n.21 above), Cic. *Att*. II 1.1 (p. 6 above).

27. Duris *loc. cit*.: *αὐτοῦ δὲ τοῦ γράφειν μόνον ἐπεμελήθησαν*. Dion. Hal. *Isocr*. 13 (cf. 2) on Isocrates and *λειότης*.

28. Cic. *leg*. I 5, 'opus . . . unum hoc oratorium maxime'.

29. Cic. *Brut*. 42: 'tuo vero, inquit, arbitratu; quoniam quidem concessum est rhetoribus ementiri in historiis, ut aliquid dicere possint argutius'. *Pace* Wardman (1976, 102), Atticus' remark is not restricted to Greek practice.

of bull's blood: 'for they could elaborate that kind of death in a rhetorical and tragic manner, whereas the banal reality offered no material for elaboration'.[30] So, Atticus concludes, since it suits Cicero's case to have Coriolanus and Themistocles alike in all respects, he will let him have even the bull and the bowl of blood for Coriolanus too, if he likes.

Tuo arbitratu . . . quare ita tibi quadrat: the orator was free to falsify the facts, if he could thereby present his argument more pointedly. It was of course only *qua* orator that he could do so. Cicero insists elsewhere that the *historian's* first rule is never to dare to say anything false;[31] it is clear that Atticus is made to cite Clitarchus and Stratocles as writing 'non tam historico quam oratorio genere',[32] and that though he allows Cicero to make his point in the argument with a historical distortion, his own account of Coriolanus' death (or Thucydides' account of Themistocles') is not thought of as being in any way impugned by it.

But how many Romans, or Hellenistic Greeks, kept the standards of history and those of oratory so separate in their minds? It has been well said that the insistence of Cicero and others on truth as the criterion of history was 'precisely because they knew the dangers of confusion, and of the misapplication to history of a principle which was valid only for rhetoric'.[33] The very nature of rhetorical education made such confusion and misapplication practically inevitable.

Take, for instance, the two *theseis* on historical themes referred to in the first chapter. The story of L. Flamininus and the bloodthirsty prostitute, which came from Valerius Antias, was entirely inconsistent with the *real* evidence for Flamininus' misconduct contained in Cato's censorial speech against him.[34] Livy describes it as a 'fabula sine auctore edita'; perhaps it had been invented by a *rhetor* to provide the theme Seneca reports, or more probably Antias himself, writing *oratorio genere* like Clitarchus and

30. *Ibid.* 43: 'hanc enim mortem rhetorice et tragice ornare potuerunt, illa mors vulgaris nullam praebebat materiem ad ornatum'.

31. Cic. *de or.* II 62: 'nam quis nescit primam esse historiae legem, ne quid falsi dicere audeat? deinde ne quid veri non audeat? ne quae suspicio gratiae sit in scribendo? ne quae simultatis?'.

32. Cic. *Brut.* 286, on Demochares; at *Brut.* 44 Cicero calls Atticus himself 'rerum Romanarum auctor . . . *religiosissimus*'. Cf. Jocelyn 1977, 342 on the difference in criteria between dialogues and history proper.

33. Walker 1952, 146 (cf. 150f on Tac. *Agr.* 10.1).

34. Livy XXXIX 42.7–12 (Cato), 43.1–3 (Valerius); Fraccaro 1911, 15–21 = 1956, 426–30.

Stratocles, had made it up out of dissatisfaction with the rhetorical possibilities of the real facts, with the schools gladly appropriating it as a *thesis*. As for Cicero's supposed defence of Popillius for parricide, that was certainly invented by the rhetoricians themselves, to provide a paradoxical case for their pupils to sharpen their skills on.[35] In just the same way they took the story of L. Metellus the *pontifex maximus*, who rescued the holy objects from the temple of Vesta when it burnt down in 241 B.C., and supposed with no historical justification that he was blinded in doing so, thus becoming arguably ineligible for priestly office.[36] When so many of the set themes belonged to an incredible world of pure fiction, it is not surprising that the historical subjects were treated in an equally fictional way.[37]

That was all very well, provided the fictions were recognized for what they were. But Popillius the parricide and blinded Metellus were accepted as historical fact within two generations of their invention in the schools,[38] and acceptance was even faster when the fiction originated with an historian who could be cited as if he were a real authority. Livy reported Antias' version of the Flamininus story at length, even though he did not believe it, and an innocent reader might well remember the false account – adorned as it is with Livy's own rhetoric – rather than the true one. Cicero too, though he must have known the authoritative version from Cato's speech, was prepared to exploit Antias' fiction in a philosophical dialogue, the *de senectute* (even attributing it to Cato himself!), just as he used the false story of Coriolanus' death in the *de amicitia*; again, why should the ordinary reader know that the 'facts' given him in a dialogue with a historical setting were subject to less stringent criteria of truth than those in a proper history? When Cato's speeches were no longer read, and Livy and Cicero were classics, Antias' *fabula* would be taken for granted as historical fact – as it is in Valerius Maximus.[39]

35. Sen. *contr.* VII 2.8, 'declamatoribus placuit parricidi reum fuisse'; Homeyer 1964, 13f, 35f.

36. Sen. *contr.* II 4; Leuze 1904, *passim.*

37. Petr. *Sat.* 1, Tac. *dial.* 35.4; Clarke 1953, 91f, etc. For popular fiction as the common background to both declamation and historiography, see Trenkner 1958, 180–6, esp. 183f.

38. Plut. *Cic.* 48.1, Pliny *NH* VII 141. Even the best historians could be led astray by rhetorical sources: see Syme 1964, 84–94 on Sallust and the 'first conspiracy', following baseless hints in Cicero's speeches.

39. Livy XXXIX 43.1–4, cf. Winterbottom 1974, 234 n.2 ('Livy, rejecting him, took the opportunity for some declamation of his own'); Cic. *sen.* 42, *amic.* 42 (cf. *Brut.* 42f, above); Val. Max. II 9.3.

Cicero himself would have had no patience with this naive attitude; he expected his readers to be sophisticated enough to distinguish the *oratorium genus* from the *historicum*. When Atticus laughs at Cicero's use of the false tradition on Coriolanus and Themistocles, it indicates a sort of professional complicity – the acknowledgment of a subtlety recognized by the *cognoscenti* but which might well mislead the ignorant.

This distinction, between those who understand the technique and those who do not, came naturally to an orator. In pointing out that the successful speaker must please the ordinary people as well as his fellow-experts, Cicero distinguishes the two parts of the audience as those who recognize what effect the speaker is having on them, and those who know *why* he is having that effect.[40] Elsewhere, more brutally, he makes Scaevola define the great orator as one who seems to the intelligent to be speaking eloquently, and to the stupid to be speaking the truth.[41] Persuasion is the orator's business, to make his case seem 'better and more probable'; the *prudentes*, by which term Cicero means anyone who understood what he was taught in the rhetor's school, know that to achieve that end the orator will not feel himself bound to stick to the truth. But he must make it *sound* like the truth, and the ignorant may be taken in.

Being 'like the truth', *veri similis*, was one of the three qualities required of *narratio* in the rhetorical handbooks. (The others were clarity and brevity.) Plausibility was what mattered. Even if the orator's narration was true, he must still make sure that it sounded plausible, and not open to any *a priori* objection on grounds of inherent improbability; if his facts were invented, of course, this was all the more necessary. Cornificius' handbook adds the caution that care must be taken in inventing *narratio* where the other side has documentary evidence or the testimony of an authoritative witness – a tactical recommendation, not an ethical one. Either truth or falsehood would serve the orator's purpose, provided he made it convincing: his *narratio*, in Aristotle's succinct formula-

40. Cic. *Brut.* 187, 'ut qui audient quid efficiatur, ego etiam cur id efficiatur intellegam'; *ibid.* 183–93 in general on the judgement of the *vulgus* and that of the *docti* and *intellegentes*.

41. Cic. *de or.* II 35 (addressing L. Crassus): 'satis id est magnum quod potes praestare, ut in iudiciis ea causa quamcumque tu dicis melior et probabilior esse videatur, ut in contionibus et in sententiis dicendis ad persuadendum tua plurima valeat oratio, denique ut *prudentibus diserte, stultis etiam vere* videare dicere'. As Clarke points out (1953, 54), Cicero does not rebut Scaevola's cynical view.

tion, was intended either to explain what happened or to make the jury suppose it had happened.[42]

Plausibility could be achieved by effective 'character-drawing', particularly of one's opponent, and for this purpose wit and ridicule were particulary useful.[43] In making that point, Cicero provides a *locus classicus* for the orator's attitude to factual accuracy. C. Caesar is discussing types of humour in book II of the *de oratore*: he cites with admiration the story invented by L. Crassus in his prosecution of Memmius (that Memmius, in a quarrel over a girl in Tarracina, had bitten his rival's arm, and that all the walls of the town bore the slogan LLLMM, for 'lacerat lacertum Largi mordax Memmius'), and points out that this type of wit is particularly valuable to the orator, whether for making up an invented *narratio*, as Crassus had done, or, if the real facts were to be used, for spraying them with a few little fibs:[44]

> Perspicitis genus hoc quam sit facetum, quam elegans, quam oratorium, sive habeas vere quod narrare possis, quod tamen est mendaciunculis aspergendum, sive fingas.

Narratio in a speech, designed to persuade, is not the same as narrative in a history, designed to report. When a historian writes *rhetorice*, he is allowed to invent as an orator invents, to add point or conviction to his story, but the reader is expected to be able to recognize what he is doing – with a laugh, perhaps, like Atticus – and assess it accordingly. Scaevola's distinction between the *prudentes* and the *stulti* applies to the historian's audience as well as the orator's.[45]

—

But the *stulti* are not only numerous, they are logically necessary. The successful orator has to convince the jury or the assembly that what he says is true; the art of persuasion does, after all, require that the audience be persuaded, and not merely by admiration of a fellow-professional's technique. The historian writing rhetorically

42. *Rhet. Her.* I 16, Cic. *de inv.* I 29, etc. Arist. *Rhet.* III 1416b36–17al (qualifying the requirement of brevity): τὸ λέγειν ὅσα δηλώσει τὸ πρᾶγμα ἢ ὅσα ποιήσει ὑπολαβεῖν γεγονέναι. See Gelzer 1935, 269f=1964,221, and (on *narratio* in general) Bonner 1977, 260–3, 291–4.

43. Arist. *Rhet.* III 1417a3–b8, in the chapter on narration; Cic. *de or.* II 241.

44. Cic. *de or.* II 240 ('salsa, ac tamen a te ipso ficta narratio'); quotation from 241. Cf. *ibid.* 237 on the limits of the use of *ridicula*: truth is not mentioned.

45. Especially as some of them were reading history (or having it read to them) precisely because of the *rhetorical* material provided by the historian: Dion. Hal. I 8.3 (p. 27 above).

is, no doubt, more concerned with exciting admiration, but he too needs his audience of non-experts: *mutatis mutandis*, his success will be the same as the orator's if he convinces them that his version of the events is the right one. So despite Cicero and Atticus, the use of oratorical tricks in history cannot be passed off with a laugh. They were designed to persuade, and the appearance of Popillius the parricide in Plutarch's *Life of Cicero*, and of blind Metellus in the elder Pliny, shows that not all readers were able to resist the persuasion.

We, the modern readers of ancient historiography, are in constant danger of being numbered among the *stulti*. It takes a substantial effort of imagination to re-create the state of mind of a Roman reader familiar with all the techniques of the rhetorical schools and conditioned to discount them.[46] When we read of Marcus Manlius hurled to his death from the very cliff the Gauls were climbing when he saved the Capitol, we must not infer that the Gauls really climbed the Tarpeian Rock, and turn the topographical evidence upside-down to justify the idea, but recognize a *mendaciunculum* invented by an historian 'ut aliquid dicere possit argutius';[47] another of the same type comes in the speech attributed to Scipio Africanus at his trial before the people, supposedly on the very anniversary of the battle of Zama.[48] The prosecution of a national hero on a charge of treason was precisely the sort of paradoxical *thesis* the schools loved to set; in historiographical terms, it provided just that sequence of vicissitudes that particularly appealed to readers; and any historian with a feeling for its rhetorical possibilities would consider himself practically *obliged* to point up the dramatic irony with an invented coincidence of time or place.

The Scipio story also provides a neat example of what happens to historical data in the rhetorical tradition. As Polybius tells it, Scipio's crushing reply to the prosecuting tribune caused the assembly to break up; in the author quoted by Gellius, the people follow Scipio to the Capitol to give thanks; in Antias' version (used by Livy), the tribunes' *scribae* and *viatores* get up and go with

46. With Tacitus, for example, we have to remember that the rhetorically-trained reader was accustomed to the exploitation of rumour (cf. *Rhet. Her.* II 12, etc), and therefore more resistant than we are to the historian's innuendoes.

47. Cf. n.29 above. See Wiseman 1979b, 37–45 on Livy VI 20.12, Plut. *Cam.* 36.8, Dio VII fr. 26.2.

48. Gell. *NA* IV 18.3 and 6, cf. Livy XXXVIII 56.5–6 (not genuine: cf. Cic. *off.* III 4, *Brut.* 77); Fraccaro 1911a, 233–9=1956, 273–7. It was invented to elaborate the account in Polybius XXIII 14.

Scipio too; and by the time we reach Valerius Maximus the prosecuting tribune himself has joined Scipio's honorific escort![49] The elder Seneca is full of examples of successive declaimers 'outbidding' their rivals' treatment of the *thesis* in just this way: when they wrote history they naturally did the same.

—

Manlius and Scipio were both examples of the rhetorical commonplace that the populace is often ungrateful to its saviours;[50] equally, Scipio's behaviour could be used to illustrate self-confidence, or Manlius' fate to exemplify heroism perverted into tyranny.[51] The exploitation of historical examples to back up a generalized *topos* was part of the regular stock-in-trade of the rhetorical schools.[52] It was a trivialization of Cicero's insistence that the orator should have a wide education, including the study of history. By bringing out instances from the past, Cicero had said, the orator gives great pleasure to his audience and adds *auctoritas* and *fides* to his speech; with his country's history at his finger-tips, he can summon a wealth of witnesses from the dead – like Appius Claudius in the *pro Caelio*, or the long line of Metelli in P. Servilius' speech to the Senate in 57 B.C.[53]

It is also clear from Cicero that *exempla* of this kind were the main value of history for the individual in his public and private life, as well as for the orator in his craft. The great *pro Archia* passage on the justification of literature (particularly history) as the source of virtue, though naturally tailored to suit the client's particular circumstances, must have been both intelligible and acceptable to the jury, not just an intellectual's fancy but part of every Roman's sense of *mos maiorum*.[54] It was said that the elder Cato had written out his *Origines*, in his own hand, in large letters for his son to read; true or not, the story illustrates the importance

49. Pol. XXIII 14.4, Gell. *NA* IV 18.4–5, Livy XXXVIII 51.12, Val. Max. III 7.1e.
50. See Fraccaro 1911a, 273=1956, 299, on Livy XXXVIII 50.7, Val. Max, V 3.2a etc; the Coriolanus and Themistocles stories exploited in the *Brutus* (p. 00 above) come under the same heading.
51. Val. Max. III 7.1 (Fraccaro 1911a, 267=1956, 296); Livy VI 20.5 (Wiseman 1979b, 47), cf. Val. Max. VI 2.1a (*de severitate*).
52. See Bonner 1949, 61f; Sen. *contr.* VII 5.13 for its abuse.
53. Cic. *orator* 120 ('commemoratio antiquitatis exemplorumque prolatio'), *Verr.* III 209; see also *de or.* I 18, 201, 256 on *exempla* as the main contribution of a historical education. *Excitare ab inferis*: Cic. *Brut.* 322; *Cael.* 33, *red. Sen.* 25.
54. Cic. *Arch.* 14 ('pleni omnes sunt libri, plenae sapientium voces, plena exemplorum vetustas' etc), cf. 28; at sections 1 and 13 he also defends Archias' *studia* as helping towards his own oratorical ability.

to the Romans of the exemplary function of history in moral education.[55]

The study of history as an incentive to virtue was a commonplace in Greek thought, associated in the historians of the first century B.C. with both the Herodotean motive of preserving great deeds from oblivion and the Thucydidean one of providing practical lessons from the past.[56] For Livy, the main value of history lay in providing examples of conduct to imitate or avoid, whether for the individual or the state; so for Tacitus too, who believed that men had to be taught by example to distinguish good conduct from evil, and therefore made it his business to record each in such a way as to encourage or deter.[57] But this noble aim, so suited to the Romans' strong ethical sense, was also an insidious temptation. When Cicero urges Lucceius, in writing his history, to praise what he approves of and blame what he does not, it is as part of a request that the historian should bend the rules, to the extent of showing more favour to Cicero himself than the truth allows: the behaviour to be reprehended was the treachery of Cicero's own enemies.[58]

Even where his own political interests are not involved, in a splendid passage on history as the light of truth and the educator of life, Cicero still insists that it needs the voice of the orator to expound it.[59] The same dilemma recurs: the orator provides a style worthy of the material, but also a technique that cannot help but distort it. Just as the criteria that apply to historical narrative are contaminated by those that apply to rhetorical *narratio*, so the *exempla* that help the individual to form his moral judgments become fatally confused with the *exempla* that help the orator to make his case persuasive.

Cornelius Nepos and Iulius Hyginus each wrote a collection of *exempla*, as well as biographies of famous men which were no doubt designed for the same purpose of moral instruction;[60] following them, Valerius Maximus composed his handbook of memor-

55. Plut. *Cato maior* 20.7: *ὅπως οἴκοθεν ὑπάρχοι τῷ παιδὶ πρὸς ἐμπειρίαν τῶν παλαιῶν καὶ πατρίων ὠφελεῖσθαι*.
56. Dion Hal. I 6.3–4 (cf. Hdt. I pref.), Diod. Sic. I 1.4–5 (cf. Thuc. I 22.4).
57. Livy pref. 10; Tac. *Ann*. IV 33.2, III 65.1 (explicit examples at *Ann*. II 32.2, IV 20.2, XIV 64.3, XV 57.2, *Hist*. I 3, etc).
58. Cic. *fam*. IV 12.3–4.
59. Cic. *de or*. II 36: 'historia vero testis temporum, lux veritatis, vita memoriae, magistra vitae, nuntia vetustatis, qua voce alia, nisi oratoris, immortalitati commendatur?'.
60. *Exempla*: Charisius I 146K, Gell. *NA* VI 18.11 (Nepos), X 18.5 (Hyginus). Hyginus' *de vita rebusque illustrium virorum*: Gell. *NA* I 14.1 (on C. Fabricius, a well-known *exemplum* of incorruptible frugality), cf. VI 1.2 on Scipio Africanus.

able deeds and sayings for the convenience of those looking for examples to learn from.[61] In pursuit of the same educative ideal as Cicero, Livy and Tacitus, Valerius produced a collection of schematic caricatures in which historical accuracy is entirely subordinated to rhetorical 'point'. In him the contamination is seen at its most extreme, but he is only the logical consequence of a view of history which saw its purpose as praise and blame. If the historian has to provide paradigms of good and evil in order to influence his reader's attitudes and behaviour, then persuasion is his business no less than the orator's.

Praise and blame were, in fact, the subject matter of one of the three basic subdivisions of oratory.[62] The epideictic *genus*, though not much practised as such in Rome, was however exemplified by the funerary oration[63] – and Roman funerals, as Polybius told his Greek readers, were above all 'incentives to virtue'.[64] So were the honorific statues, the captured spoils above the door, the busts of ancestors in consular or triumphal regalia, the inscriptions on temples and porticos put up by triumphant generals from their booty; all these were *monimenta*, 'reminders' of the virtues of the men of old which were meant to spur their descendants on to equal them.[65] It is characteristic of the Roman attitude to history that the same phrase, 'monumenta rerum gestarum', was applied equally to these visible reminders and to the works of historians,[66] which were thought of as performing essentially the same function. The aristocratic society of republican Rome gave new meaning to the Hellenistic concept of history as the best education and training for life, but it did not help the ideal that history should always tell the truth. Funerary orations and the inscriptions on portrait busts were notoriously unreliable for historical fact:[67] masquerading as objective record, they were really a means of persuasion, to convince the Forum crowd or the visitor in the *atrium* of the greatness of the

61. Val. Max. pref., 'documenta sumere volentibus'; cf. Livy pref. 10 for *documenta*, which are defined by Varro (*LL* VI 62) as 'exempla docendi causa'.
62. *Arist. Rhet.* I 1358b 12 (*ἐπιδεικτικοῦ δέ τὸ μὲν ἔπαινος τὸ δε ψόλος*): *Rhet, Her.* I 2, Cic. *de inv.* I 7, Quint. III 4.1f etc.
63. Cic. *de or.* II 341; Varro *Men.* 376B, in a satire *περὶ ἐγκωμίων*. Cf. also Dion. Hal. V 17.3–5.
64. Pol. VI 52.10, 53.9f, 54.3.
65. Sall. *BJ* 4.5–7, Pliny *NH* XXXV 7, Pliny *ep.* II 7.5 (cf. VIII 6.13), Suet. *Aug.* 31.5 ('velut ad exemplar . . .'), etc. I hope to treat this subject in more detail elsewhere.
66. E.g. Cic. *de or.* I 201, 'monumenta rerum gestarum et vetustatis exempla oratori nota esse debere'; Festus (Paulus) 123L defines *monimentum* as 'quicquid ob memoriam alicuius factum est, ut fana, porticus, scripta et carmina'.
67. Livy IV 16.4, VIII 40.4f, Cic. *Brut.* 62.

dead man, and to encourage his descendants to go and do likewise. The aims of the historian were very similar, and he was just as capable of well-intentioned misrepresentation to make his point.

At every level, then – from the conception of historiography as a persuasive art, and the assumption that only the orator could do it stylistic justice, down to the all-pervading influence of the rhetorical schools, and the techniques that practically every educated Roman had absorbed there in his formative years – in the hellenized Rome of the first century B.C. history and rhetoric were inseparable. The *prudentes*, men like Cicero and Atticus, flattered themselves that they could distinguish historical standards of truth from rhetorical ones; but the very nature of the art of persuasion made it inevitable that distortions, exaggerations and downright fictions would come to be widely accepted as historical fact, and that the reading public – and even the historians themselves – would lack the capacity to separate what deserved to be believed from what did not.

Chapter 4

UNHISTORICAL THINKING

In his great book *The Idea of History*, R. G. Collingwood defined historical thinking by adapting Francis Bacon's phrase about the natural scientist, who 'puts nature to the question'. The historian does not merely decide whether or not to believe what he is told: he puts his 'authorities' to the question, torturing them to extract answers to questions chosen by *him*. It is striking that the same metaphor occured to Thucydides, who complained that most people accept stories about their country's past *ἀβασανίστως* – not just 'without enquiry', but without the torture that was used in the ancient world to extract evidence from slaves.[1]

But Thucydides was unique. He set himself, as Professor Finley observes, a standard of accuracy unparalleled in the ancient world:

> The only possible models were among a few philosophers and among the medical writers of the school of Hippocrates, then at its height on the island of Cos. But the mere existence of parallels will not explain why Thucydides transferred their passion for accuracy to the field of history. Like all such personal matters, the question defies explanation. Whatever the reason, it left him an exceedingly lonely figure in the history of ancient historical writing, for not one man after him, among either the Greek historians or the Roman, shared his passion.[2]

If his view of historical investigation has something in common with Collingwood's,[3] then he is the exception that proves the rule.

1. Collingwood 1946, 237, 269 etc. Thuc. I 20.1; cf. 21.1, on the events of the distant past as *ἀνεξέλεγκτα*.

2. Finley 1968, 49. Perhaps one: see Bruce 1967, 3–15 on the author of the 'Hellenica Oxyrhynchia'. And Polybius may be a partial exception, in the aspiration if not in the achievement (Walbank 1965, 8f).

3. Not that Collingwood recognized it; he was more concerned with Thucydides' 'unhistorical' use of detailed narrative to affirm psychological laws, to move (in Finley's words) 'from the particular to the universal, from the concrete events to the underlying patterns and generalities . . .' (Collingwood 1946, 29f; Finley 1968, 53).

The historians of Greece and Rome did *not* 'put their authorities to the question'. They did not have the questions to put, because they were incapable of the 'historical imagination' needed for the historian to relive for himself, as Collingwood put it, the states of mind into which he enquires.[4]

Thucydides' reconstruction of archaic Greece in his *archaeologia* (I 2–19) is perhaps the nearest approach to it, but here too Thucydides stands alone. The Romans' conception of their own distant past, with Romulus' thatched hut and skin-clad senators meeting in the meadows, was indeed partly based on a real tradition (e.g. the preserved 'hut of Romulus') or correct antiquarian inference (e.g. the waterlogged Velabrum),[5] but what accurate elements it happened to include were really accidental, part of a moral stereotype of *prisca virtus* rather than the achievements of historians concerned to find out for its own sake what conditions were like in Romulus' Rome. In any case, the historians soon abandoned any imaginative grasp they may have had of the primitive settlement, narrating instead a regal and early-republican Rome either already indistinguishable from the city of their own day, or developing into it by a teleological succession of regular advances. Each approach – the 'substantialism' of which Collingwood accused Livy, or the 'philosophy of the straight-line progression' deplored by Heurgon – was equally schematic and, by our standards, unhistorical.[6]

Even Cicero, who has been rightly praised for his feeling for the past, his command of antiquarian evidence, and his care in achieving historical accuracy for dialogues set in the generation before his own,[7] could probably not have reconstructed in his imagination a historical scene further back or more distant from his experience

4. Collingwood 1946, 231ff. Dionysius' allusions to the Thucydides passage are revealing: I 74.3 (*τὴν πίστιν ἀβασάνιστον καταλιπεῖν*), IV 30.3 (*ἀταλαιπωρία*, cf. p. 48 below), referring merely to the consultation of several 'authorities' about the chronology of the regal period – including the foundation story itself. Cf. also *ἀποχρώντως* at Thuc. I 21.1 and Dion. Hal. I 8.3 (p. 27 n.1 above).

5. On which see Varro *LL* V 144, 156, Prop. IV 9.1–10, Tib. II 5.33f, Ovid *Fasti* VI 405–10, etc. *Pelliti patres*: Prop. IV 1.11–14.

6. Collingwood 1946, 43f: 'the origin of Rome, as he describes it, was a kind of miraculous leap into existence of the complete city as it existed at a later date': but see Luce 1977, 234ff (and all his chapter 7). Heurgon 1973, 187 (cf. 165), specifically on the history of the *plebs*; in the *de republica* (esp. II 22, 30, 33), Cicero conspicuously applies this teleological view to the development of the city as a whole (cf. Alföldi 1965, 141–5).

7. Rawson 1973, esp. 41 (on the variety of his sources) and 44 (on the setting of the *de oratore*).

than that of the second-century Romans whom men he knew had known. A revealing insight into the limitations of his vision is provided by his translation in the *Tusculans* of Aeschylus' passage on Prometheus nailed to the rock. It is not just that he contaminates it with post-Aeschylean matter from his philosophical source, adjusts it to suit Roman ideas of propriety, and renders the imagery into phraseology borrowed from early Latin poets;[8] much more important is the fact that 'religious notions foreign to Roman society which the older poets had failed to domesticate made Cicero helpless', and caused him to interpret the scene as a whole in Roman terms.[9] Even in responsible authors, then, we should expect as little of the reality of early Rome as Cicero here achieves of Aeschylus' world. The leap of the controlled imagination was something they were unable, or did not try, to manage.

Nowhere is this limitation more clearly seen than in the Romans' ideas about the history of their own city and its monuments. We know from Plautus that in the late third century B.C. the *cloaca maxima* was still an open channel in the Forum, yet the enclosed culvert of the late-republican city (built perhaps in the early second century) was attributed by the annalistic sources of Livy and Dionysius to Tarquinius Superbus' forced-labour programme.[10] Similarly, it was (and is) well known that the Aqua Marcia was built by the praetor Q. Marcius Rex in 144–3 B.C., yet the elder Pliny accepted a story that it was 'inaugurated', at least, by Ancus Marcius.[11] The Porticus Minucia *frumentaria* was organized in the early Empire as the distribution centre for the corn dole, yet by the time of Suetonius (or whoever was the source of the 'Chronographer of A.D. 354') the building was already attributed to Servius Tullius, and its 45 *ostia*, at which the recipients applied for their

8. Jocelyn 1973, 98ff on Cic. *TD* II 23–5; esp. pp. 99f and 109–11 (philosophical ideas), 101–4 (Roman propriety and imagery).
9. *Ibid.* 104–6; quotation from p. 104.
10. Cassius Hemina fr.15P, Livy I 56.2 (cf. 38.6), Dion. Hal. IV 44.2 (cf. III 67.5), Pliny *NH* XXXVI 107 (the elder Tarquin); Plaut. *Curc.* 476, cf. Nash 1968, 258. On the legend of the forced-labour programme, see Pais 1906, 120–2.
11. Pliny *NH* XXXI 41; *pace* Crawford (1974, 448f), I see no reason why the equestrian statue portrayed on the aqueduct by Philippus' coins in 56 B.C. should be of Ancus rather than Q. Marcius Rex. The legend of the regal ancestors of the Marcii grew out of their *cognomen*, first attested in 171 (Livy XLIII 1.12) and originally celebrating the first plebeian *rex sacrorum*, who died in 210 (cf. Scribonius Curio, Cestius Epulo, Minucius Augurinus, etc): see Münzer 1920, 80f, Heurgon 1973, 135, and Wiseman 1974b, 154f (on Plut. *Numa* 21.4, a *locus classicus* for invented genealogies).

rations, were accounted for by the number of years in Servius' reign.[12]

When King Porsenna captured the Janiculum, in one of the most famous stories of Roman history, nothing stood between him and the Capitol and Palatine except the Tiber bridge.[13] In fact, we know that the 'Servian' wall ran parallel to the Tiber; but that stretch of it had become obsolete by the early second century B.C., when it was incorporated into an embankment for defence against flooding.[14] At some time before then, probably in the third century between the Punic Wars (but not after 219, to judge by Livy's silence), the wall system had been extended across the river to incorporate the Janiculum,[15] thus removing the necessity for the stretch of wall along the Tiber bank between the Aventine and the Capitol, and releasing it for its re-use by the censors of the second century B.C. It is *this* wall system, with the riverside defences forgotten, that is presupposed by the heroic stories of Horatius Cocles and Cloelia;[16] according to the annalists, who had no conception either of the true date of the 'Servian' wall (about 380 B.C.?) or of the existence of the riverside stretch of it (still standing in the early second century), the Janiculum was brought into the fortifications by Ancus Marcius.[17]

It is quite clear that masonry only a century or two old was indistinguishable to the late-republican Romans from the work of the kings;[18] and what applied to visible remains applied also to constitutional antiquities and every other aspect of the past.[19] The favourite phrase 'in the time of our ancestors' referred to an undif-

12. Chronogr. p.144 (*MGH Auct. ant.*, *Chronica minora* vol. I, ed. Mommsen), cf. *CIL* VI 10223–5 for the numbered *ostia*. The Porticus Minucia *frumentaria* has now been identified (Cozza 1968, 9–20), and its position, partly replacing the Villa Publica, implies an Augustan date rather than the Claudian one normally assumed (Wiseman 1974c, 19f).

13. Livy II 10.4; cf. 10.1 ('alia muris, alia Tiberi obiecto videbantur tuta'), Dion. Hal. V 23.2 (*ἀτείχιστος οὖσα ἐκ τῶν παρὰ τὸν ποταμὸν μερῶν*).

14. Coarelli 1974, 22 and 279; the detailed evidence is to be published in a forthcoming issue of the *Bullettino comunale*.

15. Implied by App. *BC* I 68 (87 B.C.), III 91 and 94 (43 B.C.); see Säflund 1932, 186–93, who however dates the extension much too late.

16. So Gjerstad 1969 (esp. 149 and 154); his date for the Janiculum walls is unacceptable, but the point is not affected.

17. Livy I 33.6, cf. Dion. Hal. III 45.1, *vir. ill.* 5.2: from an anti-Etruscan source, probably Antias (Musti 1970, 80). Some writers evidently attributed the Janiculum walls to Romulus himself (Serv. *Aen.* VI 783).

18. Or even of the gods: cf. Virg. *Aen.* VIII 355–8, Festus 430L etc, on the supposed remains of Saturn's citadel.

19. Coinage, for instance: see Crawford 1976, 198 on its introduction (really in the third century B.C.) by Ser. Tullius, Numa or Saturn.

ferentiated continuum which included everything from the regal period to the generation immediately before that of the speaker's oldest living contemporaries.[20]

—

Sometimes, it is true, a genuine insight into the conditions of early Rome was achieved by the antiquarians' investigation of old inscriptions and other documentary evidence still surviving in the temples of Rome. L. Cincius, who evidently wrote a Pausanias-like guide to the antiquities of the Capitol (if not the whole city), knew that the Romans' chief magistrate in the early Republic was the *praetor maximus*, and that down to about 340 B.C. the Latin League controlled its own dominion, with Rome merely one member, bound to provide a commander for the League's forces whenever it so ordered.[21] Old laws and treaties, inscribed on bronze pillars or preserved in magistrates' archives, were known and read;[22] *elogia* and the inscribed dedications of triumphant generals could provide historical information too.[23] But the historians could not properly use the antiquarians' material, even when they understood it (which they frequently did not[24]): they had no conceptual framework in which to make sense of the *praetor maximus*, their picture of the steady growth of Rome made the evidence for the independent Latin League unusable, and when one of them did go out of his way to find and exploit contemporary evidence (Licinius Macer, with the 'linen books' and other documents), he used it not to reconstruct the real conditions of the early Republic for their own sake, but to support a schematic and polemical interpretation of the 'struggle of the orders' which suited his own political position in the 70s B.C.[25]

20. *Prisca virtus* generally ends about a century ago: cf. Ovid *Fasti* IV 157–60 (fall from *pudicitia*, 114 B.C.), Martial XI 20.10 (Augustus' *Romana simplicitas*). Cf. Rawson 1976, 710 on the naivety of Roman dating.
21. Livy VII 3.5–8, Festus 276L; Heurgon 1964, 432f on Cincius, 'diligens talium monumentorum auctor', and his *Mystagogia*.
22. Bronze pillars: e.g. the *foedus Cassianum* (Livy II 33.9, Cic. *Balb.* 53), and the *lex antiquissima* of 472 B.C. (Varro *ap.* Macr. *Sat.* I 13.21). Archives: e.g. the treaty with Carthage (Pol. III 26.1, ἐν τῷ τῶν ἀγορανόμων ταμιείῳ). Cf. Frier 1975, 79–87 on the *foedus Ardeatinum* cited by Licinius Macer (Livy IV 7.12), which he may have known *via* Cincius.
23. E.g. Cincius *ap.* Festus 498L on the gold crown dedicated by T. Quinctius Cincinnatus the dictator of 380: Heurgon 1964, 434f.
24. Cf. Heurgon 1964, 433 and 435 on Livy misunderstanding material from Cincius; at IV 34.6, Livy's embarrassment about *classis* is due to his failure to understand its original sense, as preserved in his source (cf. Ogilvie 1976, 143).
25. Frier 1975, *passim* (cf. also Pinsent 1975, 40, 50, 62 etc) on Licinius Macer; Sall. *Hist.* III 48M for his political position as *tr.pl.* 73.

Besides, the antiquarian tradition itself became contaminated with inventions of the historians. Varro, for instance, accepted from Valerius Antias the building of a house on the Palatine at public expense for M'. Valerius Maximus (supposedly dictator in 494 B.C.), and this in turn deceived Asconius, who used the item to convict Cicero of rhetorical abuse of history when he claimed in the *in Pisonem* that no-one before himself had had the building of his house paid for by the *res publica*;[26] in reality, of course, Cicero was unaware of the supposed Valerian precedent because it had not yet become part of the historical tradition.[27] This is not the only example of Varro using Antias (as indeed did Cicero himself in the later dialogues);[28] and when the greatest of the antiquarians, who 'opened the Romans' eyes to their own traditions', relies on an authority recognized even by Livy as a *fabulator*, it becomes clear that a disinterestedly empirical approach to the past was practically impossible.[29]

—

That is even true of Roman law. One would expect the jurists, whose way of thinking was essentially empirical and practical,[30] and whose procedures required a proper respect for evidence in order to establish what really happened, to have had a healthy influence on Roman historical methods. After all, the study of the Twelve Tables and other early legal texts meant that jurists were necessarily also antiquarians – 'rerum antiquarum non incuriosi', to borrow Gellius' description of one of them.[31] (On one tricky piece of archaic Latin vocabulary, for instance, Festus' source quoted both L. Cincius the collector of old inscriptions, who also wrote a work *de officio iurisconsulti*, and the great jurist Ser.

26. Asc. 13C on Cic. *Pis.* 52 ('hoc Cicero oratorio more, non historico, videtur posuisse'), quoting Antias fr. 17P, and Varro at second hand from Hyginus fr.2P; cf. Weinstock 1971, 278f.
27. I shall argue below (ch. 7) that it had not yet been invented; the alternative is that Antias had already made it up but Cicero had not yet read him.
28. Cens. *de die nat.* 17.8 and 11 quotes from Varro and Antias together, on the Secular Games and the Megalesia; and the story of Manlius Capitolinus' execution may well be another case of Varro accepting a Valerian invention (Wiseman 1979b, 49, on Gell. *NA* XVII 21.24). Cicero: see p. 119f below.
29. Cic. *Acad.* I 9 on Varro ('tu omnium divinarum humanarumque reum nomina genera officia causas aperuisti . . . '). Livy on Antias: XXXIX 43.1 (*fabula*, cf. p. 33 above); XXX 19.11, XXXIII 10.8, XXXVIII 23.6 etc.
30. Watson 1974, 124 (and all his ch. 9); *ibid.* 106f and ch. 16 on the jurists' resistance to rhetoric.
31. Gell. *NA* VII 5.1, on P. Alfenus. Cf. Cic. *de or.* I 256 on M. Iunius Congus (i.e. Iunius 'Gracchanus'? Zucchelli 1975, esp. 110f, 124): 'historiam dico et prudentiam iuris publici et antiquitatis memoriam et exemplorum copiam'.

Sulpicius Rufus, whose explanations of obscurities in the Twelve Tables Festus frequently cites elsewhere.[32]) The very prestige of the legal profession might be expected to have impressed its methods and its standards on Roman historians.[33] But no: Pomponius' history of Roman law at the beginning of the *Digest* contains details almost certainly invented by the historians of the second and first centuries B.C.,[34] and the jurists may even have added to the corpus of pseudo-historical fictions, if they were responsible for inventing the aetiological stories – to account for legal terms and procedures – which were pressed into service by the historians as part of the actual events of early Rome.[35]

One jurist who was also an historian, Q. Aelius Tubero, wrote among other things a book on the duties of a judge,[36] but it would be entirely anachronistic to infer that his historical work was necessarily marked by any more scrupulous a respect for evidence than non-judicial historiographers showed. 'Evidence' as the main preoccupation of the historian is a modern concept. So, for that matter, is evidence as the main preoccupation of the judge: 'with me, as with a good *iudex*', said Cicero, in a historical context, 'arguments have more force than witnesses' – and by arguments he meant the 'technical proofs' (*ἔντεχνοι πίστεις*) of the orator's stock-in-trade, *a priori* arguments which rely on persuasiveness rather than on the testimony of a witness.[37] We are back with the orator's *narratio*, which has to be plausible – not necessarily the truth, but *like* the truth (*veri similis*) and therefore persuasive.

'Who ever asked a historian for sworn witnesses?' Seneca was not being serious, but his question does, in fact, accurately indicate how far the ancient historiographical tradition was from the mod-

32. Festus 426–8L, cf. also 180, 232, 430, 516–8L. Watson 1974, 192f; for Cincius' work, cf. Funaioli 1907, 376f.
33. As the Hippocratic school of medicine impressed its empirical standards on Thucydides. But no other historian was so influenced, and in any case, the empirical approach in Greek medicine itself dwindled away after the third century B.C. (von Staden 1975, *passim*).
34. E.g. Hermodorus of Ephesus and the Twelve Tables (*Dig.* I 2.2.4); Cn. Flavius as Ap. Claudius' client (*ibid.* 7, cf. p. 88 below); Ap. Claudius Caecus 'Centummanus' (*ibid.* 36), clearly made up from a combination of the second-century B.C. Claudii Unimanus (Flor. I 33.16, *vir. ill.* 71.1) and Centumalus (Cic. *Off.* III 66).
35. Cf. p. 24 above. Valerius Antias was demonstrably involved in the elaboration (but not the invention) of one of the best known, Vindicius and the *vindicta*: cf. Dion. Hal. V 7.4, Plut. *Popl.* 4.5; Ogilvie 1965, 242f.
36. Gell. *NA* XIV 2.20, 'praecepta super officio iudicis'.
37. Cic. *rep.* I 59; on *argumenta*, see Arist. *Rhet.* I 1355b35ff, Cic. *de or.* II 116, Cic. *Cael.* 54 (cf. 22 *ad fin.*) etc. The logical order is neatly stated at *Cael.* 6: 'ut . . . argumento probet, teste confirmet'.

ern concept of the historian as a judge, weighing up the evidence. The narrator of Seneca's *ludus de morte Claudii* had just told the reader 'I'll say whatever comes into my mouth' – a proverbial phrase used also by Lucian on the subject of bad historians. It expresses epigrammatically the complaint Thucydides had made of historians who did not share his own standards (that is, practically all ancient writers before or after him): they are content to accept the first story they hear, without checking and cross-checking its accuracy.[38] For Thucydides, that was evidence of intellectual idleness (*ἀταλαιπωρία*) in the pursuit of truth; but surely the real point is that for people brought up on the techniques of rhetoric, the first plausible story was good enough: if it was credible, and satisfied the requirement of being 'like the truth', then there was no *need* to look further or question its accuracy.

Even a conscientious investigator like Asconius was often content with the first authority he found who gave him a satisfactory account – that is, one not self-evidently absurd or inconsistent with what he already believed. We have already (p. 46 above) found him following Valerius Antias against the clear implication of the Cicero text on which he was commenting, and there are several places where even we, with our inadequate documentation, can see that Asconius could have found other, and sometimes more reliable, data if he had looked further and not been satisfied with the first plausible version.[39] But the prevailing canons of historical investigation did not encourage him to look further. As Quintilian said in an only slightly different context, 'it is sufficient to give an account of the received version or those which are told by famous authors'.[40]

It might appear from the Romans' consistent scepticism about the reliability of Greek historiography – the 'Graecia mendax' theme[41] – that they *were* capable of exercising a critical judgment comparable to our own criteria of historical reliability. But that is not really the case: when Roman critics were not merely complaining about

38. Sen. *ludus* 1, Lucian *Hist.* 32; Thuc. I 20.3 (*τὰ ἑτοῖμα*), 22.2 (*ὁ παρατυχών*).
39. E.g. Asc. 3C/Livy XXI 25.3–5 (triumvirs' names), Asc. 3C/Vell. I 14–15 (number of colonies), Asc. 5C/Tiro *ap.* Plut. *Cic.* 41.7 (omits Furius Crassipes). I owe these examples to Dr Bruce Marshall.
40. Quint. I 8.18 (cf. 19 on *aniles fabulae*, 20 on *historia vana* etc); his main concern was with the teacher's exposition of stories in the poets (Wardman 1976, 81). Cf. Luce 1977, 102 on Livy: 'his primary task was to select the best, the most *appealing* source' (my italics).
41. On which see most recently Wardman 1976, 101ff (and all his fourth chapter).

the exaggerated importance the Greeks gave to their own past, their main objection to the Greek stories was on the familiar grounds of verisimilitude.

Valerius Maximus, for instance, says of Theseus' descent into Hades to rescue Pirithous that only an idler would tell the story and only a fool believe it.[42] The first half of that judgment contrasts the Greek tale with the Roman story of devotion Valerius had just narrated, which, being 'true', could provide serious moralists with a sounder *exemplum*; the second half clearly implies an appeal to intrinsic likelihood as the criterion of belief which the Theseus story did not satisfy. Mortals descending into Hades were simply not plausible. They would not be accepted in the rhetorical schools as part of a persuasive *narratio*.

The problem of physical impossibilities (*ἀδύνατα*) in the heroic stories had already exercised some of the Greek historians themselves, as we shall see in Part III: their solution was to rationalize the 'mythical' element away and treat what was left as the truth. A particularly clear example is Dionysius' narrative of Hercules in Italy, which distinguishes the *mythikos logos* of Geryon's cattle from the 'more truthful account' of Hercules as a great leader in charge of an invading army and fleet.[43] The 'invasion' of Attica by Dionysus (p. 151 below) is a similar case, and there are countless others,[44] treating the mythical material 'according to probability' (*κατὰ τὸ εἰκός*) and thus making it acceptable as history.[45]

Valerius Maximus would probably have accepted a version of the Theseus story doctored in this way to make it 'probable', for there was no other criterion he could have used to judge it. His criticism, trivial in itself, is worth mentioning because it contrasts so starkly with his blindness to the unhistorical nature of most of his own material. Unlike the Theseus story, his *exempla* were all 'like the truth', and that was enough.

Valerius is, perhaps, an extreme case of the unhistorical thinking with which this chapter has been concerned. But all Greek and Roman writers were affected by it to a greater or a lesser extent –

42. Val. Max. IV 7.4, 'vani est istud narrare, stulti credere'; Wardman 1976, 77.
43. Dion. Hal. I 39.1: *τὰ μὲν μυθικώτερα* (39–40), *τὰ δ' ἀληθέστερα* (41–44). Cf. Musti 1970, 15 on I 27.1, 49.2.
44. E.g. Pol. XXXIV 2–3, rationalizing Aeolus (as a master-meteorologist) and Scylla and Charybdis: Walbank 1974, 7ff.
45. Most explicitly at Plut. *Thes.* 1.5 (cf. 28). Herodotus on the Trojan War (II 120) is a particularly good example; cf. also Dicaearchus *Bios Hellados* fr. 49 Wehrli on the story of Cronos – 'by eliminating *τὸ λίαν μυθικόν* one reduces it, by reasoning, to a natural meaning'.

including the historians who provide us with nearly all our information (true or false) about the history of the Roman Republic before the age of Cicero.

Livy and Dionysius were what Collingwood called 'scissors-and-paste' historians,[46] creating their (very different) narratives out of a patchwork of what their predecessors had said about the various periods and events their subject included. They adapted this material for their own artistic purposes, and sometimes made critical judgments on their predecessors' work (though never at a more than superficial level), but essentially their historical value is no greater than that of the writers they used. They could assess the accuracy of what their sources told them only by the rhetorician's criterion of inherent probability.[47] The limitations of their historical thinking made them gullible, vulnerable to the plausible invention. They had no adequate means of detecting invented pseudo-history, even when it was historians like themselves, only a generation or two earlier, who were responsible for it.

It is regularly said of Livy that he used only one source at a time: 'his method was to follow one writer for a section, largely working from memory, and then switch to another when a particular theme had been exhausted'.[48] But it is not quite as simple as that. When two or more sources had dealt with a particular episode, he is quite capable of inserting details or motivations from one while in the main reproducing another, even where the two original versions were mutually incompatible.[49] Indeed, one might even say *especially* where they were incompatible, since part of his aim may well have been to achieve a reconstruction of early Rome by synthesizing rival interpretations. It has recently been demonstrated how Aristotle – or whoever wrote the *Athenaion Politeia* – had to reconcile conflicting traditions, stemming from writers committed either for or against the Athenian democracy, and made an imper-

46. Walsh (1961, 287) repudiates the label for Livy, but on grounds Collingwood would hardly have accepted. See Luce 1977, 143f and 149f for a good account of Livy's technique.
47. Luce 1977, 140f, and all his chapter 5. E.g. Livy I 13.5 (from Piso), VII 6.6 (from Procilius and others, cf. Varro *LL* V 148–50) on the rival explanations of the Lacus Curtius. He contradicts himself, but his second thoughts do not lead him to alter what he had already written in book I (Fraccaro 1956, 325n., cf. 404).
48. Ogilvie 1976, 25 (cf. 1965, 5–7). See Walsh 1961, 141f for a sensitive account.
49. As shown most clearly by Musti, 1970: examples at pp. 30–56 (*passim*), 74, 76, 96, 109, 116. Cf. also Wiseman 1979b on the trial of Manlius. As Luce points out (1977, 223–7, cf. 177), this is particularly true in the first decade. As D'Anna has recently shown (1975, 17–23), Virgil's technique was exactly the same.

fect job of it.[50] Livy's problem was much the same, the traditions about the 'struggle of the orders' having been elaborated with appropriate *color* by both conservative and 'popular' historians; and his solution too was much the same. What never occurred to him was to reject the elaborations to begin with.

The synthesis technique is easier to see in Dionysius, who was a much less gifted artist than Livy, and correspondingly less successful at working the inconsistent lumps into a smooth texture of his own.[51] Besides, he was not afraid of prolixity, and incorporated material from all types of source to achieve 'precise detail' (*akribeia*). He makes a great virtue of this, emphasising the usefulness of his history to philosophers and men of affairs because it goes through the events in detail, and explains the motives and pretexts which give rise to them.[52] The motives may be seen from the speeches made at the time, which persuaded the protagonists in each case to act as they did, and it is therefore the historian's duty to report them in detail too. That is all very well in the example Dionysius chooses, when the subject is the fall of Athens and the content of speeches made in the assembly is vouched for by contemporary sources;[53] but he applies it equally to fifth- and fourth-century Rome. In an earlier passage on *akribeia* and the need to report motives,[54] he had defended his lengthy account of the first conflict of the *plebs* with the patricians by pointing out that since the Romans – unlike the Corcyreans and other Greeks – had settled their political quarrels without bloodshed and by persuasion, 'I thought it necessary above all things to report the speeches which the heads of both parties made upon that occasion'.[55]

One can hardly avoid the conclusion that Dionysius regarded his speeches not just as plausible inventions to add *color* to an otherwise bare narrative, but as actually representing what was really said. They are, it is true, constructed on rigidly conventional rhetorical lines,[56] but that does not mean that the content is Dionysius'

50. Rhodes 1976, esp. 153f. For the same technique in Livy, see Luce 1977, 73 and 74.
51. Cf., as random examples, the *interreges* at V 71.3/72.3 (Pinsent 1975, 21 n.22), or the tribunes at X 8.1/4.
52. Dion. Hal. XI 1.1–5; for the philosophers and politicians, cf. I 8.3 (p. 27 above); for *ἀκρίβεια*, cf. I 5.4 etc (p. 150 below).
53. Dion. Hal. XI 1.3, *καὶ τίνες οἱ πείσαντες αὐτοὺς λόγοι* etc.
54. *Ibid.* VII 66.1–2 and 5 – to make his work *πιστός*.
55. *Ibid.* VII 66.3 (trans. E. Cary): *παντὸς μάλιστα ἀναγκαῖον ἡγησάμην εἶναι τοὺς λόγους αὐτῶν διεξελθεῖν, οἷς τότε οἱ δυναστεύοντες ἐν ἑκατέροιδ ἐχρήσαντο.* In the next sentence the phrase is *ἀπαγγέλλειν τοὺς λόγους*.
56. Cf. Ogilvie 1976, 23.

own invention. On the contrary, the verb he uses (*διεξελθεῖν*)[57] and his declared motive (of reporting what was said in order to reveal motivation) equally imply that the arguments must be, for the most part at any rate, what he found in his sources.[58] For Dionysius, the rival interpretations of, say, the struggle of the orders were not just an inconsistency to be smoothed over in the narrative: they were a godsend, providing ready-made arguments respectively *pro* and *contra* at each critical point, which a historian interested in 'agonistic' oratorical debates could exploit with a clear conscience.[59] 'Ready-made' is how they appear to us, who understand – more or less – the way his late annalistic sources went about their business. For Dionysius himself, on the other hand, they seem to have been genuine records of what was said in fifth- and fourth-century Rome. What reason had he for rejecting their authenticity? They were plausible, 'like the truth', and that was the criterion he had been taught to use.

—

This combination of unscrupulous invention on the part of the late-republican annalists and innocent acceptance of their inventions on the part of Livy and Dionysius has not been easy for modern readers to understand. We do not find it too hard to recognize the inventive technique in comparatively unimportant details, but it does not come naturally to us to expect the *big* lie as well; in that we are as gullible as the *stultus* in the Forum (p. 34 above) who accepted the eloquence of the skilled orator as truth.

Two of the greatest of modern Roman historians devoted their early years to an exposure of Valerius Antias and the way he wrote 'history'.[60] Mommsen himself had already shown the way in his *Römische Forschungen*.[61] Yet the impact was minimal; despite all the evidence that was produced, historians were reluctant to believe in the enormity of the later annalists' falsifications.[62] Nowadays we

57. Twice in VII 66.3, with (e.g.) *διελθεῖν* at XI 1.1 and 5, *ἐπεξελθεῖν* at VII 66.2. Cf. Gelzer 1964, 223f for the use of the word in Polybius' critique of Timaeus.
58. So Nitsch 1873, 23f; not, I think, refuted by Mommsen (1879, 128 n.34).
59. Cf. p. 27f above.
60. Münzer 1891, 54–71 (cf. also 14 on Antias' *colores*); Fraccaro 1911, *passim*. Münzer's work was a *dissertatio inauguralis*; Fraccaro's was described by its author as a work of 'youthful enthusiasm' (Fraccaro 1939, 3=1956, 393).
61. Mommsen 1874 *passim*=1879, 153–220 (esp. 173, 195, 218–20).
62. Münzer 1891, 14, 'etiam huius aevi homines Antiatis narrationi nimiam fidem habuerunt' (cf. 16 on Ihne and Bertolini); Fraccaro 1911a, 288=1956, 310, on the trial of L. Scipio in Antias: 'la falsificazione raggiunge qui il colmo e diviene così spudorata, che molti moderni se ne lasciarono imporre'. *Ibid.* 219=264 (footnote) on the failure to recognize that Antias' plausible fictions were invented *pour épater*

have learned to pay lip-service, at least, to the danger of accepting annalistic material as reliable, but the will to believe is still strong.[63] It has been the purpose of these first four chapters to re-state, with some new arguments, what Mommsen, Münzer and Fraccaro said long ago, and thus to warn the innocent against the lure of Clio's cosmetics.

---

le bourgeois! But they were still believed a generation later (Fraccaro 1939, 21ff=1956, 410ff).

63. Usually in the form critized by Pinsent (1971, 272): 'the reader is sometimes left with the impression, by no means uncommon in treatments of early Roman history, that any awkward notice can be explained away while those that are left are somewhat arbitrarily selected because they support an hypothesis arrived at independently'. As he goes on to say, 'for early Rome, historiographic study must precede historical' (cf. also Pinsent 1975, 19).

PART II

The Legends of the Patrician Claudii

He stalked along the Forum like King Tarquin in his pride:
Twelve axes waited on him, six marching on a side;
The townsmen shrank to right and left, and eyed askance with fear
His lowering brow, his curling mouth, which always seemed to sneer:
That brow of hate, that mouth of scorn, marks all the kindred still;
For never was there Claudius yet but wished the Commons ill.

MACAULAY, *Lays of Ancient Rome: Virginia*

Chapter 5

ATTUS CLAUSUS AND THE TWO TRADITIONS

The ingrained arrogance of the Claudian house was already a historical commonplace when Tacitus wrote his *Annals*. He used it with characteristic effect at the very beginning of his narrative, to introduce the character who would dominate the first six books – Tiberius Claudius Nero, Augustus' successor as *princeps*.[1] His contemporary Suetonius provides the fullest extant statement of the case against the Claudii; in the *Life of Tiberius*, the brief sketch of good and bad Claudii in the emperor's ancestry[2] is followed by this summary:

> It is in any case notorious that with the exception of P. Clodius, who had himself adopted by a plebeian (a man younger than himself) in order to bring about Cicero's exile, all the Claudii were *optimates* and always uniquely zealous for patrician dignity and authority, so violent and obstinate in their opposition to the *plebs* that not one of them, even in a capital trial before the people, would condescend to put on mourning according to custom, or make any supplication for favour, and some of them in their quarrels and altercations actually beat up the plebeian tribunes. There was even a Vestal Virgin who, when her brother was holding a triumph against the wishes of the people, mounted his chariot and went with him right to the Capitol, so that it would be sacrilege for any of the tribunes to forbid it or use his veto.[3]

1. Tac. *Ann.* I 4.3: 'Tiberius Nero, maturus annis, spectatus bello, sed vetere atque insita Claudiae familiae superbia'.
2. The worthy men are Ap. Claudius Caecus, Ap. Claudius Caudex *cos.* 264, C. Claudius Nero *cos.* 207 (Suet. *Tib.* 2.1); the unworthy men Ap. Claudius 'Regillianus' *Xvir*, Ap. Claudius Russus *cos.* 268, P. Claudius Pulcher *cos.* 249 (*ibid.* 2.2); the women (one of each) Q. Claudia of Magna Mater fame, and P. Pulcher's sister (*ibid.* 2.3).
3. Suet. *Tib.* 2.4: 'Praeterea notissimum est, Claudios *omnis* . . . optimates adsertoresque *unicos* dignitatis ac potentiae patriciorum *semper* fuisse atque adversus plebem adeo violentos et contumaces ut ne capitis quidem *quisquam* reus . . . deprecari sustinuerit', etc.

Generalization from a single example is a favourite technique of Suetonius',[4] and he is not afraid to commit himself to absolute terms like 'every' and 'always', even when – as here – he admits an exception.[5] So it would be enough for him if any one Claudius, on any one occasion, supposedly committed any one of the enormities in his list. In fact, the beating of tribunes and the refusal to supplicate or wear mourning are attributed in our surviving sources only to Ap. Claudius the consul of 471 B.C.,[6] though it is quite possible that the late annalists who created the pseudo-history of the early Republic made other Claudii do it as well. As we shall see, that sort of *Leitmotiv* was one of their standard techniques. Moreover, Appius' brother C. Claudius, consul in 460, is reported in Livy as dressing in mourning and supplicating the people in favour of Appius the disgraced Decemvir (so much for Suetonius' 'not one'!), and insists in the speech Dionysius gives him that the accused man would have done so himself if he had been given the chance.[7] This too is a phenomenon we shall meet again, the apologetic narrative mirroring the hostile one.

But the most important item in Suetonius' catalogue is the last. It was Ap. Claudius Pulcher, the consul of 143 B.C. (and father-in-law of Tiberius Gracchus), whose triumph was saved from the tribune's prohibition by the Vestal who rode with him in his chariot. The earliest account of the event is in Cicero's *pro Caelio*, where the validity of the triumph is not in doubt, the tribune's motive is personal enmity, and the Vestal's action is cited for praise and admiration,[8] an example of the *domestica laus in gloria muliebri* with which Cicero tries to shame the loose-living Clodia by appealing to the virtues of her forebears.[9] Here, and throughout the tradition, the arrogant patrician Claudii are a historiographical, not a historical, phenomenon. Somebody invented the legend; Livy

4. E.g., in this book, *Tib.* 30 (Tac. *Ann.* I 52.2), 51.2 (*Ann.* VI 10.1), 61.4 (*Ann.* VI 40.1), 61.5 (*Ann.* V 9.3).
5. Cf. *Tib.* 30 (*neque quisquam*), 41 (*non umquam ullos*), 46 (*numquam*, with an exception), 48.2 (*ne quidem ulla*, with an exception), 51.2 (*omnis*), 53.1 (*nec ullo*), 61.3 (*nemini*, *omne*), 61.4 (*nemo*).
6. Dion Hal. IX 48.2 and 4, 54.2, Livy II 61.5.
7. Livy III 58.1, cf. VI 20.3; Dion. Hal. XI 49.4. See p. 83 below.
8. Cic. *Cael.* 34, cf. Val. Max. V 4.6 (from the section 'de *pietate* erga parentes et fratres et patriam'; both call the Vestal Appius' daughter, so perhaps *patrem* should be read for *fratrem* in the Suetonius passage. Macr. *Sat.* III 14.14 (on Appius as a *Salius*) has no doubt that he was *vir triumphalis*.
9. Cf. Levick 1976, 12: 'proof of the survival of a favourable tradition about the Claudii and their women'. But an appeal to *prisca virtus* would be the normal way to praise the ancestors of *any* noble house, not just the Claudii.

and Dionysius exploited it on a large scale, and thanks to them it has taken root.

It was not, however, unchallenged. There was a rival legend, less dramatic and therefore less tenacious, which can also be detected by careful attention to the tradition. Since the nature of these legends can be seen most clearly in the earliest period of Claudian history, where there was practically no genuine information to complicate their authors' purposes, the arrival of the Claudii at Rome and the imagined political career of the first Appius may serve as paradigm cases.

—

Suetonius gives two versions of the arrival of the Claudii:

> The patrician *gens Claudia* . . . originated at the Sabine town of Regilli. From there it moved to Rome with a large following of clients, either shortly after the foundation of the city, on the advice of Romulus' colleague T. Tatius, or else (as the usual story has it) about five years after the expulsion of the kings, on the advice of Atta Claudius, the head of the clan. Co-opted into the patrician *gentes*, it also received at public expense a tract of land beyond the Anio for the clients, and a family burial-ground at the foot of the Capitoline.[10]

The land beyond the Anio was the nucleus of the *tribus Claudia*, one of the original 16 rural tribes in the system of citizen-registration supposedly invented by Servius Tullius;[11] the ground below the Capitoline was evidently owned by the Claudii as early as 296 B.C., when Ap. Claudius Caecus built the temple of Bellona there in the Etruscan wars, and as late as the principate of Augustus, when the ashes of P. Clodius' son 'Pulcher Claudius' were laid to rest there in an alabaster urn which has survived the destruction of the family tomb.[12] Whether the migration and the public grants were simply an aetiological tale to account for these facts, or a genuine family tradition, it is impossible to say.

10. Suet. *Tib.* 1.1: '. . . auctore Tito Tatio consorte Romuli vel, quod magis constat, Atta Claudio gentis principe . . .'.

11. Cf. Pinsent 1964, 29 and 1975, 58 for the view that the tribes were first four (the *tribus urbanae*) and then 20; *contra* Ogilvie 1965, 273 and 292. For other possibilities, cf. Badian 1962, 201.

12. Coarelli 1965–7, esp. 54–72 (cf. Wiseman 1974c, 14–17) for the Bellona temple's position; Palmer 1975, 653 nn. 3 and 5 for the urn (*CIL* VI 1282, found 'prope theatrum Marcellum sub Tarpeio') – though he regards it as an 'offering' in the temple itself.

The earlier migration-date goes back at least as far as Virgil, who in his description of Clausus, the leader of the ancient Sabines,[13] dates the diffusion through Latium of his Claudian descendants 'after Rome had been shared with the Sabines':

> *Claudia nunc a quo diffunditur et tribus et gens*
> *per Latium, postquam in partem data Roma Sabinis.*

Servius' note on this passage cites the migration-story with the *later* date, and then, commenting on the final phrase, observes 'he has taken this from a different history', and tells the tale of the rape of the Sabine women and the treaty between Romulus and Tatius.[14]

The Augustan consular Fasti also imply an early migration, for they give the first Appius, consul in 495, a citizen father called Marcus;[15] in the more usual story, however, the consul of 495 is 'Attus Clausus' himself,[16] the first of the family to be a Roman citizen. It seems probable that the 'son of Marcus' version was not that of the patrician Claudii themselves. Their family history was available for inspection in the temple of Bellona, founded by Ap. Claudius Caecus in 296, in which Ap. Claudius Pulcher the consul of 79 B.C. had the record of all his ancestors' achievements set up on shields on the wall,[17] and it is reasonable to suppose that the surviving inscriptional *elogia* of patrician Claudii go back ultimately to this source.[18] That of the consul of 495 reads simply:

> Ap. Claudius q. urb. cos. cum P. Servilio Prisco

– so succinct that it might well be a simple copy of the first of the Bellona shields.[19] Succinct or not, however, the Claudii would presumably have included Appius' filiation if he had had any; and since they did not, we may tentatively conclude that they identified the consul of 495 with the first Claudius to hold the Roman citizenship.

13. Virg. *Aen.* VII 706–9, cf. X 345. Suetonius' 'Atta Claudius' is normally 'Att(i)us Clausus', at least in Latin authors (Livy II 16.4, X 8.6, Tac. *Ann.* IV 9, XI 24, XII 25). The *Τίτος* of Dion. Hal. V 40.3 is perhaps a corruption of *Ἄττιος*.
14. Serv. *Aen.* VII 706, 'post exactos reges, ut quidam dicunt . . .'; *ibid.* 707, 'hoc de alia traxit historia'.
15. Degrassi 1947, 26–7: his son (*cos. II* 451) *Ap.f.M.n.*
16. Cf. n. 13 above.
17. Pliny *NH* XXXV 12, with an absurd attribution to the *cos.* 495; the mistake is no doubt because, like the *cos.* 79, he was the colleague of a Servilius.
18. E.g. Degrassi 1937, 19 (no.12), 49 (no.70).
19. Degrassi 1937, 43 (no. 67); the urban quaestorship is of course an anachronism, no doubt taken from some second-century historian.

In that case the 'son of Marcus' on the Augustan consular Fasti must have been someone else's invention, and the name itself betrays at least why (and perhaps by whom) the invention was made. 'Marcus' was a *praenomen* the patrician Claudii never used. The plebeian Claudii Marcelli, however, who according to Cicero were descended from a freedman of the patrician *gens*,[20] used the name regularly. It seems likely that the 'son of Marcus' version was invented to please the Claudii Marcelli – and perhaps to give Octavian's nephew C. Marcellus a more distinguished lineage. It would do that not only by challenging the traditional libertine origin of the Marcelli, but also by giving the patrician house itself a 'Romulean' origin more dignified than that of the Sabine deserters which they could be made out to be on the other chronology.[21] This motive would at least account for the existence of the story in Virgil, in the 'Capitoline Fasti', which contain other evidence of Augustan editing,[22] and in Suetonius, who had access to Augustus' files and private papers.[23]

Octavia married C. Claudius Marcellus (consul 50 B.C.) not later than 43.[24] This version may therefore be triumviral rather than Augustan in the true sense, and since Atticus wrote a genealogical account of the Claudii Marcelli, evidently at the request of C. Marcellus himself,[25] it seems likely that that was the origin of it. The first known member of the family, consul in 331 B.C., appears in the Augustan consular list as M. Claudius C.f. C.n. Marcellus;[26] the filiation perhaps suggests a supposed descent from the patrician C. Claudius *cos.* 460,[27] which would no doubt have pleased Octavia's husband by its flattering allusion to his own *praenomen*.[28]

To distinguish the two chronologies of the Claudian migration

20. Cic. *de or.* I 176, on a centumviral lawsuit 'inter Marcellos et Claudios patricios' over the rights of inheritance involved.

21. For the 'Romulization' of stories previously attributed to the later kings or the early Republic, see Musti 1970, esp. ch.3 (70 n.14 on the Claudii and Valerii).

22. Taylor 1951, 73–80. But see now Drummond 1978, 101–8.

23. E.g. Suet. *Aug.* 71.2–4, 76, 87–88, *Tib.* 21.3–6, *Claud.* 3.2–4.6.

24. Prop. III 18.15, on the age of their son.

25. Nep. *Att.* 18.4, cf. Sumner 1973, 165. He also wrote one on the Iunii, at the request of M. Brutus (*ibid.* 18.3); Marcellus' mother, still alive in 51, was a Iunia (Cic. *fam.* XV 8; cf. Münzer 1920, 406f, Wiseman 1974a, 153).

26. Degrassi 1947, 153.

27. I owe this suggestion to Elizabeth Rawson. Certainly the *cos.* 460 is treated very kindly in the tradition: p. 82f below.

28. Cf. Sumner 1976, 342 on the use of C. as a *praenomen* by the Marcelli; he assumes that the *cos.* 331's filiation is genuine. The father of the *cos.* 50 was C. Marcellus M.f., praetor in 80 and still alive in 51 (Cic. *fam.* XV 8).

is, however, only a first step, for the version which had them arriving in 504 B.C. is itself not homogeneous as we have it in our sources. It is agreed that when Attus Clausus and his five thousand dependants arrived in the infant Republic, he himself was co-opted into the patricians and given land (and perhaps a house) *sub Capitolio*, while his followers were made Roman citizens and settled on land beyond the Anio between Fidenae and a place called Picetia, the nucleus of the *tribus Claudia*. That much is common to Livy, Dionysius, Plutarch, Appian and Zonaras, as also is the motive for the migration – Clausus' opposition to the war with Rome and his prosecution by more aggressive Sabine leaders.[29] But there are important differences of emphasis which betray rival interpretations:

§i. Livy and Dionysius both describe Clausus as a deserter, with the verbs *transfugit* and *αὐτομολεῖ*; Plutarch, on the other hand, merely says that he fled from those who hated him, with no emotive phraseology except in reporting what his enemies said.[30]

§ii. Livy passes no judgment on Clausus' moral worth, and Dionysius describes him only as a noble who was powerful because of his wealth, a rather double-edged compliment; Plutarch, however, makes him not only rich and noble but also illustrious in prowess through his physical strength, a man particularly eminent both in moral worth and in eloquence.[31]

§iii. Dionysius observes that one of the grounds for his prosecution was his refusal to let the townsmen of Regillum obey the decrees passed by the general assembly of the Sabines, the implication being that he put himself above the *res publica*; Plutarch admits that his enemies accused him of aiming at tyranny, but insists that their real motive was the envy which surrounds all great men.[32]

§iv. Livy describes him as 'accompanied by a great band of clients' – an evocative phrase made more sinister by the background of *seditio*, *turba* and *factio* from which Clausus is depicted

29. Livy II 16.3–5, Dion. Hal. V 40.3–5, cf. IX 47.1, Plut. *Popl.* 21.4-10, App. *reg.* fr.12, Zonaras VII 13B.

30. Livy II 16.4, Dion. Hal. V 40.3 (cf. Alföldi 1965, 159); Plut. *Popl.* 21.6 and 8, 22.1 (*φυγὰς καὶ πολέμιος*).

31. Dion. Hal. V 40.3, *εὐγενὴς καὶ χρήμασι δυνατός* (for the wealth of the Sabines in one branch of the historiographical tradition, see Musti 1970, 71f and n.16); Plut. *Popl.* 21.4, *ἀνὴρ χρήμασί τε δυνατὸς καὶ σώματος ῥώμῃ πρὸς ἀλκὴν ἐπιφανής, ἀρετῆς δὲ δόξῃ μάλιστα καὶ λόγου δεινότητι πρωτεύων* (followed by Zonaras).

32. Dion. Hal. V 40.4, *ἐν τῷ κοινῷ μόνος ἀντέλεγε* . . . (*τὸ κοινόν* is an important recurring phrase in the Claudian legends); Plut. *Popl.* 21.5, *ὃ δὲ πᾶσι συμβαίνει τοῖς μεγάλοις οὐ διέφυγε παθεῖν, ἀλλ' ἐφθονεῖτο*.

as coming; Dionysius too describes his followers as fighting men, but Plutarch makes them the most peaceful of all the Sabines and the most accustomed to a calm and ordered way of life.[33]

§v. Dionysius makes Clausus and his followers cast themselves on the Romans' mercy as suppliants; in Plutarch, on the other hand, the consul P. Valerius Publicola *invites* Clausus to Rome as a man of honour unworthily treated, and welcomes him and his followers 'with eager goodwill'.[34]

§vi. Livy relates without comment that after his adlection into the patricians Clausus soon 'attained the position enjoyed by the leading men' at Rome; Plutarch, using almost the same phrase, adds the explanation that his influence was due to the wisdom of his policies.[35]

These differences are most easily accounted for by the assumption that two different versions of the story existed: one which made Clausus a factioneer and would-be tyrant who abjectly deserted his country for political reasons and took his strong-arm men with him, and another which saw him as a great man, wise, virtuous and eloquent, who escaped from unjust persecution with a group of like-minded compatriots and was invited to continue his admirable career at Rome. Plutarch, followed by Zonaras, preserves the favourable version most faithfully; though some of the details of it seem to reflect his own ideas of the ideal statesman,[36] it is highly unlikely that he himself would have totally recast an existing hostile tradition to achieve this. He must have had the choice between a hostile and a favourable version, with his preconceptions leading him – unlike Dionysius and Livy – to believe the latter and tacitly to reject the former as being motivated by malice.[37]

The logical order of the two versions is, I think, revealed by the fact that the favourable account evidently presupposed the hostile

33. Livy II 16.4, 'cum . . . a turbatoribus belli premeretur, nec par factioni esset, ab Inregillo magna clientium comitatus manu Romam transfugit'; Dion. Hal. V 40.3, *τοὺς ὅπλα φέρειν δυναμένους*; Plut. *Popl.* 21.9, *ὅπερ ἦν ἐν Σαβίνοις ἀθόρυβον μάλιστα καὶ βίου πρᾴου καὶ καθεστῶτος οἰκεῖον* (including women and children).

34. Dion. Hal. IX 47.1 (in a speech against a later Appius); Plut. *Popl.* 21.7–9 (*φιλοφρόνως καὶ προθύμως*), followed by Zonaras.

35. Livy II 16.5, 'in principum dignationem pervenit'; Plut. *Popl.* 21.10, *ἀρχὴν πολιτείας λαμβάνοντα ταύτην, ᾗ χρώμενος ἐμφρόνως ἀνέδραμεν εἰς τὸ πρῶτον ἀξίωμα καὶ δύναμιν ἔσχε μεγάλην.*

36. Cf. Wardman 1974, 49ff, esp. 69–78 on envy (n.32 above), 79–86 on wealth (n.31 above).

37. Wardman 1974, 190f and 195 on Plutarch and malice; Hillard 1976, 185–7 on Plutarch's reluctance to believe ill of his subjects.

one: it admitted the background of political chicanery and had to insist that Clausus was the innocent party, something that would not have been necessary if the factional struggle had not already become part of the tradition. Similarly, the insistence on the law-abiding nature of Clausus' followers seems to imply a pre-existing version which made them just the opposite.

It is quite likely that the details of the story were even *invented* by the author of the anti-Claudian version. The Claudii themselves presumably knew – or believed – that their *gens* had migrated to Rome from the Sabine country, and no doubt identified the leader of the migration with the first known Appius, the consul of 495; but did they know how and when it happened? It is perhaps more likely that the event was pinned down to a convenient Sabine war (inferred from the triumphal *fasti*?) by a writer who wanted to portray the family as renegades, and make their arrival in Rome as inauspicious as possible.[38] The 'Augustan' version of the story, putting the migration in the time of Romulus, shows that the date '504 B.C.' was not canonical in the family's own tradition;[39] on the other hand, the unanimity with which the other sources accept it shows that it *became* canonical, presumably because some historian who influenced all the later tradition made it so, by spelling out the supposed circumstances of the migration. The author of the anti-Claudian version, with his 'deserter' theme, is the most likely candidate, in which case the acceptance of his chronology by the author of the apologetic version is another indication of his priority.

In rhetorical terms, that is, the first of our authors took as his *thesis* the bare tradition of a Claudian migration and developed it with the *colores* of faction, desertion, etc., filling in (as the rules of the rhetorical game allowed) as many fictional details as he liked, provided only that they were not inconsistent with his basic data.[40] His successor had a more difficult task: for him, the details had now become part of the *thesis*, and the application of an apologetic *color* could only be achieved by imputing different motives, and a different moral character, to the chief protagonist.[41]

It is important to recognize this fundamental principle in the

38. Mommsen (1864, 293f) thought the tradition originally undated; so too Ogilvie (1965, 273) and Alföldi (1965, 159f); *contra*, Münzer 1899, 2663.
39. Nor is it likely that the date of the origin of the *tribus Claudia* was known (Badian 1962, 201); Fabius Pictor, Vennonius and probably Cato (Dion. Hal. IV 15.1) evidently assumed that it existed in the time of Ser. Tullius.
40. See p. 26 above.
41. Cf. p. 7 above.

writing of annalistic pseudo-history:[42] you have to accept the 'facts' which your predecessors have invented and which have thus become part of the tradition, but you are still at liberty to interpret them however you like, and make them tell quite a different story by changing the motivation of the characters. The technique can be seen very clearly in the further career of Attus Clausus, after he became Appius Claudius the consul of 495.

—

He first appears in the tradition in 498, where Dionysius sets out a debate on the plebeians' reluctance to fight in the Latin War because of their grievances about debt – a crisis which eventually resulted in the creation of the dictatorship. The two main speakers in the debate are M. Valerius, the son of Publicola, and Appius Claudius Sabinus.[43]

Appius' speech is reasonable, not violent. He points out first (§66) that the abolition of debts would be dangerous, in that the aggrieved party would then no longer be the poor, who cannot themselves destroy the state, but the rich and powerful, who can. Even if the creditors accepted it without a fight, such a cancellation of contracts would lead to the breakdown of communal life and of all work, trade and useful activity, because the rich would no longer risk their money, and the resulting conditions would be a breeding-ground for sedition. Secondly (§67), it would be a very bad precedent to give in to the wishes of the masses, whose desires are insatiable and who will follow every concession with further demands. They must be checked now, while they are weak, or Rome will suffer the fate of Greek cities who gave away too much too soon.[44] As the soul must not be subject to the body, so the reason must not be subject to the passions, nor the wise to the senseless element in the state. As for the plebeians' military strike, it has no significance since the poorest citizens are armed only with slings and are militarily negligible. Finally (§68), sympathy for the debtors is misplaced. Why are they in debt? In most cases, because of their own improvidence. Any cases of genuinely undeserved hardship should be relieved piecemeal by the generosity of indi-

42. Cf., as random examples of the principle at work, Gabba 1976, 91–4 on Aeneas' flight from Troy; Jocelyn 1971, 51–60 (esp. 53) on the Romulus and Remus story; Musti 1970, 90 on Ser. Tullius and the sons of Ancus Marcius.

43. Dion. Hal. V 63–69 (Appius' speech at 66–8).

44. At this point (V 67.3), I think Dionysius' phraseology betrays his method: *παραδείγμασί τε πολλοῖς εἰς τοῦτο ἐχρήσατο πόλεων Ἑλληνίδων ἔργα διεξιών, ὅσαι . . . κτλ.* (Cf. p. 52 above on *διεξελθεῖν*). His source probably gave the *exempla* in full.

vidual creditors; relief for all alike would be unjust because the worthless would be made equal with the deserving. It is intolerable that the Romans should not be able to do what is best and in the common interest of all, but be forced to act against their judgment, as if in a conquered city. Do not obey those who are useless to the state, and throw away *Fides Publica* for mere sling-throwers;[45] let those who will not accept a justice common to all citizens get out, and good riddance. The senseless element in the state will just become arrogant if it is flattered.

That, I submit, is not *superbia Claudiana*. It is the conservative position rationally stated, quite unlike the crude violence of the tradition Suetonius reports. The emphasis is on the common good,[46] and the justification is in terms of the superiority of justice over injustice,[47] self-control over self-indulgence,[48] hard work over idleness,[49] wisdom over senselessness,[50] and general moral excellence over its opposite.[51]

Where does this *color* come from? There is one detail, early in the speech, which may indicate its origin. In arguing that aggrieved creditors could be a danger to the state, Appius is made to say that 'cities are not overthrown by those who are poor and without power, when they are compelled to act justly, but by the rich and those able to conduct public affairs, when they are insulted by their inferiors and fail to obtain justice'. The last phrase sounds very much like the situation of Attus Clausus before his migration, according to the favourable version recorded by Plutarch.[52] Dionysius himself, in his narrative of the migration, does not share that view of Clausus; if therefore the reference in the speech is to the speaker's own previous experience, as it seems to be, then the speech itself is not likely to be Dionysius' own invention, but is presumably taken from the apologetic version of Claudian history

45. V 68.4, with a cross-reference to II 75.3, Numa's foundation of the *ἱερὸν Πίστεως δημοσίας* and its attendant sacrifices.
46. *τὸ κοινόν*: V 67.3, 67.5, 68.1, 68.3, 68.5; cf. 66.3 (*κοινὸς βίος*), 67.1 (*τὰ κοινά, ἐν κοινῷ*), 68.2 (*κοινὴν βοήθειαν*), 68.5 (*κοινωνεῖν*).
47. V 66.2, 66.4 (*δίκαιος* also at 66.3, 68.5).
48. *σωφροσύνη* V 66.2, 68.5; *ἀκολασία* 66.4; *ἡδονή* and *ἐπιθυμία* 67.1–2, 67.5, 68.1.
49. *φιλεργοῦντες* V 66.2, 66.4; *ἐργασία* 66.3.
50. *ἄφρων* V 67.1, 67.4; *ἀνόητος* 67.2, 68.5.
51. *τῷ χείρονι μέρει τοῦ πολιτεύματος χαρίζεσθαι . . . τοῦ κρείττονος ὑπερορᾶν* (V 66.2); *ἧς ἐξ ἴσου μεθέξουσιν οἱ πονηροὶ τοῖς χρηστοῖς* (68.2); *πονηρός* also at 66.1, 66.2, 67.1, 67.3, 68.1. Cf. Polybius II 21.7–8 on C. Flaminius; Bernstein (1978, 177f) plausibly suggests that similar arguments were used against Ti. Gracchus.
52. Dion. Hal. V 66.2, cf. Plut. *Popl.* 21.5f and 7f.

– an example of those 'wise policies' by which Appius became so influential.[53]

If, so, there are three points to be noticed for future reference: first, the concern about the future and the evil precedent of giving in to the demands of men who will go on to demand other concessions; second, the related idea of the arrogance of the *plebs*, which will be made worse by giving in to them and can only be checked by firmness; and finally the simultaneous appeal to the gods and to *mos maiorum*, where Appius invokes that *Fides Publica* 'which our ancestors have honoured with a temple and sacrifices throughout the year'.[54] We shall meet all these themes again.

The next scene is Appius' consulship three years later. The *nexi*, complaining about the burden of debt, cause a disturbance in the Forum; the consuls intervene to put down the *seditio*; a senatorial debate follows, in which Appius urges that the matter be simply dealt with by the *imperium consulare* ('just arrest one or two of them and the others will keep quiet'); his colleague Servilius inclines to milder remedies.[55] Meanwhile, a campaign against the Volsci is called for; Servilius, promising debt relief, leads the army to battle, but after his victory Appius frustrates the debtors' hopes by giving the harshest possible judgments on cases of debt, 'both because of the inbred arrogance of his character and in order to destroy his colleague's credit';[56] the whole *factio nobilium* supports him, and Servilius is frustrated. Then a Sabine war threatens, and the plebeians, despairing of help from consuls or Senate, refuse to enlist and demonstrate again in the Forum. Appius furiously attacks his colleague's inactivity and concern for his own popularity[57] – 'but the Republic is not entirely deserted, the consular *imperium* not wholly thrown away: I alone will stand up for my authority and that of the *patres*'. With that Appius arrests one of the ringleaders, and pays no attention when he appeals to the people. The crisis continues until the consuls go out of office at the end of the year, Appius 'patribus mire gratus'.

Thus Livy. Dionysius' version is much the same, except that it is prefaced by a speech of Appius insisting on a hard line against the debtors. It is much shorter than the earlier Appian speech in

53. Plut. *Popl.* 21.10 (ἐμφρόνως); cf. n.44 above on Dionysius' source for the speech.
54. Dion. Hal. V 66.4 (future danger), 67.1 (dangerous innovation), 67.2 and 68.5 (arrogance), 68.4 (*Fides*).
55. Livy II 23.15 (Appius 'vehementis ingenii vir').
56. Livy II 27.1, 'et insita superbia animo et ut collegae vanam faceret *fidem*'.
57. Livy II 27.10 – *ambitio* and *populare silentium*.

Dionysius, and though he again appeals to *mos maiorum* and *σωφροσύνη*, and points out the danger of tyranny,[58] the context here is quite different. Appius is introduced as harsh and arrogant, a phrase repeated in his altercation with Servilius;[59] he considers the people disgracefully pampered because they are no longer subject to corporal punishment and taxation as they were under the kings, and he relies on superior strength – in particular, that of the patrician youth – to frighten the *plebs* into submission.[60] In Dionysius' narrative, too, some of the details confirm the clear impression of a hostile source: in the first Forum disturbance, Appius flees ignominiously from the scene in fear of physical assault; after Servilius' defeat of the Volsci he flogs and executes 300 hostages, and then succeeds in denying Servilius a well-deserved triumph.[61]

The following year the crisis went on. There was uproar in the Senate when debt relief for the *plebs* was debated. Appius took the hard line, being harsh by nature 'and borne aloft by the hatred of the plebeians and the applause of the *patres*'. His diagnosis was that this tumult was due entirely to the institution of *provocatio*, which turned the consular *imperium* into mere threats. What was needed was the election of a dictator, from whom there was no appeal – 'then let one of them strike a lictor, when he knows that the man whose *maiestas* he has offended has the power to flog or kill him'.[62] This view prevailed – by unfair means, according to Livy[63] – and Appius was almost made dictator himself. In the end, however, Publicola's brother Manius Valerius was appointed.

In all of this Livy consistently follows the 'violence and arrogance' tradition, which appears also in the narrative of Dionysius, where the younger senators get Appius' motion carried by force.[64] In the speech Dionysius gives him, however, Appius appears much more sympathetic, refusing to yield to what is not lawful or honourable,[65] insisting on free speech,[66] warning that concession

58. Dion. Hal. VI 24.1 (*κατὰ τοὺς πατρίους ἐθισμοὺς*), 24.2 (*τῷ σωφρονοῦντι μέρει τῆς πόλεως*), 24.3 (tyranny).
59. VI 24.1 (his *γνώμη αὐστηρὰ καὶ αὐθάδης*), 27.1 (Servilius calls him *αὐστηρὸν καὶ αὐθάδη*).
60. VI 24.2 (*πέρα τοῦ μετρίου τρυφῶσι*), 24.3 (*ἰσχὺς, ὅπλον, κράτος*).
61. VI 26.3, 30.1–2 (though here the *color* is anti-Servilian).
62. Livy II 29.9–12.
63. II 30.1, 'factione respectuque rerum privatarum'.
64. Dion. Hal. VI 39.1, *βίᾳ πολλῇ*.
65. VI 38.1, *ὅ τι μὴ νόμιμον μηδὲ κάλον*.
66. VI 38.1 *ad fin.*

would mean the overthrow of the state,[67] putting the city's security before his own,[68] and again invoking *mos maiorum*.[69] 'You may', he says, 'call my attitude nobility or arrogance, as you please . . . the result of wisdom or of madness'.[70]

The inconsistency of Dionysius' account stems, I think, from his habit of using pairs of full-scale speeches at each critical point in the narrative. He wants to give each side a good case, and so he uses his pro-Claudian source for Appius' speech, while the narrative, and his own comments on it, largely reflect the hostile version. Indeed, the reason Appius keeps coming in at all is presumably because the pro-Claudian source gave him a succession of dignified speeches. There is surely no other reason why Dionysius keeps giving the honest-conservative viewpoint in the debates to Appius; considering the way Appius appears in his narrative, it would have been more consistent to give it to someone else, if Dionysius' historiographical conscience had allowed him such a liberty.

Livy, on the other hand, is much more sparing and less mechanical with his speeches. He gives Appius the brutal consul just a few well-chosen words, mostly in *oratio obliqua*,[71] and then leaves him out, thus preserving the artistic unity of his story. After his consulship, Appius comes into Livy's narrative only once more, with a brief appearance in 480. In Dionysius, however, he appears several more times – luckily for us, who are interested in his sources, but with a disastrous effect on the consistency of Dionysius' own historical picture.

—

The patchwork nature of Dionysius' history is shown clearly in Appius' next intervention, at the conclusion of the first secession of the *plebs*. A long speech is given to Menenius Agrippa;[72] then a short one to Manius Valerius, who attacks the cruel and arrogant creditors for creating a faction with Appius at its head, 'an enemy of the people and a champion of oligarchy';[73] and finally a long speech to Appius himself, replying not to Menenius but to Valerius.

Appius is introduced as the leader of the faction that opposed the

67. VI 38.2 (cf. *τὸ κοινόν* in 38.3).
68. VI 38.3, *οὐ τὸ ἴδιον ἀσφαλὲς ἀλλὰ τὸ τῆς πόλεως*. Contrast n.63 above.
69. VI 38.3, opposition to *τὰ μὴ πάτρια πολιτεύματα*.
70. VI 38.2, *εὐγενὲς εἴτε αὔθαδες*; 38.3, *ἀπὸ τοῦ φρονίμου εἴτε διὰ μανίας τινος*.
71. Livy II 23.15, 27.10f, 29.9–12.
72. Dion. Hal. VI 49–56.
73. VI 58.3, *μισόδημον ἄνδρα καὶ ὀλιγαρχικόν*. The creditors are accused of *ὕβρις*, *πλεονεξία*, *ἀδικία*, *ὠμότης* and *ὑπερηφανία*, and carefully distinguished from the *σωφρονοῦν μέρος* of the patricians (*ibid.*).

people, and as a man 'with an arrogant opinion of himself'[74] – justly so, Dionysius immediately adds, for his private life was sober and dignified,[75] and his political attitude was noble and such as to protect the dignity of the aristocracy.[76] Evidently the historian is trying to have it both ways. The speech itself is sober, rational and responsible, very much like the first speech attributed to Appius at V 66–8, and repeating many of the same arguments.

He begins by defending himself against the charge of cruelty towards his fellow-citizens,[77] defying Valerius to produce the victims and insisting on his personal generosity as a creditor; if he is called an enemy of the people and champion of oligarchy, it is only because the Romans' ancestral government is preferable to democracy, the worst of all known constitutions in that it leads to tyranny – and tyranny is what Valerius seems to be aiming at, with his demagogic proposals.[78] The Romans must keep their ancestral traditions, and 'faith, a holy thing', and not give in to unjust demands,[79] for the *plebs* will just ask for more and more, wanting to be made equal with the *patres* and enjoy their privileges.[80] The rest of Appius' argument is an assessment of the present danger, pointing out the weakness of the seceders' position.[81] The whole speech clearly shows how consistent with his earlier pronouncements Appius' position is made to be, in such themes as his personal generosity to individual debtors,[82] the far-sighted fear of worse things to come,[83] the plebeians' arrogance and mindlessness,[84] and the value of *mos maiorum* and *Fides*.[85]

That the consistency stems not from Dionysius but from his

74. VI 59.1, *μέγα φρονῶν ἐφ' ἑαυτῷ* (cf. V 68.5 for *μεγάλα φρονεῖν* used by Appius of the *plebs*).
75. *Ibid.*, *σώφρων καὶ σεμνός*.
76. *Ibid.*, *ἥ τε προαίρεσις τῶν πολιτευμάτων εὐγενὴς* . . .
77. VI 59.2, *ἐπιτήδευμα οὔτε πολιτικὸν οὔτ' εὐπρεπές*; 59.3, *ὠμότητα ἢ φιλοχρηματίαν*, etc.
78. VI 60.1 (quoting Valerius at 58.3), 60.2–3 (with reference to points made by Valerius at 58.1 and 3). 61.1 marks the end of the counter-attack against Valerius himself (announced at 59.2).
79. VI 61.1, *πίστιν, ἱερὸν χρῆμα*.
80. VI 61.2–62.1 (with a brief reference at 62.1 to Menenius, as *σώφρων* but misguided).
81. VI 62.2–64.3.
82. VI 59.3, 63.3; cf. V 68.2.
83. VI 61–2; cf. V 67.
84. *αὐθάδεια*: VI 60.4, 61.4, 62.1, 62.5, 64.3; cf. V 67.2, 68.5. *ἄνοια* etc: VI 60.4, 61.1 (*ἀγνώμων*), 61.3 (*ἀμαθής, ἄφρων*), 61.4, 64.3; cf. V 67.1–2, 67.4, 68.5. For general moral worthlessness (cf. n.51 above), see especially VI 60.1–3.
85. VI 60.1, 61.1; cf. V 68.4.

source, the pro-Claudian annalist, may perhaps be deduced from the next occasion we see Appius in action, restating his position with dignity when the *patres* finally vote for Menenius' concessions:[86]

> I shall not abandon my original opinion, or willingly desert my post as a citizen. The more I am abandoned by those who once shared my policy, the more I shall one day be honoured by you. You will praise me while I live, posterity will remember me when I am gone. Do you, Capitoline Jupiter, and you gods and heroes who keep watch over our city, grant that the return of the fugitives be fair and advantageous to all, and that I may be mistaken in the forebodings I have about the future; but if misfortune should come on the city as a result of these measures, may you yourselves quickly correct them and make our affairs safe and secure. And may you be favourable and propitious to me, who never chose to say what was agreeable instead of what was useful, and who will not now betray the state (*τὸ κοινόν*) to secure my own safety.

When the plebeians accept the ambassadors' terms and the Senate ratifies the concessions, Appius again calls the gods to witness and foretells how many evils will follow.[87] The revealing thing in his first prayer, however, is the way Dionysius translates the formulae 'quod felix faustumque sit' and 'quod faxitis deos velim fortunare' – suggesting, I think, that he had a Latin original in front of him.

Appius' prayers were, of course, in vain. After a brief appearance in 492 at the head of the senators who wanted to resist 'the arrogant and ignorant multitude',[88] we next find him opposing the tribune Decius on the matter of Coriolanus' trial before the people. This speech is a counterpart to Appius' appeal to the gods at the end of the secession, for he is made to say that despite his prayers things have turned out not as he had hoped, but as he expected.[89] Once more he puts the welfare of the state before his own safety, all the more defiantly, considering how dangerous free speech has proved

86. VI 68.2–3.
87. VI 88.3, mercifully not a full-length speech.
88. Dion. Hal. VII 15.2–3, *ὄχλον αὐθάδη καὶ ἀμαθῆ* (cf. VI 60.2–3 on those – like Valerius – who 'court the people'); at VII 15.3 it looks as though Dionysius' narrative source had a violent scene, evidently provoked by Appius, which he omits.
89. VII 48.1–2; cf. VI 68.2.

for Coriolanus.[90] 'But while I have life, no fear shall deter me from saying what I think.'

The plebeians, he says, have not been satisfied with their gains, but have demanded more – naturally, since they are hostile to the established constitution and are trying to turn it into a democracy, just as Appius had forecast.[91] They are not content with the ancestral form of government, and if the *patres* had not resisted their attack on Coriolanus, everything the ancestors had built up would have been lost.[92] Their treatment of Coriolanus shows their arrogance,[93] so no more concessions must be made, or things will just get worse. The rest of the speech is concerned with the particulars of the situation, but the arguments he uses are all reasonable ones, with no crude threats or appeals to the consular *imperium*. It is true that at the end he admits the possibility of freeing the slaves and making common cause with Rome's enemies if the plebeians force an armed showdown; but he immediately goes on:

> O Jupiter and all you gods who guard the Roman state, may there be no occasion for anything of this kind! Rather may these terrible threats go no farther than words and result in no deplorable act![94]

The continuity with the themes of earlier Appian speeches is obvious,[95] even to the extent of another reference to that *Fides* which the patricians' original concessions on debt had violated.[96]

—

At Appius' next appearance, in the context of Spurius Cassius' agrarian bill in 486, we have a most extraordinary hybrid which can only have been produced by Dionysius' attempt to synthesize the speeches in his sources.

Cassius proposed to divide among the people a tract of public land which certain wealthy patricians were occupying, and in addition to include the Latins and the recently-conquered Hernici in the share-out. Uproar in the Senate followed, with bitter opposi-

90. VII 48.3–4, *τῆς κοινῆς ὠφελείας* (cf. VI 68.3).
91. VII 49.1, *τῇ καθεστώσῃ πολιτείᾳ*; 49.3, *τῷ κόσμῳ τῆς πολιτείας* (cf. VI 61.1).
92. VII 50.2, *τὸν πάτριον κόσμον τῆς πολιτείας*; 50.4.
93. VII 51.3 (*αὐθάδεια*), cf. 50.1 (lack of *σωφροσύνη*), 51.2 (*ὕβρις* as of drunkenness or madness), 50.2 and 51.6 (*πλεονεξία*). The plebeians' *παρανομία* is a constant theme: 50.2, 50.4, 50.5 (twice), 51.4, 51.5, 52.1.
94. VII 53.6 (trans. E. Cary).
95. He praises the *γενναιότης* of the *patres* (VII 50.4, 51.2, 51.4); cf. his earlier speech at VI 62.2, 64.3.
96. VII 49.2; cf. V 68.4, VI 61.1.

tion not only from Cassius' consular colleague Verginius, but also from the oldest and most honoured senators, particularly Appius Claudius, who accused him of stirring up sedition. Then one of the tribunes got Cassius to split his proposal, and got Verginius to admit the desirability of dividing the public land, but not that of admitting the Latins and Hernici.[97] That was the situation when Appius' opinion was called for in the ensuing senatorial debate.

To begin with the speech goes entirely according to expectation. Appius opposes any division of the public land, on the same grounds that he had used to oppose abolition of debts at the time of the secession, namely the undesirability of idleness, which is what would result from giving the plebeians a free hand-out of what belonged to the state: public property should remain public property.[98] Besides, even if the *patres* did agree to the division of land, it was the dangerous Cassius, not they themselves, who would get the credit. So far so good, but Dionysius continues: 'after saying this and other things to the same effect, he ended by giving them the following advice' – and the advice that follows, far from being a mere peroration, takes up three times as much space as what has gone before, and has quite a different tone.

Appius now advises the election of a commission of ten senators to restore to the state any public land illegally occupied, to sell part of it and rent out the rest on five-year leases. For at present, he observes, the poor are quite *rightly* aggrieved at the unjust occupation of public land. It is true that the emphasis is on the rented part of the land, the income from which is to be used for the payment of soldiers and the purchase of war supplies (public property thus remaining public property);[99] but even so, his proposal is a concession, and not at all what one would have expected from the familiar conservative Appius at the beginning of the speech.

Further confusion follows. The next contribution to the debate comes from A. Sempronius Atratinus, who praises Appius at length for all the virtues we have come to associate with the favourable tradition as represented in Appius' speeches – wisdom, farsightedness, fearlessness and so on[100] – and concurs entirely with his

97. Dion. Hal. VIII 69.3–73.1. Appius: 71.1, cf. 69.2 on the *πρεσβύτατοί τε καὶ τιμιώτατοι*.

98. VIII 73.2; cf. V 66.2–4 on idleness, n.46 above on *τὸ κοινόν*.

99. VIII 73.4: *ὁ φθόνος τῶν πενήτων . . . δίκαιός ἐστι* (for *τὰ κοινὰ ὄντως κοινὰ γινόμενα*, see previous note).

100. VIII 74.1: *φρονῆσαι πρὸ πολλοῦ τὰ μέλλοντα* (cf. V 66.4–67.1, VI 61.2–62.1, 68.2, 88.3, VII 49.4); *οὐ φόβῳ εἴκοντα* (cf. VI 38.3, 68.3, VII 48.3–4); *τὸ φρονιμόν* (cf. n.35 above); *γενναιότης* (cf. n.95 above).

proposal.[101] He only adds, as a small detail left out by Appius, that the senatorial commission be empowered to determine how much of the marked-out land should be leased, and how much should be divided up among the plebeians.[102] But Appius had not suggested that at all; the very first thing in his speech had been a demand that the land be *not* divided up among the plebeians,[103] and he had gone on to propose the *sale* of the unleased part of it, his motive being to give the new owners, and not the state, the trouble of defending their title against the lawsuits of the previous occupiers (73.3).

Sempronius' 'additional detail', which is loudly applauded by the *patres* and immediately voted into effect, evidently implies an Appian proposal which had conceded the main point entirely. So we have three different Appii here: the familiar conservative trying to hold the line against disastrous innovations, then a more flexible figure admitting the justice of the plebeians' complaints, and finally a ghostly reforming Appius whose proposal to divide the land among the people appears in the debate from nowhere.

For all his faults, Dionysius cannot be personally responsible for this farrago. It must result from his simultaneous use of discrepant versions, and it is not hard to guess what they were. The working-up of the Sp. Cassius episode, with the agrarian reformer as would-be tyrant, is generally agreed to be a contribution of historians influenced by the tribunate and death of Tiberius Gracchus in 133 B.C. Many of the details show it – the disputed proposal to include allies in the distribution, the Gracchan-type boundary stones which the commission is to use,[104] and so on – and the very idea of a Sempronius agreeing with an Appius Claudius on the distribution of *ager publicus* among the poor must surely belong to that stratum of the tradition, reflecting the time when Ti. Sempronius Gracchus and his father-in-law Ap. Claudius Pulcher (the consul of 143) proposed just that. Even the supporting arguments in the debate can be used as evidence for real issues and controversies of the Gracchan period.[105]

Dionysius, then, had at least two rolls open on his desk as he

101. *Ibid.*: *γμώμην τε οὐχ ἑτέραν, ἀλλὰ καὶ αὐτὸς τὴν αὐτὴν ἀποδείκνυμαι.*
102. VIII 75.3, with *προστίθημι* referring back to *μικρὰ ἔτι προσθεὶς* at 74.1; cf. also 74.3 for explicit agreement with Appius.
103. VIII 73.2, *οὐκ εἷα συγχωρεῖν τῷ δήμῳ τὴν διανομήν.*
104. VIII 73.3, cf. *ILLRP* 467–75. For the allies, cf. Bernstein 1978, 145–8, who argues independently that Ti. Gracchus originally included the Italians among the beneficiaries of his agrarian law, but then cut them out to prevent opposition when the bill came to the vote.
105. E.g. Gabba 1974a, 135–8 on VII 73.5 etc; cf. Lintott 1968, 180.

worked on this episode: one of a pro-Gracchan annalist from whom he took Atratinus' speech and the picture of a reforming Appius which it implies (Licinius Macer, perhaps?), and one of the author he had used for Appius' earlier speeches, portraying him as a responsible conservative, from which he took the first part of Appius' speech. It is possible that the rest of the speech was Dionysius' own attempt to reconcile the two versions he was using.[106]

The third roll – the one Livy preferred to use – seems to have slipped under the desk, for we get very little of Appius the arrogant factioneer. A few chapters later, however, there may be a hint of it, where the plebeians, resentful at Cassius' death and the contemptuous patricians' refusal to carry out the promised division of land, suspect that a dictator will be appointed to tyrannize over them,[107] and fear that it will be the 'harsh and stern' Appius.[108] This detail, coming significantly in Dionysius' *narrative*, sounds much more like the Appius of VI 24 (p. 68 above) than the brave and wise conservative his readers have become accustomed to in the intervening books.

Appius' final appearance comes in 480. We find him in Livy, reassuring the *patres* that the power of the tribunes can be defeated from within: there would always be one tribune who would be prepared for the country's good to seek a personal victory over his colleagues and thus win the approval of the better sort. All the *patres* had to do was to get one or more such tribunes on their side, and their veto would do the rest. They followed his advice, and that year's threat of an agrarian law was foiled.[109]

With that, our knowledge of the fictional career of the first of the Claudii comes to end. Wearisome though Dionysius' speeches are, it is worth struggling through them[110] if only to see how completely imaginary the story is. With the one exception of the Sp. Cassius episode – where there was already a well-established, though equally factitious, tradition to be fitted in (at whatever cost to coherence and consistency) – the whole picture is evidently drawn

106. VIII 74.4, in Atratinus' speech (*ἄλλης τινὸς . . . θεραπείας μετρίας*), may betray his unease: this was not supposed to be a different proposal from Appius' (cf. n. 101 above).
107. VIII 81.1 (*θρασύτεροί τε καὶ ὑπεροπτικώτεροι*), 81.3 (*τυραννικὴν . . . ἐξουσίαν*).
108. VIII 81.4, *πικρὸν ὄντα καὶ χαλεπόν*. See p. 78 n.12 below for the first of these adjectives.
109. Livy II 44.2–5, 'exemplo in perpetuum' (see p. 84 below on Dion. Hal. X 30.5).
110. *Pace* Mommsen (1864, 289, on their 'intolerably insipid wordiness'!).

from the use of one or other of the two sources identified in the story of the migration of the *gens*: one that made the Claudii savage and arrogant factioneers, relying on the consular *imperium* and the strong arms of their lictors to try and overthrow the plebeians' just demands, and the other which emphasized wisdom and nobility, attributing the arrogance and the factioneering to the plebeians themselves, and making out that only the Claudii were clear-sighted enough to realize, and courageous enough to say, that concession would mean the loss of traditional standards and the downfall of the Republic.

The rival sets of characteristics were evidently imputed to the Claudii as a family, not just to Attus-Appius; for both legends follow his descendants right down at least to the second century B.C. Genuine historical tradition, beyond the mere inference from names in the *fasti*, had to be taken increasingly into account after about the end of the fourth century, as did rival legends invented for other purposes, as is clear from the case of the Sp. Cassius episode. The legends, therefore, are not always in such a pure form as we can see them in the early days, but the continuity of the main themes is, I think, demonstrable.

Chapter 6

CLAUDIAN ARROGANCE AND CLAUDIAN WISDOM

The Appius who 'stalked along the Forum' in Macaulay's poem was the tyrannical and libidinous Decemvir, the villain of the Verginia story.

The Decemvirs were elected in 451, when Appius was consul; the Augustan consular Fasti for the year mark it as his second consulship and give him the filiation 'Ap.f. M.n.', thus identifying him as the first Appius' son, who had been consul in 471.[1] It is likely enough that the members of the Board of Ten appointed to draw up Rome's law code were senior senators, and the Fasti may well represent historical reality. In the tradition followed by Livy and Dionysius, however, the consul of 471 and the Decemvir are two quite separate characters;[2] their differentiation allows the Decemvir to be a comparatively young man and therefore more plausibly lustful,[3] and leaves room for a popular trial and death in prison for the consul of 471, whose supposed assault on the tribunes and refusal to supplicate were expanded by Suetonius into the characteristic behaviour of all Claudii.[4]

The career of the second Appius consists of five episodes: an unsuccessful candidature for the consulship in 483;[5] opposition, as consul-elect in 472 and consul in 471, to Volero Publilius' bill to have the tribunes elected by the tribal assembly;[6] a disastrous campaign against the Volsci;[7] opposition to an agrarian law in the

1. Degrassi 1947, 26–7: 'Ap. Claudius Ap.f.M.n. Crassinr[i]gill. Sabin. II T. Genu[cius L.f.L.n.] Au[gu]rinus abdicarunt ut de[c]emviri consular[i imperio fie-r]ent. Decemviri consular[i imp]erio legibus s[cribundis fact]i eod. anno Ap. Claudius Ap.f.M.n. Crassin[rigill. Sab]in. qui cos. fue[rat] T. Genucius L.f.L.n. Augurin[us q]ui cos. fuerat . . .'. For Appius' *cognomina* ('Crassinus Regillensis'?), see Münzer 1899, 2663 and 2699.

2. Livy and Dionysius also differ from the Fasti on Appius' *M.n.* filiation: see p. 60 above.

3. Livy III 35.6 ***minimus natu*** (inconsistent with *ea aetate* at 35.3?).

4. Suet. *Tib.* 2.4; p. 58 above.

5. Dion. Hal. VIII 90.

6. *Ibid.* IX 42–49, Livy II 56–57.

7. Dion. Hal. IX 50, Livy II 58–60.

year after his consulship;[8] and finally his trial before the people and his death.[9] Though Livy ignores the first of these and passes over Appius' part in the fourth, it is clear that his account and Dionysius' draw on the same source material.[10] It is equally clear, from the repetition of themes and key words from one episode to another,[11] that the authors they used had conceived his career as an artistic unity, and one which reflected the characteristics and preoccupations imputed to his father.[12]

Authors, in the plural – for here, just as much as in the first Appius' career, traces of both a hostile and a favourable version can be detected, inadequately synthesized by Dionysius and Livy. In the main, the hostile tradition prevails: Appius' arrogance is emphasized from the start,[13] and his anger, violence and cruelty are duly exemplified in his behaviour as consul, both in attacking the tribune Laetorius over Volero's bill, and in dealing with his mutinous troops in the Volscian campaign.[14] But the same characteristics are also attributed to his plebeian opponents,[15] and responsibility for the transition from words to deeds, which led to the violent confrontation between Appius and his lictor on one side and Laetorius and his tribunician *viator* on the other, is symmetrically apportioned by Dionysius to each of them.[16] Besides, how violent *was* the confrontation? Dionysius' narrative insists that Laetorius was struck, and describes his bruised face to prove it;[17] Livy, in a context emphasizing plebeian *vis* and *ira* (and describing Appius by no more harsh a word than *pertinax*), only says that there would

8. Dion. Hal. IX 52–3, Livy II 61.1–2.
9. Dion. Hal. IX 54, Livy II 61.3–9.
10. Münzer 1899, 2698. Compare, for instance, Livy II 56.9 and 59.8 with Dion. Hal. IX 48.1 and 50.4 (rhetorical *sententiae* from a common source).
11. E.g. young patricians (Dion. Hal. VIII 90.1, IX 48.2, Livy II 56,10), *ἐπιείκεια* of Appius' opponents (Dion. Hal. VIII 90.1 and 4, IX 44.4 twice, 50.2), clients (Dion. Hal. VIII 90.1, IX 41.5, 48.1, Livy II 56.3), *concordia* (Dion. Hal. IX 45.1, 49.3, Livy II 57.2–3, 60.2 and 4), determination to deprive Appius of *honores* (Dion. Hal. VIII 90.6, IX 50.4, 53.4).
12. Explicitly at Dion. Hal. IX 42.3, 47.1 and 4, Livy II 56.5 and 7, 58.5, 61.3. For his *πικρότης*/*acerbitas* (Dion. Hal. IX 42.3, 44.6 and 8, 47.4, Livy II 58.9), cf. Dion. Hal. VIII 81.4 on his father. Cf. also V 68.1f and IX 52.4 (piecemeal remedies).
13. *αὐθάδεια*: Dion. Hal. VIII 90.1 and 3, IX 49.1, cf. 44.5 (*ὑπερηφανία*). *Superbia*: Livy II 56.7.
14. *Ira*: Livy II 58.6, cf. 61.3. *Vis*: Livy II 59.4, cf. Dion. Hal. IX 48.1–2 and 4. *Crudelitas*: Livy II 56.7. *Saevitia*, *ferocitas*: Livy II 58.4 and 6, 59.4, 60.1, cf. Dion. Hal. IX 47.4 (*τὸ θηριῶδες*).
15. Livy II 56.13–16 (*ira*, *saevientem*, *irae*, *vim*), Dion. Hal. IX 44.5 (anger), 45.1 (violence), 44.7 and 54.6 (tyranny and *hybris*: cf. 46.2 and 47.2).
16. Dion. Hal. IX 45.2, 47.4 (with a deliberate cross-reference).
17. *Ibid.* 48.2 and 4.

have been bloodshed if Appius' colleague had not got him out of the way and made a successful appeal for calm.[18]

Predictably, it is the speeches attributed to Appius by Dionysius that reveal the favourable tradition most clearly. In a short address as consul-elect, and in the long speeches opposing Volero's bill as consul and the agrarian law the next year, many of the familiar themes are brought out: the good of the state as opposed to private advantage,[19] the excellence of the ancestral constitution,[20] the dangers of idleness among the *plebs*,[21] the abolition of *Fides* and the arrogance and lawless behaviour of the tribunes.[22] His foresight is emphasized: he sees the whole range of plebeian demands, past, present and future, and prays to the gods to avert their effects.[23] At the end of his last speech comes the very characteristic Appian *topos* that some people nowadays call dignity arrogance, justice stupidity, courage madness, and self-control naivety;[24] correspondingly, what used to be thought vices are now prized as virtues, but Appius will continue to speak out against them with sincerity and frankness.[25]

Glimmers of the favourable version are also visible in Livy's account of Appius' trial and death, with its reference to his *constantia* in the face of the threatening plebeians.[26] Livy reports his death by natural causes, though in Dionysius and Zonaras he kills himself before the trial resumes.[27] The tribunes tried to prevent his son from delivering the customary *laudatio* at his funeral, but the people were unwilling to deny this last honour to 'so great a man'.[28]

18. Livy II 56.15 (cf. n. 15 above). The 'ould have . . . if' formuluation is a commonplace in the Claudian legends: see p. 102 below for a particularly shameless example.
19. Dion. Hal. IX 43.2, 49.1, 53.7.
20. *Ibid*. 44.1 and 7, cf. 50.7. *ὁ κόσμος τοῦ πολιτεύματος* (cf. VI 61.1, VII 49.3) had already appeared in the narrative of Appius' unsuccessful candidature in 483 (VIII 90.3), and may be alluded to in the speeches at 53.4 (*ἀκοσμία*, twice) and 53.5–6 (*κοσμεῖσθαι*, *ἐπικοσμεῖν*).
21. *Ibid*. 43.2, 52.5, cf. 51.5.
22. *Ibid*. 44.7, 45.1.
23. *Ibid*. 44.7, 52.5–6, 53.2 and 7; Livy II 57.4 (a clear allusion to a theme worked out more fully in Dionysius).
24. Dion. Hal. IX 53.6: *αὐθάδεια μὲν ἡ σεμνότης καλεῖται πρὸς ἐνίων, μωρία δ' ἡ δικαιοσύνη, μανικὸν δὲ τὸ ἀνδρεῖον, καὶ ἠλίθιον τὸ σῶφρον* (cf. VI 38.2–3).
25. *Ibid*. 53.7, *μετὰ πάσης ἀληθείας καὶ παρρησίας* (cf. VI 38.1).
26. Livy II 61.5–7, cf. 56.14 (*pertinacia*); also Dion. Hal. IX 54.3 (nothing *ἀγεννές* – cf. p. 72 n.95 above).
27. Livy II 61.8; Dion. Hal. IX 54.4–5 (natural causes an invention of his relatives), Zonaras VII 17.
28. Livy II 61.9, cf. Dion. Hal. IX 54.5–6. The favourable version no doubt gave the eulogy in full; Dionysius, presumably, was not tempted to reproduce it because it was not an 'agonistic' speech.

The son, in this version, must have been Appius the later Decemvir. His evil career, superimposed on to the interlocking stories of the Twelve Tables, the second secession and the attempt on the virtue of Verginia,[29] is expounded with all the familiar *colores* of Appian arrogance, cruelty and violence.[30] Several themes recur from the career of his 'father' – notably the reliance on lictors,[31] patrician youth,[32] and Appius' own faction and clients[33] – but on a greater scale, appropriate to the Decemvir's quasi-tyrannical position. *Dominatio*, *regnum* and *tyrannis* are the key words now, with Tarquinius Superbus as the natural point of comparison.[34]

The characteristics of the tyrant had been part of the stock in trade of Greek political philosophy ever since the age of Herodotus and Euripides,[35] and it was agreed that he exemplified irresponsible power aimed at the gratification of his personal appetites.[36] Through the influence of Hellenistic rhetorical theory, he had become, by the age of Cicero, a standard element in the practice declamations used for the training of budding orators.[37] His characteristic vices were *vis*, *superbia*, *crudelitas* and *libido*, all of which duly appear in the political invectives of Cicero and his contemporaries at the end of the Roman Republic.[38]

Any Appius was automatically guilty of the first three of these; Appius the Decemvir now personified the fourth as well.[39] Moreover, the typical Greek tyrant reached his position by demagogy:[40] the account in Livy and Dionysius of Appius campaigning

29. The Verginia story was evidently a pre-existing 'folk-tale'; cf. Münzer 1899, 2700–1 on Diod. Sic. XII 24.2 (the characters not named), and p. 107 below.
30. Livy III 33–58, Dion. Hal. X 54–XI 46.
31. E.g. Livy III 36.3–5, 41.3, 45.7, 46.4, 48.3, 49.3–4, 56.6 (tribunician *viator*), 57.3; Dion. Hal. X 59.5, XI 37.3 etc.
32. E.g. Livy III 37.6 and 8, 49.2, 56.2; Dion. Hal. X 60.1, XI 2.1 and 4; Zonaras VII 18. Cf. n.11 above, both for this and for the *concordia* theme (Livy III 32.8, Dion. Hal. X 54.6, 60.5, Zonaras VII 18).
33. E.g. Livy III 56.2; Dion. Hal. X 60.1, XI 32.1 (cf. VIII 90.1–2 for the *cos.* 471).
34. E.g. Livy III 38.2, 39.3–7, 44.1 53.7, 58.5; Dion. Hal. XI 35.5, 37.2, 41–2 *passim*.
35. Hdt. III 80.2–5 (Otanes' speech), Eur. *Suppl.* 444–55 (Theseus' speech), etc.
36. The classic expositions are in Plato *Rep.* VIII 562a–IX 580c, and Aristotle *Pol.* IV 1295a and V 1310b–1315b (cf. also Xen. *Hiero*).
37. Cic. *de inv.* II 144, *Att.* IX 4 (which shows how relevant a topic it could be); Juv. *Sat.* VII 15.1, Petr. *Sat.* 1.3, etc; Bonner 1949, 10, 27f, 34.
38. Dunkle 1967, esp. 159f. For *libido* and *hybris*, see Hdt. III 80.5, Eur. *Suppl.* 452–5, Plato *Rep.* II 360cl, Arist. *Pol.* V 1311a25–b36, 1314b23–27, 1315a14–24.
39. Alföldi 1965, 154. See especially Livy III 44.1–2 and 6, with 44.4 'crudelem superbamque vim'; *libido* also at 36.7, 45.8, 50.7, 51.7, 57.3; Dion. Hal. XI 1.6, 35.4–5 etc.
40. Plato *Rep.* VIII 565c9–566d4, Arist. *Pol.* V 1310b12–31.

for re-election to the decemvirate corresponds exactly to Plato's classic description.[41] Tyranny had already made an unobtrusive appearance in the treatment of Appius the consul of 471,[42] but it is only now that the theme is worked up in detail. The author of the hostile version was an artist, with a firm grip on his material well in advance. (The same mastery appears in his casual reference to Appius the Decemvir as one who despised the gods:[43] impiety was a typical tyrant's crime,[44] and if this Appius was not conspicuously guilty of it, some of his descendants were, and the seed had to be sown in the reader's mind in good time.)

Finally, the 'client' theme. The reliance of the Claudii on their personal dependants is implicit in the hostile tradition of Attus Clausus' migration, as it is in the opposition of Appius the consul of 471 to Volero Publilius' proposal about the election of tribunes, which was designed to frustrate the patricians' influence on the elections through their clients.[45] Now for the first time we see this reliance in action, in the person of the Decemvir's odious client M. Claudius, who acts as Appius' pimp by falsely claiming Verginia as his own slave. He is the first of a long series of Claudian clients written into the historical tradition as the agents of their masters' despotic arrogance.

How could the author of the favourable version counter this devastating indictment? He evidently did his best, by imputing unworthy motives to Appius' opponents,[46] applying the *color insaniae* to his lust for Verginia,[47] giving him a defence speech insisting that his early popularity was deserved,[48] and attributing his death in prison to foul play by the plebeians.[49] But in the end, the Decemvir was irredeemable. His family's reputation could

41. Plato *Rep.* VIII 566d8–e4; Livy III 33.7, 35.3–6, 36.1–2; Dion. Hal. X 54.7, 57.4, 58.3. Appius' demagogy is accepted as (genuine?) early tradition by Mommsen (1864, 298f); also by Münzer, though he recognized the artificiality of the 'tyrant' *color* (1899, 2700, cf. 2701).

42. Dion. Hal. IX 47.2 (Laetorius' speech); cf. 43.2, where Appius urges war as a means of keeping the *plebs* quiet, a characteristic tyrant's gambit (Plato *Rep.* VIII 566e6–567a9, Arist. *Pol.* V 1313b28–9).

43. Livy II 56.4 (*impie*), 57.2 (*deorum hominumque contemptor*), both from speeches by Verginius.

44. E.g. Plato *Rep.* VIII 568d7–8, IX 574d24, 575b12.

45. Attus Clausus: p. 62f above. Volero's bill: Livy II 56.3, Dion. Hal. IX 41.5 (cf. VIII 90.1–2).

46. E.g. Livy III 51.8 (Icilius' *popularis* ambitions), Dion. Hal. XI 22.2–3, 23.6 (Valerius' and Horatius' factions).

47. Livy III 47.4, 48.1; Dion. Hal. XI 35.4.

48. Livy III 56.8–13, cf. Dion. Hal. X 55.1, 57.4 etc.

49. Dion. Hal. XI 46.3, cf. *vir. ill.* 21.3. The parallelism with the consul of 471 (rival

only be saved by producing a counter-Claudius to prove him untypical.

Gaius Claudius, consul in 460, was the younger son of the first Appius ('Attus Clausus') and brother of the second (*cos.* 471). Introduced by an essentially formulaic comment on inborn hatred of the *plebs*,[50] Dionysius' version of his career before and after the Decemvirate provides the usual mixture of arrogance (mostly in the narrative)[51] and conservative wisdom (mostly in the speeches),[52] with appropriate echoes of his father and his brother.[53] In the decemviral episode itself, however, the favourable view is unchallenged. Livy preserves the artistic unity of Gaius' character by omitting his earlier and later appearances;[54] Dionysius, who was less sensitive to internal contradictions, could easily have incorporated hostile material here too, if there had been any. In both authors alike, the role of C. Claudius in the story of the Decemvirate is a wholly honourable one, and that is presumably because only the author of the favourable version brought him in at this point at all. The reason is clear: to dilute the effect of Appius the Decemvir and make him out to be uncharacteristic of the Claudian house.

Gaius is supposedly the Decemvir's uncle, and 'constantissimus in optimatium causa'.[55] He is given a long speech in the Senate, pleading with Appius to remember the constitutional Republic in which he was born rather than the career of *hybris* and tyrannical self-gratification into which his desire for pleasure has led him.[56] Gaius has inherited the ancestral Claudian policy of putting the public advantage before his own, and speaking out without fear;[57] he begs Appius to emulate his ancestors, who were honoured in

accounts of his death) appears also in the repetition of *tantus vir* at Livy II 61.9 and III 57.6.

50. Dion. Hal. X 9.2: *ἔμφυτον τὸ πρὸς τοὺς δημοτικοὺς ἔχοντα μῖσος διὰ προγόνων* (cf. IX 47.4, Livy II 56.5, 58.5, IV 36.5, V 2.13, VI 40.2, IX 33.3).

51. E.g. Dion. Hal. X 9.2, XI 55.2, 60.1.

52. E.g. X 12–13, 30.3–4, XI 55–56.

53. Explicitly at X 30.3 and 5, XI 55.2; implicitly at X 13.6 (cf. IX 45.2), 15.5 (cf. VII 53.5) etc. Cf. also *τὸ ἀνόητον* (X 13.4, 30.3), *παρρησία* (X 13.6, XI 56.5), *ὁ κόσμος τοῦ πολιτεύματος* (XI 55.2, 60.2).

54. Cf. Livy III 15.1, 17.1, 19.1, 21.7, IV 6.7 – no elaboration.

55. Livy III 35.9, on Appius preventing his election to the decemvirate; cf. II 60.7 (*constantia* of the *cos.* 471).

56. Livy III 40.2–5, Dion. Hal. XI 7–15. *Civilis societas*: Livy III 40.3, Dion. Hal. XI 7.2, 8.2–3 (*ὁμονοία, εὐκοσμία, κόσμος πολιτικός*, etc). Tyrant's appetites: Dion. Hal. XI 13.1–3, cf. 10.4, 11.2, 13.5, 15.4; *hybris* against citizens' wives and daughters at 10.3 (cf. 2.2–4, an example of the *αὐθάδεια* of the young patricians).

57. Dion. Hal. XI 9.1 and 3 (cf. 30.3, 55.2), with cross-reference to VI 68.3, VII 48.3f, IX 33.7 etc.

their lifetime and praised after their death,[58] and calls on the shade of his dead brother (Appius' father) in the course of an elaborate appeal to the gods and to the spirits of his forefathers.[59] Although the *topos* is not emphasized in either Livy or Dionysius, it is clear that he ended with the characteristic far-sighted Claudian prophecy of disasters to come – in this case the popular rising which would force the Decemvirs to abdicate.[60]

Ignored, Gaius retires to Regillum with his relatives and dependants, leaving Appius in guilty isolation and thus freeing the Claudii and their clients (presumably sober and virtuous citizens, in this version) from any suspicion of connivance in his villainy.[61] They do not return until the Decemvirs have been forced out of office and Appius is in prison, waiting to go on trial for his life before the tribal assembly. Then they appear *en masse* to plead for him with the people, urging his past merits and appealing to *concordia*,[62] in a demonstration which is not only a proof of the family's *pietas* but also a deliberate contrast with the arrogant refusal (in the hostile version) of Appius the consul of 471 to humble himself and plead at *his* trial.[63] The point is underlined in a later speech by C. Claudius in the Senate, where he accuses Appius' enemies of having had him killed in prison precisely in order to *prevent* him from appealing to the peoples' compassion in this way – and also to prevent him from invoking *Fides*, a detail which surely betrays the origin of the speech in the favourable version.[64]

The Decemvirate episode allows the rival interpretations of Claudian history to be distinguished with particular clarity. If proof is still needed that these represent two different sources whose *colores* imposed themselves on Livy and Dionysius alike, it is available in a detail from a senatorial debate in 457 B.C. in which C. Claudius opposes the increase in the number of tribunes to ten. Cincinnatus reminds him of a political insight of his father, who had observed that the more tribunes there were, the better for the

58. *Ibid.* XI 13.3 (cf. 15.4), with cross-reference to VI 68.2.
59. *Ibid.* XI 14.3, Livy III 40.3.
60. Livy III 40.4, 'magnas excitari ferme iras; earum eventum se horrere'; Dion. Hal. XI 15.4, *οἷα μαντεύομαι*.
61. Dion. Hal. XI 15.4, 22.4; Livy III 58.1 (cf. p. 63 above for the clients). His resolve to do so is praised by the Senate for its *γενναιότης*: Dion. Hal. XI 15.5. But cf. Luce 1977, 263f.
62. Livy III 58. 1–4, cf. Dion. Hal. IX 49.4 (*πολλὰ τὸ κοινὸν εὖ πεποιηκώς*).
63. Livy III 58.1, VI 20.3 (*sordidatus, prensare*); cf. II 61.5, Dion. Hal. IX 54.3–4. *Pietas*: Livy III 58.5.
64. Dion. Hal. XI 49.4, *ὅρκους τε καὶ πίστεις ἐπιβοώμενος*. Cf. n.49 above.

common good, since they were then more likely to disagree among themselves. Now, the first Appius had indeed made this point, in a debate attributed to the year 480 – but Dionysius had not reported it. It comes in Livy (p. 75 above), and it is Livy again who makes a later Appius bring out this *vetus ac familiare consilium* to free the Senate from a similar dilemma in 416.[65] The recurring motifs of each version appear equally in both authors, who transmit the rival themes with only such selection or change of emphasis as Livy's moralizing artistry and Dionysius' spurious *akribeia* demand.

From the year 443 onwards, Dionysius survives only in excerpts. Even from Livy alone, however, we can see how the Claudii continued to be portrayed, with the same factitious themes recurring.

The next two Appii are consular military tribunes in 424 and 403 respectively: each is introduced with a reference to his ancestral opposition to the *plebs*; each is left in Rome to face the tribunes while his colleagues are at the front, just as the Decemvir had been in 449; each successfully opposes a move to have plebeian consular tribunes elected.[66] In the next generation, C. Claudius 'Inregillensis' is made dictator in 337 and nominates C. Claudius Hortator as his master of horse, but after an objection on religious grounds both abdicate from office; Livy's laconic reference *could* be a genuine 'archival' item, but there must be a strong suspicion that he is summarizing an invented episode in which an arrogant Claudius appointed one of his own clients to high office, as his grandson P. Claudius Pulcher was supposed to have done in 249.[67]

Of these three Claudian generations, Livy treats only the second at length, giving the consular tribune of 403 an improbably long career (dictator 362, consul 346) with important interventions at the time of the war with Veii and during the crisis of the Licinio-Sextian 'rogations'.[68] His speeches, which clearly represent the favourable tradition,[69] are full of recurring themes which look

65. Dion. Hal. X 30.5, Livy II 44.2–5 (*exemplo in perpetuum*), IV 48.5–9, V 2.14.
66. Livy IV 36.5 ('iam inde ab incunabulis imbutum odio tribunorum plebisque'), V 12.13 ('imbutum iam ab iuventa certaminibus plebeiis'), cf. III 41.8.
67. Livy VIII 15.5–6; cf. *epit.* 19, Suet. *Tib.* 2.2, Degrassi 1947, 42f.
68. Livy V 3–6 (403), 20.5–6 (396), VI 40–41 (368). He ignores the tradition that it was Appius, perhaps as quaestor, who objected to Brennus' weighing-out of the gold for the Gallic ransom (Festus 510L, cf. Dion. Hal. XIII 9).
69. But note the introduction to the third one, at VI 40.2: 'Ap. Claudius Crassus, nepos decemviri [cf. IV 48.5], dicitur *odio* magis *iraque* quam spe ad dissuadendum processisse'. The content of the speech hardly bears out this hostile characterization, which Livy perhaps disowns with his *dicitur*. I cannot see why Ogilvie (1965, 670 and 673) calls the second speech 'demagoguery . . . violent and declamatory'.

forward as well as back, to Appius the censor and his descendants as well as Appius the Decemvir and his ancestors.

He defends *mos maiorum* against continuous plebeian demands,[70] he appeals to *concordia* and *Fides*,[71] he insists on the virtues of hard work and discipline,[72] he wants public income to benefit all the citizens through the *aerarium*,[73] and he contrasts the free republican state with the tribunes' tyrannical domination.[74] All that is familiar; what is new, called for by the plebeians' demand for the consulship, is the emphasis on *religiones* and *auspicia*, the 'contempt of the immortal gods' which would be involved in electing plebeian consuls who had no traditional right to take the auspices.[75]

> Let Sextius and Licinius mock religious scruple if they will: 'What does it matter if the sacred chickens don't eat, if they come out of their cage too slowly, if some bird has given an ill-omened call?' These are small matters – but it wasn't by despising those small matters that your ancestors made this republic great![76]

There has been only one earlier hint of this theme, where Appius the consul of 471 complained that the tribunate had been introduced into the state without benefit of omens and auspices, but it is entirely consistent with the god-fearing Claudii of the favourable tradition, who despairingly invoked the favour of heaven just as this Appius does now, signing off his final speech with 'quod faxitis deos velim fortunare'.[77]

The grandson of this outspoken conservative was the most famous Appius Claudius of all, the censor of 312 B.C. Three, perhaps four, of the acts attributed to him are certainly historical: as censor, he had the Via Appia laid out from Rome to Capua, and saw to the construction of Rome's first aqueduct; as consul in 296, he fought

70. Livy V 3.2–3, 6.17, 20.5 ('largitio *nova*'), VI 41.4 and 8.

71. V 3.5 and 10, VI 41.11.

72. V 4.4, 6.1 and 17, 20.6 (*urbani otiosi*): for the idleness theme, cf. pp. 65f above.

73. V 20.5–6 (cf. VI 41.11 for *praedari*); p. 73 above on *τὸ κοινόν*.

74. *Civilis*: V 3.9, VI 40.15 (cf. III 40.3). *Libertas*: VI 40.6–7 and 12. *Regnum*: VI 40.7 and 10, 41.10. *Seditio* of tribunes: V 3.2, 6.11–13, VI 40.3. Their treachery: V 6.10 and 15.

75. VI 41.4, cf. 41.9 *nefas*; religious *color* also at 40.7 (*si dis placet*), 40.11 (*portentum*).

76. VI 41.8. Imagined quotation in *oratio recta* is a feature of these Appian speeches (V 3.7, 4.7; VI 40.8–13, 40.15 and 19).

77. Dion. Hal. IX 45.1 (*παροῦσα συν οἰωνοῖς τε καὶ ὀττείαις*); Livy VI 41.12 (cf. Dion. Hal. VI 68.3, VII 53.6).

against the Etruscans and built the temple of Bellona as a result of a vow made in the campaign; and according to a tradition at least as old as Ennius, in 280, though old and blind, he dissuaded a wavering Senate from making peace with Pyrrhus.[78] His career was very thoroughly worked over in the historiographical tradition – perhaps as early as Fabius Pictor, since Q. Fabius Maximus Rullianus is very conspicuous in Livy as an opponent of Appius' schemes.[79] Certainly Livy had a wide range of sources to draw on, including Piso, Licinius Macer, Aelius Tubero and probably Claudius Quadrigarius,[80] each of whom will have interpreted the existing facts, and invented new ones, according to his own preoccupations. Among them – not necessarily among the four names that happen to be mentioned – was the anti-Claudian annalist.

The traces of his work are unmistakable throughout almost the whole of Livy's treatment of Appius' censorship. After a brief reference to the excellence of Appius' reputation, thanks to the road and the aqueduct, Livy immediately cancels out its effect by saying that he completed them as *sole* censor, his colleague having abdicated in shame at their disgraceful revision of the senatorial membership.[81] Though Livy uses no stronger a word than *pertinacia*, the formulaic nature of his description of Appius' motivation no doubt reveals his source,[82] as does the resumption of the subject under the following year, which is introduced by the observation that though there had been no dispute between tribunes and patrician magistrates for very many years, one now arose 'from that family which seemed to be fated to cross swords with the *plebs* and its tribunes'.[83] The dispute was an attempt by the tribune P.

78. Cic. *Cael.* 34, *sen.* 16 (cf. p.109 below), cf. Degrassi 1937, 19 (no. 12) and 59 (no. 79). See also pp. 59–60 on the Bellona temple.

79. E.g. Livy IX 42.1–2, 46.13–15 (origin of *cognomen* 'Maximus'), X 15.7–10, 25–26. Cf. also IX 36.2: the two identifications of Fabius' officer sent into northern Etruria (K. Fabius or C. Claudius) must reflect rival accounts exalting the respective families. Pictor is cited by name at X 37.14.

80. Livy IX 44.3f (Piso), 46.3 (Macer), X 9.10–12 (Macer, Tubero, Piso); IX 46.8–9 corresponds closely to Piso fr.27P (Gell. *NA* VII 9.5f). Quadrigarius: IX 5.2 (321 B.C.), X 37.13 (294). *In quibusdam annalibus*: IX 42.3, 46.2, X 17.11, cf. 25.12f, 26.5f. *In trinis annalibus* (with a fourth version implied): X 18.7.

81. Livy IX 29.5–8. Frontinus (*de aq.* 5.1–3) makes it clear that he held on to office in this version precisely in order to complete his projects – just as the Decemvir had done (Livy III 40.12).

82. Livy IX 29.8, 'iam inde antiquitus insitam pertinaciam familiae gerendo'.

83. Livy IX 33.3: 'ex ea familia quae velut fatales cum tribunis ac plebe ⟨simultates agere deb⟩ebat'. The emendation is by Walters and Conway (*OCT* app. crit.); '⟨simulates exerc⟩ebat' Mueller, '⟨inimicitias ger⟩ebat' Walter. The MSS. have '. . . plebe erat'.

Sempronius – otherwise unknown – to force Appius to resign the office he persisted in clinging to, complete with a long speech in which Claudian arrogance is dwelt on at length, with particular reference to the Decemvir. Sempronius orders Appius to be imprisoned; Appius appeals to the other tribunes, finds three to support him, and carries on with his one-man censorship amid the detestation of all classes.[84]

It is all quite unhistorical: the illegally prolonged censorship is unknown to the Fasti and incredible in the light of Appius' later career, and the story has too many significant details and dramatic ironies to be anything but a rhetorical historian's invention.[85] It also involves the equally fictitious legend of the Potitii, supposedly a family of immemorial antiquity who had been entrusted with the rites of Hercules by the god himself, but who now, persuaded or bribed by Appius, handed over their sacred responsibility to public slaves; the angry gods wiped out the Potitii and later robbed Appius of his sight.[86] Sempronius the tribune makes great play with this in his speech, the proof of Appius' impiety culminating in a reference to his 'contempt for gods and men' which precisely echoes a phrase used of the Decemvir in Livy's third book.[87]

It is of course possible that all this *color* is the work of Livy himself, but the demonstrable existence of the 'hostile source' makes it an unnecessary hypothesis. It is more likely that Livy sometimes used the available anti-Claudian material, as here, and sometimes rejected it, as in the comic story of the flute-players' strike. (This was an aetiological tale, to explain the masked revelry of the fluteplayers at the Quinquatrus festival, which was pressed into service as another example of Appius' interference with religious matters; Livy reports it, with apologies, as an event of the year of Appius' censorship, but he does not mention his involve-

84. Livy IX 33–34. Decemvir: 34.1–3. Claudii in general: 34.3–6, 34.15 ('familia imperiosissima et superbissima'), 34.22 (*superbia, audacia*), 34.16 (*regnum*), 34.24 (*pervicacia, superbia*). Cf. IX 42.3, *vir. ill.* 34.8: the hostile source evidently alleged that Appius stayed in office for five years, until his consulship in 307.

85. E.g. the consuls' complaint that the *lectio senatus* was 'ad gratiam ac *libidinem* facta' (IX 30.2); Appius' legalistic self-defence (33.8–9, cf. II 56.11–12 on the *cos.* 471, 'contemptim de iure disserendo'); the appeal (34.26), like the Decemvir's *provocatio* at III 55.5–8.

86. Livy IX 29.9–11; the bribe is specified in Festus 270L, *vir. ill.* 34.2, *origo gentis Rom.* 8.4–6, Macr. *Sat.* III 6.13 (from Asper). The Potitii were never a patrician *gens*, and the censors had no authority over state religious cults: see Palmer 1965, 293–308 and 320, rightly attributing the invention to an anti-Claudian annalist.

87. Livy IX 34.18f and 22: 'virtutem in superbia, in audacia, in contemptu deorum hominumque ponis' (cf. III 57.2 'deorum hominumque contemptor').

ment in it.[88]) When we find on two separate occasions – his consulship in 307, his praetorship in 295 – that Appius spent his year of office in Rome instead of on campaign, just like the Decemvir and the two consular tribune Appii,[89] then I think we are entitled to detect the hand of the anti-Claudian annalist, working up another of his characteristic themes.

The city and the Forum are Appius' spiritual home: it is there that his skills are applied, in ambitious factioneering and self-enrichment.[90] He is portrayed as a clever, fast-talking urban politician, inept and terrified in war, trying to sabotage the military efforts of Fabius Rullianus, whose valour the Republic needs much more than Appius' eloquence.[91] It is a portrait hardly to be reconciled with the victory over the Etruscans which was firmly (and genuinely) anchored in the historical tradition by the temple of Bellona,[92] but one which could be made plausible by attaching Appius to the aedile Cn. Flavius, supposedly a freedman's son, who published the *ius civile* and calendar *fasti* in 304 B.C. There is no sign of Appius in Piso's account of Flavius, which fortunately survives, and it is easy to see the point at which Livy turns from Piso to an author who made Appius the aedile's patron, with a retrospective account of his censorial adlection of freedmen's sons into the Senate and his supposed distribution of *humiles* (i.e. freedmen?) throughout the 31 tribes.[93] The latter act is regularly assumed to be historical,[94] but the context in which it is reported must arouse

88. Livy IX 30.5–10, Ovid *Fasti* VI 653–94 ('Claudius' at line 685: Palmer 1965, 309f), *vir. ill.* 34.1. See Palmer 1965, 308–19 for its unhistorical character (with a very speculative reconstruction of what may have been the reality behind it).
89. Livy IX 42.4; X 22.7, 25.9; see n.66 above.
90. Livy IX 42.4, 46.11 (*urbanae artes, opes*), 46.10 and 13 (*forensis factio*), 46.14 (*forensis turba*), X 22.7 (*urbi ac foro praeses*). Cf. X 15.2 on his *civiles artes*, wrongly, I think, accepted as basically historical by Mommsen (1864, 292 and 303f): 'It is remarkable how in this respect he walks in the steps of his great-great-grandfather, the decemvir' (Mommsen 1864, 304) – but that is in itself enough to arouse suspicion.
91. Livy X 15.8 (*ambitiosus*), 18.6 (inept), 19.6 (*cavillans*), 25.8 (terrified). Eloquence: X 15.12, 19.6f, 22.7. Generals needed, not orators: X 19.8, 22.6. Speeches against Fabius: X 25.13, 26.6. Cf. Mommsen 1864, 303, with 291f on the unmilitariness of the Claudii as a supposedly genuine tradition: he resorts to special pleading to explain away their triumphs.
92. Livy X 19.16–19, attributing the change to Bellona's inspiration. But what about the *memor deum ira* (IX 29.11)? (At X 21.8 some soldiers in Appius' army are struck by lightning.)
93. Piso fr.27P (Rawson 1976, 712f); Livy IX 46, with the change of source at 46.10; cf. 29.7, 30.1f on the *prava lectio senatus*.
94. E.g. by Taylor 1960, 133–7 and Treggiari 1969, 38–42, 54–7 – the standard works on the tribes and on freedmen respectively. Cf. Mommsen 1864, 305f and

suspicions that it is no more than plausible *color* for a demagogic Appius.[95]

Being selective, Livy sometimes drastically abbreviated his source.[96] Two likely examples of this are Appius' *interregnum* in 299, when he refused to accept a plebeian candidate for the consulship, and his own election as consul two years later, when he tried to get two patricians – himself and Fabius – elected. The former case produced an exchange of speeches with the tribune M'. Curius (ignored by Livy), and the latter a magnanimous refusal by Fabius to preside over his own election as Appius the Decemvir had supposedly done.[97] Both look very like the author of the hostile version extending his arrogant-patrician theme to the very last available historical context.

The author of the favourable version evidently did the same with the wise-conservatives theme, though the loss of Dionysius makes it harder to detect. Livy had no room for an Appius who stood for ancestral custom in religious matters; when the priesthoods were opened to plebeian membership in 300, he attributes the objections to 'the patricians' in general, without naming a spokesman. But their arguments (which he minimizes) sound very much like those of Appius the consular tribune in 368, ending with the familiar hope that the innovation may not prove disastrous, while the tribune's answer (which he gives at length) is directed at Appius by name.[98] It is likely that one of his sources gave Appius a conservative speech, which could not be included without ruining the consistency of his own account.

After 293 B.C. Livy fails us too. The generation of Appius

Münzer 1899, 2683, both of whom I think greatly underestimate the extent of annalistic invention in Caecus' career.

95. Cf. Plut. *Popl.* 7.5 (δημαγωγῶν ἔδωκεν Ἄππιος); Livy's story (at IX 46.14) implies that the four urban tribes were only created in 304. The distribution also appears in Diodorus (XX 36.4), who is generally assumed to have used only good early sources for Roman history; in fact, it can be demonstrated that he also used late annalists, particularly in this section on Caecus (see p. 115 below). The distribution of freedmen throughout the tribes was a contentious issue in the first century B.C.: see Livy *epit.* 77 (P. Sulpicius in 88), Dio XXXVI 42.2 etc. (C. Manilius in 66), Asc. 52C (P. Clodius in 53).

96. E.g. the quasi-*contio* at X 18.5, with *orationes longiores* by Appius and Volumnius (cf. Dio VIII fr.36.27).

97. Livy X 11.10 (cf. Cic. *Brut.* 55, *vir. ill.* 34.3), 15.7–12 (cf. III 35.7-8, 40.12). Rightly recognized as fictitious by Mommsen (1864, 312); cf. Alföldi 1965, 163.

98. Livy X 6.9–11 (explicitly linking it with the demand for the consulship in 368), cf. VI 41.4–12; X 7–8 (speech of P. Decius Mus against Appius), esp. 7.5, 8.4–6.

Caecus' sons saw seven Claudian consuls,[99] the foundation of the two great *stirpes* of Pulchri and Nerones,[100] and, no doubt, the *real* origins of Claudian power and influence; but both the facts and the legends are very largely lost with Livy's second decade.[101] One of the few exceptions – in the latter category – I think we owe to the fertile imagination of the 'hostile source'.

Livy's nineteenth book evidently covered the years 250–241 B.C. Two of the episodes in it are reported by his epitomator as follows:

> Claudius Pulcher the consul [in 249] set out contrary to the auspices – he ordered the chickens to be drowned when they would not eat – and fought an unsuccessful naval battle against the Carthaginians. Recalled by the Senate and ordered to nominate a dictator, he nominated Claudius Glaucia, a man of the lowest rank, who was forced to abdicate, but afterwards attended the games in his *toga praetexta*. . . . Claudia, sister of the P. Claudius who had lost the battle through contempt of the auspices, was pressed by the crowd on her way back from the games [evidently in 243],[102] and said 'I wish my brother were alive, to lead another fleet'; she was fined for this.[103]

Cicero, Valerius Maximus and Suetonius report Pulcher's *bon mot* about the chickens ('if they don't want to eat, let them drink'), and add that he was put on trial before the people.[104] The Augustan consular Fasti call the disgraceful dictator M. Claudius C.f. Glicia, an ex-scribe; according to Suetonius, he was Pulcher's own *viator*.[105]

99. M. Claudius Marcellus 287, C. Claudius Canina 285 and 273, Ap. Claudius Russus 268, Ap. Claudius Caudex 264, P. Claudius Pulcher 249, C. Claudius Cento 240. Canina triumphed in 273; triumphs were also attributed to Russus and Caudex (Eutrop. II 18.3, Sil. It. *Pun.* VI 661f; Degrassi 1947, 74–5), not without dispute in the sources, as I hope to explain elsewhere.
100. Suet. *Tib.* 3.1 for Caecus' son Ti. Nero.
101. Cf. Val. Max. VI 5.1 on an early third-century P. Claudius whose *fides* (in enslaving the defeated Camerini) was supposedly repudiated by the Senate.
102. Reported between the foundation of Fregenae and Brundisium in 245–4 (Vell. I 14.8) and the consulship of A. Postumius in 242; Ateius Capito, however (quoted in Gell. *NA* X 6.4) dated the event to 246.
103. Livy *epit.* 19 (cf. XXII 42.9 for a reference back); Suet. *Tib.* 2.2, essentially the same.
104. Cic. *ND* II 7 (cf. *div.* I 29, II 20, 71); Val. Max. I 4.3, VIII 1.abs.4; Suet. *Tib.* 2.2.
105. Degrassi 1947, 42–3; Suet. *Tib.* 2.2 (MSS *Ilycian*, i.e. *Glycian*?). Pulcher's pride is astonishingly interpreted by Mommsen (1864, 317) as essentially 'democratic'.

We have already noted the 'client theme' in the hostile tradition (p. 81 above); Cn. Flavius the aedile of 304 has provided a further example of it, and he too was an ex-scribe.[106] But the contemptuous nomination of Claudius Glicia is a comparatively minor item; it is the story of the chickens that reveals the true talent of the anti-Claudian annalist. There is, of course, no sign of it in Polybius, who merely reports Pulcher's defeat and later fine and condemnation by the people.[107] The rhetorical nature of the story is made clear by Florus, who says that Pulcher's ships were sunk at the very time and place that he had drowned the chickens,[108] and its origins are not hard to find. Pulcher was an arrogant man,[109] his defeat was unexpected, and his colleague was L. Iunius Pullus ('Chicken').[110] The type of source we are dealing with is revealed by the name of one of the tribunes who supposedly put Pulcher on trial before the people, a name unknown among Roman magistrates before the mid-first century B.C., but rich in possibilities for rhetorical epigram: the tribune was called *Pullius*.[111]

The elaboration of Claudius Pulcher's defeat is, I think, the hostile annalist's masterpiece, approached only by the story of Appius Caecus and the Potitii, which similarly became a standard historical *exemplum* as soon as it was written. Both illustrate the theme introduced by the description of Appius the Decemvir as *deorum hominumque contemptor*, and with such effect that the

106. Piso fr. 27P, Cic. *Att.* VI 1.8, *Mur.* 25, Livy IX 46.2–3, Val. Max. II 5.2, Pliny *NH* XXXIII 17, Macr. *Sat.* I 15.9. His profession was already in the earlier tradition; with the insertion of Appius into the story, he becomes 'ipse scriba Appi Caeci' (Pliny *loc. cit.*).

107. Pol. I 49–51 and 52.2–3; cf. Diod. Sic. XXIV 1.5. Münzer (1899, 2858) is tempted to accept it as genuine.

108. Flor. I 18.29: 'non ab hostibus sed a dis ipsis superatus est, quorum auspicia contempserat, ibi statim classe demersa ubi ille praecipitari pullos iusserat, quod pugnare ab iis vetaretur'.

109. Naevius *Bell. Pun.* fr.45M ('superbiter contemptim conterit legiones') may possibily refer to him; cf. Pol. I 52.2, *ἀλογίστως τοῖς πράγμασι κεχρημένος*.

110. Iunius too is supposed to have lost a fleet, in a storm: Cic. *ND* II 7, *div.* I 29, II 20, Val. Max. I 4.4.

111. Schol. Bob. 90St: 'ob id factum dies ei dicta est perduellionis a Pullio et Fundanio tr.pl.'; cf. Ogilvie 1975, 122 for the annalists' invention of appropriate names. In this account, his trial was interrupted by a storm and not resumed, thanks to the intervention of some other tribunes on Pulcher's behalf (Schol. Bob., cf. Val. Max. VIII 1.abs.4). It is noticeable that both Appius Caecus and Appius the consul of 185 are represented as benefitting from favourable tribunes (Livy IX 34.26, XXXIX 32.13), a fact which must surely be connected with the 'Claudian tactic' of splitting the tribunician college (Dion. Hal. X 30.5, Livy II 44.2–5, IV 48.5–8, V 2.14). Not that it helped in the end: *actione mutata*, the tribunes imposed a severe fine (Schol. Bob., cf. n.114 below; Cic. *ND* II 7, 'a populo condemnatus est').

author of the 'favourable version' must have considered it the main target of his refutation. Certainly it explains the emphasis on the gods in the speeches of the wise-conservative Claudii of the fifth and fourth centuries; in particular, it accounts for the way in which Appius the ex-consular tribune opposed the idea of plebeian consuls in 368 (p. 85 above). His creator was evidently trying to cancel out the effect of the notorious chickens well in advance.[112]

—

The sequel to Pulcher's sacrilege and defeat introduces another theme, unfortunately ill-documented: the women, and the goddesses, of the Claudii.

Claudia's arrogant and impious prayer[113] that her brother might come back to life and drown another fleet-full of Roman citizens resulted, according to Livy's epitomator, in a fine. Gellius specifies that the plebeian aediles C. Fundanius and Ti. Sempronius (i.e. Ti. Gracchus, the later consul of 238) fined her 25,000 *asses*,[114] and a later reference in Livy suggests that Sempronius was perhaps supposed to have used the money to build a shrine of *Libertas* on the Aventine.[115] It would not be surprising if her punishment were presented as another in the schematic series of plebeian victories against the overbearing patrician house.

The activity of the plebeian aediles at this time was evidently interpreted in this light in at least one version. The Publicii, for instance, lived up to their name by punishing powerful landowners who had contemptuously defied the law and occupied public land;

112. Perhaps even with the same phraseology: compare Livy VI 41.8 ('si ex cavea tardius exierint [*sc.* pulli]') and Val. Max. I 4.3 on Pulcher ('cum pullarius non exire cavea pullos nuntiasset'). The invention, by a post-Ciceronian historian, of a Vestal Claudia who dedicated a temple to the Bona Dea (Ovid *Fasti* V 155–6, Rawson 1977, 355) may perhaps be attributed to the author of the 'apologetic' tradition.
113. Gell. *NA* X 6.1 ('voces petulantiores'), 6.3 ('verba tam improba et tam incivilia'), Val. Max. VIII 1.damn.4 ('votum impium'); cf. Suet. *Tib.* 2.3.
114. Gell. *NA* X 6.3; note the parallel with Schol. Bob. 90St on Pulcher, fined 120,000 *asses* after a prosecution by the tribunes Pullius and Fundanius – the latter now reappearing in a later magistracy. In Claudia's case too, the penalty should have resulted from a trial before the people, the largest fine a magistrate could impose by his own *coercitio* being traditionally 3000 *asses* (Festus 220L, cf. 268–70L; cf. Crawford 1976, 200f); in fact, Valerius Maximus and Suetonius (previous note) refer to a trial, and Ateius Capito (*ap.* Gell. *NA* X 6.4) discussed Claudia's case in a commentary on *iudicia publica*. For aedilician prosecutions, see Bauman 1974, esp. 252f.
115. Livy XXIV 16.19: 'in aede Libertatis quam pater eius in Aventino ex multaticia pecunia faciendam curavit dedicavit'. Cf. also Festus 108L for the supposed temple – hardly genuine, since it is inconceivable that none of the accounts of C. Gracchus' last stand on the Aventine in 121 would have referred to so significant a family *monumentum* on the hill if it had really existed.

from the fines they exacted they built the Clivus Publicius to the Aventine, established the festival of Flora, and perhaps founded the goddess's temple as well.[116] It is possible that the report is genuine, from the records of the plebeian aediles,[117] but its interpretation in the historical tradition is so patently artificial as to raise the suspicion that the story of the Publicii is mainly an aetiological explanation for the name of the Clivus.[118] After all, the Clivus Pullius was accounted for in the same way: its supposed constructor was presumably 'Pullius the tribune of 249', now advanced to the plebeian aedileship.[119]

That the public honour paid to 'the people's men' was a late-republican notion is suggested by the travertine monument of C. Publicius Bibulus at the foot of the Capitol, which cannot be earlier than the first century B.C., but purports to be the tomb of a third-century plebeian aedile built on land granted to him at public expense.[120] Bibulus himself is no doubt a genuine historical character, but the honour may well be a later invention, the corollary of his identification as one of the Publicii who built the Clivus and founded the Floralia.[121]

Somehow, though the details escape us, the Claudii were involved in this tale. A later C. Publicius Bibulus, tribune of the *plebs* in 209, is made to attack M. Claudius Marcellus in an episode which bears all the hallmarks of first-century rhetorical historiography;[122] the tomb below the Capitol corresponds in position to that of the patrician Claudii on the south side;[123] the Claudii of the first century B.C. claimed some honorific connection with Flora,

116. Ovid *Fasti* V 277–294, emphasizing the arrogance of the rich and the boldness of the *vindices populi* (cf. pp. 72–4 above for the *ager publicus*); Varro *LL* V 158, Festus 276L (Clivus), Tac. *Ann.* II 49 (temple).

117. Cf. Livy X 23.13 (296), XXVII 6.19 (210), 36.9 (208), XXXIII 25.2–3 (197).

118. Varro *LL* V 158: 'clivos Publicius ab aedilibus plebei Publiciis qui eum *publice* aedificarunt'. Ovid *Fasti* V 285–94: *publica . . . Publicios . . . populus . . . publica . . . cura . . . Publiciumque vocant.*

119. Varro *loc. cit.*: 'simili de causa Pullius at Cosconius [*sc.* clivi], quod ab his viocuris dicuntur aedificati'. Cf. *ILLRP* 449, 463 for plebeian aediles as road-builders, *CIL* I² 593.20–52 for plebeian and curule aediles as *curatores viarum.*

120. Nash 1968, II 319f; *ILLRP* 357, 'C. Poplicio L.f. Bibulo aed.pl. honoris virtutisque caussa senatus consulto populique iussu locus monumento, quo ipse postereique eius inferrentur, publice datus est'. The aedileship must be before 216 B.C., since it is not recorded by Livy.

121. Their identification as L.M. Publicii Malleoli stems from a different version, which made them *curule* aediles (Festus 276L, Tac. *Ann.* II 49).

122. Livy XXVII 20.11–21.4, Plut. *Marc.* 27.

123. Cf. p. 59 above: Publicus' tomb was outside the Porta Fontinalis, that of the Claudii outside the Porta Carmentalis.

perhaps through C. Claudius Cento the consul of 240;[124] the Claudia episode, and the last appearance of the scandalous Claudius Glicia, take place during festival games which drew a huge crowd, as the first Floralia must have done.[125] Though the suggestion can be no more than guesswork, it is conceivable that the Floralia were founded in Claudius Cento's consulship, and that the anti-Claudian annalist composed a plausible rival version, pressing into service whatever aetiological material he could find, or invent, to give the credit to the heroes of the *plebs* and make the Claudian contribution to the occasion merely a characteristic display of arrogance and contempt for the people.

This speculation may, perhaps, be justified by comparison with the next appearance of a Claudian lady in the historical tradition, also in connection with the establishment of one of the great festivals of the Roman religious year. With Quinta Claudia, however, the problem is not too little information but too much.[126]

The first of each year's festival games were the Megalesia in April, in honour of the Great Idaean Mother of the Gods. A much more formidable divinity than Flora, she occupied a unique and ambiguous position in the Roman pantheon: on the one hand, her exotic worship appealed above all to the masses, and could appear as a paradigm case of religious awe induced by the emotional means traditionally shunned in Roman cult;[127] on the other hand, the story of her transfer from Phrygia to Rome in 204 B.C. involved

124. *Aurei* and *denarii* of C. Clodius cf. Vestalis, 41 B.C.: Crawford 1974, 521 (Plate LXII no.512); cf. 447 (Plate LI no.423) for the obverse design. Crawford rules out an allusion to Cento on the grounds that the Floralia were founded in 238 (Pliny *NH* XVIII 286); but Velleius dates them to 241 (Vell. I 14.8), and the chronology of the early *ludi* was notoriously disputed (Cic. *Brut.* 72, 'est enim inter scriptores de numero annorum controversia'). Atticus dated Livius Andronicus' first production to 240 (Cic. *Brut.* 72, *sen.* 50, *Tusc.* I 3; cf. Gell. *NA* XVII 21.42), implying the introduction of *ludi scaenici* in that year.

For three reasons, it is more likely than not that the moneyer was – or claimed to be – descended from Cento: (i) he evidently belonged to the patrician *gens* (if the reverse design is rightly interpreted) but was not a Nero or a Pulcher; (ii) both he and his father used the *praenomen* C.; and (iii) he was patron of Forum Clodi (*CIL* XI 3310a, 3311), which must have been founded when the Via Clodia was built in the third century; Cento is one of the possibilities as constructor of the Clodia (cf. Wiseman 1970b, 137 and 140, where his name should be added to those of the *coss.* 287 and 285, and Rawson 1977, 342f).

125. Livy *epit.* 19, Gell. *NA* X 6.2; cf. nn.102 and 124 above for the uncertain chronology.

126. The various traditions are analysed by Schmidt 1909, 1–30 (esp. 10–17).

127. Lucr. II 618–23, with Wiseman 1974a, 28f; in general, see Bömer 1964, esp. 135–8.

the prestige of several aristocratic Roman families, and her festival was an annual showpiece of self-advertisement for the curule aediles who were responsible for it.[128] As a result, the historical tradition on the introduction of her cult is particularly complex, the predictably tendentious annalistic accounts being further confused by more popular traditions, which evidently stemmed from the dramatic performances of the Mother's 'sacred story' at her festival and from the votive offerings and other works of art dedicated in her honour.[129]

Our earliest evidence is in Cicero's attack on Clodius for his handling of the Megalesia as aedile in 56:

> At the Sibyl's instigation, when Italy was exhausted by the Punic War and plagued by Hannibal, our ancestors sent for those rites from Phrygia and established them in Rome. They were received by the man who was judged to be the best of the Roman people, P. Scipio, and the woman who was considered the most chaste of the *matronae*, Q. Claudia – whose old-fashioned strictness your sister is thought to imitate extraordinarily well! Did your ancestors' connection with these rituals have *no* effect on you, then? . . .[130]

A month or so earlier, attacking Clodius' sister at the trial of Caelius, he had made her ancestor Appius Caecus cite Quinta as a paragon of virtue whose example Clodia should follow.[131] The story was clearly well known; the archaic feminine *praenomen* Q. – converted into a *cognomen* by later authors – suggests that it is probably authentic;[132] and Quinta's role in it was evidently as the

128. Bömer 1964, 131f, with 132ff on the paradoxical 'boycott' of the Mother by the Roman aristocracy; Wiseman 1974a, 159–61 on the *ludi Megalenses* and the aediles.

129. Ovid *Fasti* IV 326, 'mira sed et scaena testificata loquar'; cf. Arnob. *adv. nat.* VII 33 (with Wiseman 1974a, 168f), Schmidt 1909, 13f. Julian *or.* V 2, 161b; his account confirmed *ὑπὸ πλείστων ἱστοριογράφων καὶ ἐπιχαλκῶν εἰκόνων ἐν . . . Ῥώμῃ*.

130. Cic. *har. resp.* 27 (cf. 22): 'quae [sacra] vir is accepit qui est optimus populi Romani iudicatus, P. Scipio, femina autem quae matronarum castissima putabatur, Q. Claudia . . .'.

131. Cic. *Cael.* 34: 'nonne te . . . ne progenies quidem mea, Q. illa Claudia, aemulam domesticae laudis in gloria muliebri esse admonebat?' She is a paragon of *prisca virtus* also in Plut. *Mor.* 145E.

132. Cf. Varro *LL* IX 60, *CIL* I² 1765, 1785, 1837, 1839 etc for Secunda, Tertia and Quarta as women's *praenomina*. 'Claudia Quinta' in Livy (XXIX 14.12), Ovid (*Fasti* IV 305), Tacitus (*Ann.* IV 64), etc; 'Quinta Claudia' in Valerius Maximus (I 8.11). For Quintus (masc.) as a *praenomen* occasionally used by the Claudii, cf. Rawson 1977, 349.

feminine counterpart of P. Scipio Nasica and an example of old-time morality.

The first account in a historian is that of Diodorus, who provides the same elements with one remarkable exception:

> It was found written in the Sibylline oracles that the Romans should establish a temple for the Great Mother of the Gods, that her sacred objects should be fetched from Pessinus in Asia, and be received by a muster of the whole populace going forth to meet them, that the best of the men and likewise the [best?] of the women [. . .], and that they should lead the welcoming procession, when it took place, and receive the sacred objects of the goddess. When the Senate proceeded to carry out the instructions of the oracle, Publius Nasica was selected as the best of all the men and Valeria as the best of the women.[133]

Whatever the explanation of the change of name,[134] the 'choice of the best' and the parallelism with Nasica are essentially the same as in Cicero.

Already, however, a more dramatic version was current, known to Propertius and expounded at length by Ovid, who knew it from the theatre.[135] The 'muster of the whole populace' meets the goddess's ship at the mouth of the Tiber and begins to tow it upstream, but the ship grounds in the shallows. 'Claudia Quinta', a beautiful patrician whose smart dress and ready tongue had given her an undeserved reputation for immorality, steps out from her place among the *matronae*, prays to the goddess to vindicate her chastity, and easily pulls the ship off the sandbank single-handed. The procession resumes, with Quinta at its head, and delivers the goddess to Nasica in the city, amid rejoicing and festivity.

This 'popular version' quickly became canonical. Practically all the post-Augustan sources follow it, with appropriate embellishments. (Quinta pulls the ship with her girdle, the ship miraculously overtakes her, and so on; finally, Quinta becomes a Vestal Vir-

133. Diod. Sic. XXXIV 33.2, in F. R. Walton's Loeb translation – except for the crucial passage in the middle, where he translates an emended version. The received text runs: *καὶ τῶν τε ἀνδρῶν τὸν ἄριστον καὶ γυναικῶν ὁμοίως τὴν ἀγαθήν καὶ τούτους ἀφηγεῖσθαι τῆς ἀπαντήσεως κτλ*. There must be a lacuna after *τὴν ἀγαθήν*, which is itself evidently corrupt; the final sentence, however, shows what the sense must be. See Schmidt 1909, 15 n.5, who reads '. . . *ὁμοίως τῶν ἀγαθῶν* ⟨*τὴν ἀρίστην ἐξαιρεῖσθαι*⟩ *καὶ τούτους* . . .'.
134. Münzer (1899, 2899) thought it a mere slip.
135. Prop. IV 11.51–2, Ovid *Fasti* IV 247–348 (cf. n.129 above).

gin.[136]) Some recollection of the earlier 'choice of the best' does survive,[137] but essentially the story was changed for ever in the Augustan period.[138]

Livy's account seems to mark a half-way point. He has Nasica receive the goddess from the ship at the Tiber mouth and bring her to land, where the *matronae* receive her in their turn:

> Among them one name is notable, that of Claudia Quinta; it is said that though her reputation had hitherto been doubtful, she made her chastity more famous to posterity by so holy a service.[139]

Quinta has been dropped from the 'choice of the best', which is made much of by Livy in Nasica's case,[140] but though she appears in the scene at the Tiber, as in the 'popular version', she does not do anything there to justify her moral vindication. Nor can she, for Livy's narrative, which differs at many points from the 'popular version' as Ovid reports it,[141] is particularly inconsistent with it in having the goddess brought to *land* at the Tiber mouth, thus giving Quinta no opportunity to do anything.

Indeed, Livy elsewhere says that Nasica brought the goddess all the way from the sea to the city himself, which leaves no room for any contribution by the *matronae*.[142] Nasica has his own developing legend,[143] which helps to confuse the tradition; to a

136. Seneca *de matr.* fr.80H, Pliny *NH* VII 120, Stat. *Silv.* I 2.245–6, Sil.It. *Pun.* XVII 1–45, Suet. *Tib.* 2.3, App. *Hann.* 56, Herodian I 11.4, Lact. *div. inst.* II 8.12, Julian *or.* V 2, *vir. ill* 46.1–2, Solinus I 126, Macr. *Sat.* II 5.4. See Bömer 1964, 146–51 on the growth of the 'Vestal' legend.

137. App. *Hann.* 56 (*δι' ἀνδρῶν καὶ γυναικῶν ἀριστῶν*), Pliny *NH* VII 120 (*pudicissima femina*).

138. Cf. Bömer 1964, 138–42 on the importance of the Augustan age in the development of Cybele's legend. The miracle of the unburnt statue (Val. Max. I 8.11, Tac. *Ann.* IV 64) probably dates from then: Bömer 1964, 149.

139. Livy XXIX 14.12: 'inter quas unius Claudiae Quintae insigne est nomen . . . cui dubia, ut traditur, antea fama clariorem ad posteros tam religioso ministerio pudicitiam fecit'.

140. Livy XXIX 11.5–8, 14.5–9, XXXV 10.9, XXXVI 40.9, *epit.* 49. 'Qui vir optimus a senatu iudicatus est' is a formulaic description of Nasica from Cicero to St Augustine: Cic. *har. resp.* 27, *fin.* V 64, Vell. II 3.1, Pliny *NH* VII 120, Sil. It. *Pun.* XVII 5–7, *vir. ill.* 44.1, Aug. *CD* II 5.

141. E.g. the goddess's origin, Pessinus or Troy (Livy XXIX 10.5, 11.7; Ovid *Fasti* IV 249f, 264, 273f); Attalus' attitude, hostile or friendly (Livy XXIX 11.7; Ovid IV 286); the name of the dedicator of the temple (Livy XXXVI 36.4; Ovid IV 347). Cf. Schmidt 1909, 5 etc.

142. Livy XXXVI 36.3 (falsely dating the event to 205 B.C., when Africanus was consul: a pro-Scipionic version?).

143. Schmidt 1909, 10, 29f. In the 'popular version', he probably received the

certain extent he and Quinta are rivals for the 'star role' in this episode.[144] A version that exalted one might well have to demote the other.

Somebody, at some stage, introduced the idea of Quinta's bad reputation, which is entirely foreign to Cicero's picture of her. (If there had been any doubt at all about Quinta's morals, he could not have used her as an *exemplum* in the Caelius case.) On the other hand, by the time of the 'popular version' her bad reputation had been accepted and neutralized, as it were, by the goddess's miraculous vindication. Somewhere in this confused succession of legends the familiar anti-Claudian annalist and his rival must have given *their* accounts, and though here too the attempt cannot be anything but speculative, a reconstruction is possible.

C. Claudius Nero was censor in 204, when the Great Mother came to Rome: he and his colleague let the contract for the building of her temple.[145] If the Sibylline Books required the Senate to choose the best Roman of each sex to receive her,[146] his influence might well have resulted in the *optima matronarum* being a patrician Claudia. I tentatively suggest that this was the original, and no doubt genuine, tradition (as in Cicero); that the 'hostile' annalist made Q. Claudia a loose woman, and therefore replaced her in the 'choice of the best' with another patrician lady (as in Diodorus);[147] that the apologetic annalist insisted that her bad reputation was undeserved, and therefore allowed her a place among the *matronae* in the honorific escort (as in Livy); and finally that the 'popular version', concerned less with the dignity of the Claudii than with the miraculous power of the goddess, was evolved from the two

goddess into his own house: Val. Max. VIII 15.3, Juv. *Sat.* III 137f, *vir. ill.* 44.1, 46.3 (*hospes*), cf. Ovid *Fasti* IV 347. In reality, she was housed in the Aedes Victoriae on the Palatine: Livy XXIX 14.14 (probably an 'archival' item).

144. Even rivals in moral excellence. The early annalists gave no reason for the choice of Nasica (cf. Livy XXIX 14.9), but in Val. Max. VIII 15.3 he is *sanctissimus*, in Dio fr.61 εὐσεβὴς καὶ δίκαιος, virtues which correspond to the lady's *castitas*.

145. Livy XXIX 37.2, XXXVI 36.4 (cf. Rawson 1977, 353).

146. As in Diodorus; if we insist on the distinction between *iudicatus* and *putabatur* in Cicero, perhaps the 'best woman' emerged some other way (named by the *matronae*?).

147. He may even have provided another *pudicissima matrona*, if he is responsible for the story about Sulpicia (the wife of Q. Fulvius Flaccus *cos IV* 209) and the temple of Venus Verticordia: see Val. Max. VIII 15.12, Pliny *NH* VII 120, Solinus I 126 – almost certainly fictitious, since according to Obsequens 37, the temple was founded in 114. The Sibyl's involvement in the Verticordia story (Ovid *Fasti* IV 157–62), and the fact that Valerius Maximus calls Nasica *sanctissimus vir* and Sulpicia *sanctissima femina* (VIII 15.3 and 12), are tantalizing hints of a connection of which the details escape us.

rival stories by a dramatist of considerable imaginative powers, and immediately made all other accounts obsolete.

If that hypothesis approximates to the truth, then the story of Quinta Claudia is one of the few occasions where the anti-Claudian annalist met his match in the invention of pseudo-history.

—

In the later books of Livy, where he had more varied sources to draw on, the hostile or favourable Claudian *colores* are less easily detectable. Where the patrician Claudii occur, they are often secondary figures in tendentious narratives composed with other purposes in view.

In 217, for instance, C. Claudius Cento was *interrex*, followed by P. Cornelius Asina; there was a confrontation between the patricians and the plebeians over the consular *comitia* at which C. Terentius Varro was elected.[148] It sounds a familiar Claudian scene, but according to Livy the dispute arose in Asina's *interregnum*, not Cento's. His source is likely to have concentrated on the wretched Varro, supposedly the son of a butcher and damned for ever by losing the battle of Cannae the following year, with a patrician Cornelius – and a Scipio at that – as the other protagonist.[149] Similarly in 211, at the fall of Capua, Ap. Claudius Pulcher *cos.* 212 is only marginally involved in the various accounts of his colleague Q. Fulvius Flaccus' execution of the Campanian senators;[150] and in 169 the stormy censorship of his son C. Claudius Pulcher and the elder Ti. Gracchus is expounded with an emphasis on the excellence of Gracchus (and the villainy of the *publicani*) rather than the virtues or vices of Claudius himself.[151]

There are, however, some episodes where we hear the authentic tones of the man who created the arrogant patrician Claudii of the

148. Livy XXII 34.1: 'interreges proditi a patribus C. Claudius Appi filius Cento, inde P. Cornelius Asina: in eius interregno comitia habita magno certamine patrum ac plebis' (of which an extended account follows).

149. The *Chronicon Paschale* and *Fasti Hydatiani* (on the year of Asina's consulship) call him Scipio: Degrassi 1947, 442.

150. Livy XXII 15.3, 16.1.

151. Livy XLIII 14 and 16, XLIV 16.8–11, XLV 15; cf. Cic. *rep.* III 2, *inv.* I 48, Val. Max. VI 5.3, *vir. ill.* 57.3. For the *publicani*, cf. Badian 1972, 17–20 on the late-annalistic *color* applied to the events of 213; those of 169, however (*ibid.* 42, on Livy XLIII 16), he regards as essentially historical: 'It could no doubt be argued that this might still be rewriting in the late Republic. However, we are now in the full light of history, when men like Cato were recording the events of their own day . . .'. Compare Badian 1966, 21 on Valerius Antias: 'his disregard for facts is clear from his handling of the trials of the Scipios, in what should have been the full light of history . . .'.

fifth and fourth centuries. (Ap. Claudius Cento, sent as legate to Illyria in 170, is a minor example: led by greed to attack the town of Uscana, he suffers a humiliating defeat entirely inconsistent with the Polybian version of the campaign, innocently reported by Livy eight chapters later.[152])

Ap. Claudius Pulcher was consul in 185, his brother Publius in 184. According to Livy's account, Appius' colleague should have returned to Rome to hold the elections, but Appius himself got back from his campaign first in order to preside and help his brother. With three more distinguished competitors for the one place open to patricians, Publius was not expected to get in; but Appius, instead of preserving an objective neutrality, canvassed for him in the most shameless way, 'flitting about the Forum' (the very phrase used of Appius the Decemvir in his campaign for re-election) and refusing to be put off despite the general indignation at his behaviour.[153] The tribunes of the *plebs* were greatly exercised by it, some opposing the consul and others strenuously defending him – no doubt as a result of the application of the 'Claudian tactic' of splitting the college.[154] Several times the elections were broken up, until Appius succeeded and got his brother in. Any doubt about the origin of this unlikely tale, which is quite inconsistent with Livy's portrayal of Appius elsewhere as a model of senatorial *dignitas*, is surely dispelled by the report of the election of Publius' colleague: the plebeian candidates behaved with moderation, and not with 'Claudian violence.'[155]

Recognition that the hostile annalist is alive and well and on Livy's bookshelves may help to explain the odd treatment of C. Claudius Pulcher the consul of 177, and his campaign in Histria. Both his predecessors, M. Iunius and A. Manlius, were in Histria already, without official authority and in defiance of opposition from the tribunes;[156] Claudius, who was properly authorized to take over the war, went there and ordered them back to Rome.

152. Livy XLIII 9.6–10.8 (cf. 18.5–21.1); esp. 10.3, 10.5 and 11.1 on Cento's *cupiditas*, *neglegentia* and *temeritas*. Cf. Walsh 1961, 146–50 on Livy's 'doublets' and their cause.
153. Livy XXXIX 32.5–13, esp. 10 'toto foro volitando' (cf. III 35.5; *volitare* occurs practically nowhere else in Livy).
154. Livy XXXIX 32.12, 'magnis contentionibus tribunorum quoque plebis, qui aut contra consulem aut pro studio eius pugnabant'; cf. IX 34.26, the same motif in the hostile portrait of Ap. Caecus, and n.111 above.
155. Livy XXXIX 32.13, 'moderatis studiis, non vi Claudiana, inter plebeios certatum est'. For Livy's view of Appius elsewhere, see esp. XXXIX 36.3, 37.19. Lintott (1968, 71, 74, 176, 209) evidently accepts the electoral scene as genuine.
156. Livy XLI 1–7.

According to Livy, however, he left Rome suddenly at dead of night without the due formalities, made a fool of himself in Histria (where Iunius and Manlius refused to accept his authority), got the same boat back to Aquileia, returned to Rome so fast that he nearly caught up a despatch he had sent to his colleague, went hurriedly through the proper formalities and returned to Histria in just as headlong a manner as before.[157]

The passage is clearly written for laughs, with ironical emphasis on the official formula *votis nuncupatis*, *paludatis lictoribus*,[158] and a conspicuous alliteration at beginning and end to help the reader make his effect at the *recitatio*.[159] Livy must have enjoyed writing it, but can hardly have invented the material himself. It is inconsistent with his favourable picture of Claudius in the campaign proper – a colourful account which no doubt owes much to the sixteenth book of Ennius' *Annales*[160] – and it goes against the moral he draws in the next book, in an extended passage on the *vota nuncupata* before the war with Perseus.[161] It cannot be historical: Claudius fought both in Histria and in Liguria, according to the triumphal Fasti,[162] and there would hardly have been time for all this travelling to and from Rome. It must be simply irresponsible invention by an author determined to put the worst complexion on whatever Claudius did.[163] The emphasis on lictors, and on the consular *imperium*,[164] perhaps suggests some of the anti-Claudian annalist's early-republican themes, now transposed into a different key.

Finally, Ap. Claudius Pulcher the consul of 143. Left in Rome while his colleague went off to fight (that in itself is enough to arouse suspicion[165]), he made a campaign for himself by wantonly provoking the Gallic Salassi in the foothills of the Graian Alps. He suffered a defeat in the ensuing war and lost 5,000 men, but in a

157. Livy XLI 10.5–13.
158. Livy XLI 10.5, 10.7, 10.11, 10.13.
159. 10.5 'nocte profectus praeceps in provinciam abiit', 10.13 'in provinciam aeque ac prius praecipiti celeritate abiit'.
160. Livy XLI 11–18. Cf. XLI 1.7 on the tribunes T.C. Aelii in Manlius' army; Ennius reputedly added *Annales* XVI because of his admiration of 'T. Caecilius Teucer and his brother' (Plin *NH* VII 101) or of 'the tribune C. Aelius' (Macr. *Sat.* VI 3.3).
161. Livy XLII 49.1–8, esp. 49.5 on *temeritas* leading to *clades*, *prudentia* to success.
162. Degrassi 1947, 80–1.
163. It recalls another tendentious episode, that of Flaminius' *vota non nuncupata* in 217, before Trasimene (XXI 63.5ff).
164. Livy XLI 10.7 and 9: Claudius' authority defied.
165. Cf. notes 66 and 89 above.

subsequent battle killed 5,000 of the enemy, supposedly the minimum number for a triumph.[166] With true Claudian arrogance, though knowing full well he had won no victory, he assumed that the triumph was his for the asking, and requested the funds for it; they were refused, so he triumphed *iniussu populi* at his own expense.[167]

Against that background, the story of the Vestal Virgin who defended her father's triumph against a hostile tribune could be turned from an example of *laus* and *pietas* (which is how Cicero knew it[168]) into yet another shocking case of Claudian contempt for the Roman people. Even at this late date, within two or three generations of his own time, the author of the hostile version evidently kept up his attack. He is at his best in the account of Appius' censorship in 136: Appius' harshness *would* have led him to do many outrageous things, had it not been for the mildness of his colleague Q. Fulvius Nobilior, who always gave in to him and thus gave him no opportunity for anger![169]

Meanwhile, what of his rival? It is notoriously easier to portray vice than virtue, and the recurrent themes of the pro-Claudian tradition are less conspicuous. But they are detectably there, and in the same author whose treatment of Attus Clausus' migration led us to postulate the pro-Claudian tradition in the first place.

Plutarch twice refers to Appius the consul of 143 as one of the wisest and most excellent of the Romans of his age, in the context of his marriage-alliance with, and political support of, Tiberius Gracchus.[170] That might simply be praise by association, so to speak, from a pro-Gracchan source, were it not for a similar and more revealingly explicit description of him in the *Life of Aemilius Paullus*. When Appius stood unsuccessfully against Scipio Aemilianus for the censorship of 142, he is supposed to have said 'O Paullus, groan beneath the earth as you see your son escorted down to the Forum by Aemilius the crier and Licinius the tax-

166. Val. Max. II 8.1; cf. Cic. *Pis*. 62 ('minus magnum bellum', of M. Piso in Spain), who does not quote a figure.
167. Dio fr. 74.1–2 (*πρὸς τὸ γένος ὠγκωμένος . . . τοσαύτῃ ὑπερηφανίᾳ . . .*), Oros. V 4.7 ('infami impudentia atque ambitione usus') – both no doubt from Livy, though there is no trace of this *color* in the very sketchy epitome of book LIII; Obsequens (21) also mentions the defeat inflicted by the Salassi. *Iniussu populi*: Suet. *Tib*. 2.4.
168. Cic. *Cael*. 34, Val. Max. V 4.6; p. 58 above.
169. Dio fr. 81; cf. n.11 above for *ἐπιείκεια*: *τραχύς* no doubt translates whatever word Dionysius rendered as *αὐστηρός* (Dion. Hal. VI 24.1, 27.1).
170. Plut. *TG* 4.2 (*πολὺ φρονήματι τοὺς καθ' αὑτὸν ὑπεραίρων*), 9.1 (one of *οἱ πρωτεύοντες ἀρετῇ καί δοξῃ*).

farmer!'[171] The two men were 'the greatest in the city', but while Scipio's influence was based on his personal glory and popularity with the people, Appius had the Senate and the *optimates* behind him – 'for that was his family's ancestral policy'.[172]

Not only is there a clear echo of the 'wise policies' by which Attus Clausus had reached the same pre-eminent rank in the Roman state,[173] but Scipio's disgracefully demagogic escort, unworthy of a noble and a patrician, is very reminiscent of the way Appius Claudius the Decemvir campaigned for his re-election in the story Livy relates.[174] It looks like an example of something we have seen already with the sacred chickens: the author of the favourable version doing his best to cancel out the more damaging details that went to make up his predecessor's account, in this case by attributing them to Appius' opponent.

In Valerius Maximus' collection, under the heading 'Wise Sayings', an Appius Claudius is credited with the opinion that activity is better for the Roman people than idleness, since it gives an opportunity for the exercise of *virtus*: the danger of idleness was, of course, one of the first recurring themes in the speeches Dionysius borrowed from the 'favourable source'.[175] We do not know to which Appius this pearl of wisdom was attributed, but that in itself is significant: it could have been any of them. The wise conservative Claudii were as schematic and repetitive an invention as the cruel and arrogant ones. If the impact of the repetition was less effective, it was perhaps because their creator did not have the imagination – and the sheer effrontery – of his predecessor.

171. Plut. *Aem. P.* 38.3-5, *Mor.* 810B.

172. Plut. *Aem. P. 38.3: ὁ μὲν τὴν βουλὴν ἔχων καὶ ἀρίστους περὶ αὐτόν. αὕτη γὰρ Ἀππίοις ἡ πολιτεία πάτριος.*

173. Plut. *Popl.* 21.10 (p. 63 above), where *τὸ πρῶτον ἀξίωμα* is also echoed in Plut. *TG* 4.2.

174. Plut. *Aem. P.* 38.4: *ἀνθρώπους ἀγεννεῖς* (cf. n.26 above) *καὶ δεδουλευκότας, ἀγοραίους δὲ* (cf. n.90 above) *καὶ δυναμένους ὄχλον συναγαγεῖν καὶ σπουδαρχίᾳ καὶ κραυγῇ πάντα πράγματα βιάσασθαι* (also 38.5 *Λικίννιος Φιλόνεικος*). Livy III 35.4f: 'ipse medius inter tribunicios, Duillios Iciliosque, in foro volitare (cf. n.153 above), per illos se plebi venditare . . .'.

175. Val. Max. VII 2.1, cf. Dion. Hal. V 66.2–4, VIII 73.2 (and n.72 above).

Chapter 7

THE DATE OF COMPOSITION

When Theodor Mommsen read his paper 'The Patrician Claudii' to the Prussian Academy in March 1861, at the very outset he put his finger on the crucial point:[1]

> We are accustomed to regard this Claudian *gens* as the very incarnation of the patriciate, and its leaders as the champions of the aristocratic party and of the conservatives in opposition to the plebeians and the democrats; and this view, in fact, already pervades the works which form our authorities. In the little, indeed, which we possess belonging to the period of the Republic, and particularly in the numerous writings of Cicero, there occurs no hint of the kind . . . It is in Livy that we first meet with the view which is now current.

'No hint of the kind' is a slight exaggeration, since Mommsen rightly recognized that the story in Cicero's *Brutus* of Appius Caecus refusing to accept a plebeian consul must be fictitious, part of the schematic view of the family as blindly reactionary patricians.[2] (He might have added the story of P. Claudius Pulcher and the chickens in the *de natura deorum* and *de divinatione* – but he evidently believed that to be historical.[3]) At the end of the paper, therefore, the statement is modified:[4]

> If the notice in Cicero's *Brutus* has been correctly estimated above, this series of falsifications must already have existed in Cicero's time; but the 'Claudian arrogance' was certainly not yet at that time generally recognised and familiar, otherwise assuredly Cicero would not have allowed so suitable a handle

1. Mommsen 1864, 287 (trans. W. P. Dickson).
2. Cic. *Brut.* 55 (p. 89 above); Mommsen 1864, 311f.
3. Cic. *ND* II 7, *div.* I 29, II 20, 71 (p. 90 above); Mommsen 1864, 317.
4. Mommsen 1864, 314f.

for invective against his mortal enemy Clodius wholly to escape him.

How long does an invention take to become 'generally recognised and familiar'? It was presumably by taking advantage of the chronological flexibility offered by the phrase that Mommsen was able tentatively to assign authorship of the 'Claudian arrogance' legend to Licinius Macer.[5]

For Mommsen, it was the optimate Claudii of the Sullan period – particularly C. Claudius the consul of 92, whose *potentia* is frequently mentioned by Cicero – who made it plausible for a contemporary historian to interpret their ancestors as arrogant patricians.[6] He is followed by Klingner, who does not suggest an author for it (though Antias is hinted at),[7] and also by Ogilvie, who specifies Antias as the author (though with some ambiguity about his motives).[8]

Meanwhile, however, an entirely different date and context for the invention of the legend had been proposed by Hermann Peter; he thought the author was Fabius Pictor, and his motive the hostility between Appius Caecus and Fabius Rullianus during the Samnite Wars.[9] Tentatively accepted by Walsh,[10] this idea has since been taken up with great energy by Alföldi, as part of his much-criticized theory that practically all the annalistic tradition on the regal period and the early Republic is basically Fabian.[11]

Yet all these suggestions, including Mommsen's own, fail to satisfy the *terminus post quem* Mommsen established over a cen-

5. Mommsen 1864, 315f. Mommsen believed that the *real* early-republican Claudii were 'the predecessors of the Gracchi and of Caesar' (1864, 318) – a view based on the demagogy of Appius the Decemvir and Appius Caecus, which he considered essentially historical (cf. pp. 81, 88 above) – and that the *popularis* Macer wished to deprive them of the credit for this.
6. Mommsen 1864, 315; cf. Cic. *Planc.* 51, *Brut.* 166, *Verr.* IV 133. Mommsen is wrong, however, to say (*ibid.*) that *all* the Claudii were 'in the oligarchic camp': cf. App. *BC* I 68 on the Appius who owed Marius a favour.
7. Klingner 1965, 83 (evidently also accepting Mommsen's view of a previously favourable tradition); *ibid.* 84 on Antias 'bringing the Claudii back within bounds' by having Publicola invite them to Rome.
8. Ogilvie 1965, 15: 'it is Antias alone who is responsible for the picture of those proud patricians the Claudii', in the context of his pro-Sullan bias ('it is no accident that one of Sulla's staunchest allies was Ap. Claudius Pulcher', *cos.* 79). *Ibid.* 295 and 376 for Antias' *hostile* portrait of early Appii, 273f for the 'migration in 504' tradition as an invention (by Antias) to make the Claudii sound republicans.
9. Peter 1914, xlviii–lii (cf. p. 86 above).
10. Walsh 1961, 89f (but cf. 90 n.1).
11. Alföldi 1965, 154 and 159–64; for criticism of Alföldi's overall view, see (e.g.) Gabba 1967, 139–142 and Poucet 1976 *passim* (esp. 201, 209f).

tury ago. Except in his late work,[12] Cicero is completely unaware of the 'family character' of the Claudii that Livy took for granted.

—

In his defence of C. Cornelius in 65 B.C., Cicero gave a rapid sketch of the history of the tribunate, of which a few quotations, and Asconius' commentary, survive. He dealt among other things with the second secession of the *plebs* and the end of the power of the Decemvirs, and the commentator observes:

> Only the names are not added – who among the Decemvirs it was who granted the claim against liberty [*sc.* by upholding his client's claim that the girl was his slave], and who was the father against whose daughter the decision was given – obviously because everyone knows that Appius Claudius was the Decemvir in question, and L. Verginius the girl's father.[13]

'Everyone knows' is a dangerous argument.[14] According to the Argives, the Trojan image of Athena, whose loss brought about the fall of the city, was brought to Argos; Pausanias refused to believe it when he was shown round, because '*it is known* that the Palladium was brought to Italy by Aeneas'.[15] But Diomedes stole the Palladium: where else would the Greeks have brought it back but Argos? The Aeneas story depends on Diomedes' loot being only one of two, or only a copy;[16] by the second century A.D., thanks to the Roman empire, this secondary version had prevailed, and it was hard for anyone to conceive the possibility that it had not always been accepted. Similarly with the Decemvir's name: everyone knew it, because of Livy. It does not follow that Cicero knew it too.

A much fuller account than the thumbnail sketch in the *pro Cornelio* is given in the second book of the *de republica*, but even here Appius is not named. Cicero describes the despotic rule of the second board of Decemvirs, and the revolt against their injustice, cruelty and *libido*:

> Of course the story is well known, and celebrated in many literary works – how a certain Decimus Verginius killed his

12. The *Brutus* belongs to 46 B.C., the *de nat. deorum* and *de div.* to 44.
13. Asc. 77C: 'scilicet quod notissimum est. . .'. Other names omitted by Cicero are supplied by Asconius on the same page.
14. Cf. Suet. *Tib.* 2.4 (p. 57 above), and Mommsen 1864, 292: 'Von dem Decemvir Appius Claudius rührt *bekanntlich* das römische Landrecht her' (my italics).
15. Paus. II 23.5: *τὸ μὲν δὴ Παλλάδιον . . . δῆλόν ἐστιν ἐς Ἰταλίαν κομισθὲν ὑπὸ Αἰνείου.*
16. Dion. Hal. I 69, etc.

virgin daughter with his own hand, in the Forum, because of the lust of one of the Decemvirs . . .

Diodorus too says simply, 'One of their number had conceived a passion for a poor girl of good family . . .', without naming any of the characters.[17] It has been convincingly inferred that originally the characters *had* no names (as was often the case in popular narrative), 'that the very name Verginia was simply a hypostatization of *virgo*, and that the identity of her father as Verginius and the names of the remaining characters were all gradual embellishments'.[18] If so, the variant *praenomen* of Cicero's Verginius suggests that the process was still under way when he wrote; it is quite possible that in 51, when the *de republica* came out, the lustful Decemvir had not yet been identified as Appius. By 45, however (the date of the *de finibus*), Appius has been named, and his victim's father is *Lucius* Verginius, as in Livy.[19]

It may be objected that the 'many literary works' Cicero refers to could hardly have left the villain without a name – though it is worth noticing that Cicero does not specify historical works: poetry, fable, popular philosophy and collections of *exempla* are all possible. It may also be argued that when he wrote the *de republica* Cicero was anxious not to offend his more influential contemporaries, because of a projected campaign for the consulship by his brother,[20] and might have left the Decemvir anonymous so as not to annoy Appius Claudius the consul of 54. So the argument from silence is not quite foolproof in the Verginia story; but the case does not rest on that alone.

On 15 May 61 B.C., just after Clodius' acquittal at the trial for sacrilege arising out of his invasion of the rites of the Good Goddess, Cicero delivered in the Senate his speech *in Clodium et Curionem*.[21] In the published version, he incorporated the *altercatio* between himself and Clodius in the House, during the course of which Clodius had mocked him for staying at his Campanian villa: 'what has a man of Arpinum, *agrestis et rusticus*, to do with Baiae?' In his reply, Cicero dwells on Clodius' obtuseness in not realizing that his defence counsel, C. Curio, owned a villa at Baiae

17. Cic. *rep.* II 63 ('nota scilicet illa res et celebrata monumentis plurimis litterarum'), Diod. Sic. XII 24.2.
18. Ogilvie 1965, 477; cf. Münzer 1899, 2700f and p. 80 above.
19. Cic. *fin.* II 66. For the dates, cf. *Att.* V 12.2, *fam.* VIII 1.4 (*de rep.*); *Att.* XIII 19.4, 32.2 (*de fin.*).
20. Wiseman 1966, 109f.
21. Cic. *Att.* I 16.8–10, Schol. Bob. 85–91St.

which had once belonged to the Arpinate Marius. In missing this point, he says, Clodius was so blind that it is obvious he must have looked at something he was forbidden to see – a reference to the Good Goddess's rites, with the suggestion that the gods must have blinded him for his sacrilege.[22]

The scholiast helpfully observes that Clodius' family was descended from 'Appius the Blind', and it is conceivable that Cicero was alluding to Caecus. Not, however, to the story that his blindness was the punishment meted out by the gods for bribing the Potitii to give up their care of the rites of Hercules (p. 87 above). Cicero shows no knowledge of that, and the pretended blinding of Clodius is alluded to without any specific reference, merely as the sort of thing that would happen to anyone who saw too much, as in the story of Teiresias.[23]

The point is made most clearly in the *de domo* four years later, where Cicero asks whether any of Clodius' ancestors, in their private worship or their public priesthoods, had ever been present at the rites of the Good Goddess. Of course not – not even he who became blind. So popular beliefs are evidently wrong, if Appius Caecus, who never knowingly looked at what he ought not to see, lost his sight, while Clodius, who polluted secret rites 'not only by looking at them but also by sacrilegious sexual offences', was struck only with blindness of the intellect. Similarly in the *de haruspicum responso*:

> Do you think that your blind lust is preferable to blindness of the eyes, not realizing that the sightless eyes of your ancestor are more to be desired than the burning eyes of your sister?

The contrast there is a different one, based on lust rather than obtuseness, but it is still a contrast. Appius the censor and Publius Clodius have, for Cicero, nothing in common at all.[24]

In the *pro Caelio*, where Cicero impersonates Appius the censor as a means of attacking Clodia's immorality, his blindness is referred to again (in the throw-away line 'it won't hurt him, he won't see

22. Schol. Bob. 88St: 'ita fuit caecus ut facile appararet vidisse eum quod fas non fuisset'.

23. E.g. Val. Max. I 1.ext.5 on Alexander's soldiers, blinded for entering Ceres' temple at Miletus, from which men were forbidden. Cf. (in general) Devereux 1973, esp. 40–45.

24. Cic. *dom.* 105, *har. resp.* 38. Appius the demagogue (who could surely have been used against Clodius) is also unknown to Cicero: Cn. Flavius is treated as an independent agent at *Mur.* 25, while at *Att.* VI 1.8 Cicero does not even know his date.

her'), but there is no hint anywhere that the old censor was anything but a heroic example of old Roman *gravitas*,[25] brought on to *contrast* with the behaviour of his great-great-great-great-granddaughter. There is exactly the same picture of him in the *de senectute*, where Cicero's quotation of Ennius shows that it was a traditional one.[26] It is reasonable to infer that until the author of the hostile version invented the arrogant and sacrilegious aspects of his career, Appius the censor had been a stainless example of old Roman virtue.[27] That was what he was to Cicero, who adduced him not as a precedent, but as a contrast, to the blinding of Clodius' intellect by the angry gods.

The *pro Caelio* passage, as we have seen above,[28] also proves that Q. Claudia was still free from any taint of immorality, and Appius the consul of 143 just a *triumphator* with a loyal daughter, not a monster of arrogance and illegality, when Cicero wrote the speech in 56 B.C. As Mommsen said, *could* he have failed to use the hostile version of Claudian history against Clodius and Clodia, if it had existed in his time?

The question is raised in an acute form by a later passage of the *in Clodium et Curionem*, where there is a splendid word-picture of Clodius getting into his disguise before going to the Good Goddess's celebrations:

> When you were winding the bands round your feet, when you were having the head-dress fitted on, when with difficulty you were putting your arms into a sleeved tunic, when the breast-band was being carefully tied round you, in all that time did you never remember that you were Appius Claudius' grandson? Even though lust had perverted your whole mind, yet did you not . . . [lacuna, presumably containing a reference to Clodius' father]. But I suppose that when they brought you the mirror you realized you didn't belong to the Pulchri after all.[29]

Though Cicero only goes back two generations, no doubt because he did not want to spoil the boudoir scene, here too Clodius' ancestors are brought in as a contrast, as the scholiast duly

25. Cic. *Cael.* 33: 'ille austerus mos ac modus'.
26. Cic. *sen.* 16, 37: 'vigebat in illa domo mos patrius et disciplina'.
27. Hence Cicero writes to Ap. Claudius in 50 B.C. 'in censura, si iam es censor, ut spero, de proavo multum cogitato tuo' (*fam.* III 11.5).
28. Pp. 58, 95f, 98.
29. Schol. Bob. 89St: '. . . longe te a pulchris esse sensisti'.

observes.[30] For 'lust perverted your whole mind' one would have thought the Decemvir was an almost inevitable *exemplum*.[31] But he was not used, because Clodius' ancestors were evidently better exploited as being all that he was *not* – a tactic that would have been extraordinarily perverse and self-defeating if the hostile version had yet existed.

Quoting the final pun on *pulchri*, the scholiast tells the story of P. Claudius Pulcher – the first to bear that name – and his defeat in the naval battle at Drepanum. The fact that he chooses this point to do so, without cross-reference to any other passage, clearly indicates that Cicero did not refer to Pulcher anywhere in his speech. But the speech was delivered immediately after, and as a result of, the trial of a Publius Claudius for sacrilege, during the course of which evidence had been given about the misbehaviour of one of his sisters;[32] if Cicero had known the story of another Publius Claudius, who threw the sacred chickens in the sea, who was brought to trial as a result of the ensuing defeat, and whose sister was indicted for her 'impious prayer' that Publius might lose another fleet, I submit that it is inconceivable he would have made no allusion to it.

On this subject the argument from silence seems compelling: the hostile tradition, with its theme of the arrogance of the Claudian *divum contemptores*, exemplified above all by Appius the Decemvir, Appius Caecus the censor, and his son Publius Pulcher, cannot have been current in 61. Nor, I think, can it have been current in 57 or 56, since it does not appear in the *post reditum* speeches, even where religious matters are the main issue; for example, it would have been an ideal moment to exploit the *divum contemptor* theme at the point in the *de haruspicum responso* where Cicero exclaims at the paradox that Clodius, of all men, is complaining about offences against religion.[33] Finally, the hostile tradition can hardly have been current even in 52, or we should expect to find it in the *pro Milone*.[34]

30. *Ibid.*: 'maiorum suorum dissimillimum contestatus est'; Cic. *dom.* 83f on Clodius' father, 'civem medius fidius egregium *dissimilemque vestri*'.
31. Cf. p. 80f above; the standard vices of the tyrant (including *libido*) are attributed to Clodius by Cicero just as they are to the Decemvir by Livy: see Dunkle 1967, 163 and 167 (comparing Cic. *Mil.* 76 with Livy III 45.8).
32. Cic. *Mil.* 73, Plut. *Caes.* 10.5, *Cic.* 29.3–4; cf. Wiseman 1969, 53–5.
33. Cic. *har. resp.* 8 (on the rebuilding of Cicero's house): 'Publius, inquam, Clodius sacra et religiones neglegi violari pollui questus est!'
34. Particularly in the context of Clodius' attempt to prevent Milo becoming consul (Cic. *Mil.* 24–5): the Ap. Caecus of *Brut.* 55 would have been a useful weapon there.

However, the story of Pulcher and the sacred chickens *was* known to Cicero when he wrote the *de natura deorum* and *de divinatione* in 44. The *de natura deorum* was written first,[35] and it is interesting to see how Cicero's treatment of the story differs in the two works. In the earlier one, Lucilius' speech on proofs from divination contains this:[36]

> Shall we then take no notice of P. Claudius' rashness in the first Punic War? Even though he was joking when he mocked the gods – because the chickens wouldn't eat when released from their cage, he ordered them to be thrown in the sea, so that they could drink if they didn't want to eat – when his fleet was defeated, that joke brought great grief on himself and a great disaster on the Roman people.

The way the story is spelt out perhaps implies that it was not a familiar one which could be briefly alluded to. In the *de divinatione*, on the other hand, the story is referred to succinctly without explanation.[37] In the meantime, perhaps, it had become part of the tradition.

That hypothesis is at least consistent with the other Ciceronian evidence. If he became aware of the lustful Decemvir between 51 and 45,[38] of the reactionary Caecus between 52 and 46,[39] and of the sacrilegious Pulcher between 56 and 44 (perhaps precisely in 44 itself), it strongly suggests that the hostile annalist was publishing his early-Republic books in the late 50s or the early 40s of the first century B.C.

—

If that is the case, then the author of the 'favourable version', who evidently invented his wise and god-fearing conservative Claudii in order to counter the effect his predecessor had made, must be dated between the middle 40s B.C. and the period – probably in the 20s – when Livy and Dionysius had begun to publish. It is quite possible that the appearance of his early books overlapped in time with that of the hostile author's later ones – and, indeed, his own later ones with the beginnings of Livy and Dionysius. But the late 40s and the 30s must be roughly his *floruit*.

But Caecus appears only as a contrast (*Mil.* 17). Cf. *Mil.* 85f for Clodius as an offender against the gods.

35. Cic. *div.* II 3.
36. Cic. *ND* II 7.
37. Cic. *div.* I 29, II 20, 71.
38. Cic. *rep.* II 63, *fin.* II 66; n.19 above.
39. Cic. *Mil.* 17, *Brut.* 55: n.34 above.

There are just two details which may help to confirm this date. Firstly, Plutarch, as we have seen (p. 62f above), evidently used the favourable version for his account of the arrival of Attus Clausus and his followers at Rome in 504. For him, Clausus was not a factious deserter, but a man of great moral worth, rich, noble, eloquent – and illustrious for his physical strength.[40] That is an unexpected quality: courage, yes, but why strength? The answer may be that the author of the favourable version wanted to emphasize the ancestry of the lesser branch of the patrician Claudii, the Nerones, whose *cognomen* meant 'strong' in the Sabine language.[41] It was precisely in 38 B.C. that the Claudii Nerones became more important than the Pulchri for the first time in Roman history, when Octavian married Livia Drusilla and Ti. Claudius Nero and his unborn brother became the Triumvir's stepsons.

Secondly, there is a recurring *topos* in the speeches of the conservative Appii, that the same characteristics may be described in different terms, as virtues or as vices, according to one's partisan commitment.[42] The classic account of that phenomenon is in Thucydides' analysis of the *stasis* at Corcyra – and Thucydides, after centuries of neglect, had suddenly been 'rediscovered' at Rome in the middle forties B.C., as part of the controversy about the 'Attic' style of oratory.[43] Sallust, writing the *Catiline* about 40 B.C., was notoriously influenced by Thucydides, and the Corcyra passage in particular:[44] perhaps, in his different way, the author of the 'favourable version' felt the same influence about the same time.

The dates of our two historians, then, can be established with some degree of probabality. Their characteristics are all too clearly apparent. But what are their names? and why did they do it?

40. Plut. *Popl.* 21.4: *ἀνὴρ χρήμασί τε δυνατὸς καὶ σώματος ῥώμῃ πρὸς ἀλκὴν ἐπιφανής.*
41. *Fortis*, *strenuus*: Suet. *Tib.* 1.2, Gell. *NA* XIII 23.7.
42. Dion. Hal. VI 38.2–3, IX 53.6.
43. Thuc. III 82.4ff; Cic. *Brut.* 287f, *orator* 30–2; Syme 1964, 52f and 245, Earl 1972, 854f.
44. Sall. *Cat.* 52.11f; Syme 1964, 117 and 255 (cf. 127–9 on the date).

Chapter 8

—

AUTHORS AND MOTIVES

But for one awkward fact, we could confidently name the author of the hostile version straight away. The obvious identification is with Valerius Antias. Unfortunately, however, the one testimony we have on Antias' date puts him unequivocally in the 80s or 70s B.C.[1]

It has long been recognized that the schematic picture of the brutal and arrogant Claudii is systematically correlated with the opposite, but equally stereotyped, family character of the Valerii.[2] Again, Macaulay sums it up:[3]

> *Ah! woe is me for the good house*
> *That loves the people well!*

After delivering his *horrida et atrox sententia* on the necessity of appointing a dictator to suppress plebeian complaints, the first Appius is very nearly made dictator himself, but finally Manius Valerius is appointed – much to the relief of the *plebs*, 'who feared no grim arrogance from *that* family'.[4] The contrast is repeatedly pointed by a series of fictional debates in which the plebeian and patrician points of view are put forward by a Valerius and a Claudius respectively: Dionysius has the first Appius oppose Marcus Valerius on the debt question in 498, Manius on the same subject in 495, 494 and 493, and Manius again on the trial of Coriolanus in 491;[5] Publius Valerius, son of Publicola, opposes both the second Appius in 472, according to Dionysius, and his consular colleague C. Claudius in 460, according to Livy;[6] and the main opponent of Appius the wicked Decemvir is, of course, L. Valerius Potitus.[7]

1. Vell. II 9.6: 'vetustior Sisenna fuit Coelius, aequalis Sisennae Rutilius Claudiusque Quadrigarius et Valerius Antias'.
2. Münzer 1891, 56f, attributing it to Antias; Peter 1914, cccxii, apparently assuming Valerian insertions (by Antias) into an existing hostile tradition (from Pictor, cf. his pp. xlviii–lii).
3. *The Battle of Lake Regillus* xvii (on the death of M. Valerius).
4. Livy II 30.6 – because of his brother Publicola's *provocatio* law.
5. Dion. Hal. V 64–68, VI 23–24, 38–41, 58–64, 88.3, VIII 48–56.
6. Dion. Hal. IX 49, Livy III 18.
7. See esp. Livy III 38–41, 49–55, Dion. Hal. XI 4–6, 19–22, 38–39 etc.

If these fictional confrontations (particularly in Dionysius) do not always portray the Claudii in a bad light, it is, I think, because Dionysius was interested in giving each side a good case, at whatever cost to consistency, and so used the apologetic source for most of his Claudian speeches.[8] But the *fact* of the pairing-off of Claudii and Valerii in this way must surely go back to the hostile version; as always, the apologist does not alter the substance of his predecessor's account, but has to change the motivation as revealed in the speeches, making the Claudii responsible and far-sighted, and occasionally hinting at over-zealous democracy leading to tyranny on the part of the Valerii.[9]

The same thing no doubt happened with the story of the arrival of Attus Clausus in Rome: the hostile version, as we saw above, had him come as an abject suppliant in the year of Valerius Publicola's consulship, while the favourable one made Publicola invite him and welcome him. It is likely that the hostile annalist drew a contrast between the Sabine origins of the two families: as we know from Plutarch's *Life of Publicola*, it was supposedly the first of the Valerii who urged the reconciliation of Romulus' Romans and Tatius' Sabines, and stayed behind with Tatius in Rome, with all his relatives and clients.[10] How different that statesmanlike reconciler of strife could be made to seem from Clausus the party boss who deserted his country and fled to Rome! The favourable version accepted the circumstances of Clausus' migration, but altered the emphasis to exculpate Clausus himself and give him the same virtues of wisdom and persuasiveness attributed to the original Valerius. (Plutarch, who had his own ideas about the virtues of a statesman, predictably adopted an account that made Clausus eloquent and wise without impugning Publicola's magnanimity.[11])

In the later narrative, too, Valerian items can be found in the Claudian legends. The most blatant example is in the episode of the Great Mother's installation at Rome: not only is one patrician Valerius – invested with the fictitious dignity of *two* past consulships – the senior member of the senatorial delegation sent to Attalus to request the goddess's transfer, and another the junior member, sent back to Rome to announce to the Senate the success

8. Cf. above, pp. 52, 69.
9. E.g. Dion. Hal. VI 60–61.
10. Plut. *Popl.* 1.1, Dion. Hal. II 46.3.
11. *Pace* Münzer (1891, 9f), Plutarch's biography of Publicola is not taken *entirely* from the author of the Valerian legend; cf. Plut. *Popl.* 9.9, 10.1–3, for traces of a version that hinted at Publicola's 'regal power', and 14.6–8 for M. Valerius' dishonest attempt to trick Horatius over the Jupiter-temple dedication.

of the embassy,[12] but the palm of female excellence, in the choice of the best Roman of each sex to receive the goddess on her arrival, is given not to Quinta Claudia, as in the version Cicero knew, but to a Valeria.[13]

There is no question about the authorship of the Valerian legend. It was the work of Valerius Antias.[14] And if the arrogance of the patrician Claudii was an inseparable corollary of it, as it evidently was, then that must surely be Antias' work as well.

Certainly the unscrupulousness of the inventions, in each case, strongly suggests that the same hand was responsible for both. In particular, the substitution of Valeria for Quinta Claudia in Diodorus, which seems to guarantee the interdependence of the two contrasting family legends, is irresistibly reminiscent of the assertion reported by Plutarch – clearly from Antias – that the statue in the Sacra Via of the courageous girl who escaped from Lars Porsenna was not of Cloelia at all, but of Publicola's daughter Valeria.[15] Scholars have been reluctant to attribute Diodorus' Valeria to Antias as well as Plutarch's,[16] but only because of the undefended assumption that Diodorus used exclusively early material for his Roman narrative; in fact, it is quite clear that he also used first-century sources, including at least one that must have been practically contemporary with himself.[17]

Diodorus reports the supposititious Valeria in the course of a history of the Scipiones Nasicae, who were descended from Africanus' uncle Cn. Scipio (consul 222) – they were the consul of

12. Livy XXIX 11.3, 11.8, 14.5, XXX 23.5. Cf. Münzer 1891, 63f on the invention of M. Valerius Laevinus' consulship in 220, *ibid.* 57–61 on invented Valerian *legationes* in general; Schmidt 1909, 12 on the Attalus embassy.
13. Diod. Sic. XXXIV 33.2; p. 96 above.
14. See Münzer 1891, *passim*; rightly taken for granted by Walsh (1961, 88f), Ogilvie (1965, 14), etc.
15. Plut. *Popl.* 19.5 and 8 (Münzer 1891, 58); *contra* Livy II 13.11, Dion. Hal. V 35.2, etc.
16. See especially Münzer 1891, 64 and 1899, 2899; but Schmidt (1909, 16) draws the natural conclusion. For a spirited rejection of the *Einquellenprinzip* in Diodorus, see Borza 1968, esp. pp. 44–5.
17. Most obviously in his treatment of Appius Caecus: his dating of Cn. Flavius was unknown to Cicero in 50 B.C., despite the research Cicero had been doing on early republican history for the *de republica* (Diod. Sic. XX 36.6, Cic. *Att.* VI 1.8, cf. IV 14.1); and his description of the stone-paved Via Appia can hardly be earlier than the first century B.C. (XX 36.2, cf. Wiseman 1970b, 141 and 149f). Similarly, his version of the Gauls' attack on the Capitol is probably no older than Claudius Quadrigarius (XIV 66, cf. Wiseman 1979b, 40f: the account Cicero took for granted was quite different), while the treatment of Ascanius' son Iulus as the ancestor of the *gens Iulia* must be from a source of Caesarian date (VII 5.8, cited by Eusebius).

191, chosen as *vir optimus* to receive the Great Mother; the consul of 162, who opposed Cato over the destruction of Carthage; the consul of 138, who as *pontifex maximus* led the senators to kill Tiberius Gracchus; and finally the consul of 111 B.C. The context is significant, because Antias had a special interest in the Nasicae, and particularly in the consul of 191 himself.[18] According to Antias, and probably him alone, it was in that Nasica's consulship that the Megalesia were instituted and the first-ever theatrical games held.[19] When a Valeria appears in such company – along with the Valerian *legati* noted above as inserted into the Great Mother narrative – the identity of her creator, who thereby demoted Quinta Claudia, can hardly be in doubt.

(We do not know, unfortunately, how Antias dealt with the death of Tiberius Gracchus. But if, as is likely, he portrayed Nasica the *pontifex maximus* as a heroic tyrannicide, then Appius the consul of 143, as Tiberius' father-in-law and supporter, must have been among the villains of his piece.[20])

The institution of the Megalesia fits into another known Valerian theme, the origins of the Roman festivals. From the original Volesus Valerius' *ludi* in honour of Dis and Proserpina,[21] through a succession of invented *ludi saeculares* in Valerian consulships, down to the separation of senatorial seats at the *ludi Romani* in 194 (Scipio Africanus' consulship), Antias' devotion to the subject was unremitting.[22] His treatment of the introduction of the Floralia,

18. Münzer 1901, 1495: '[Antias] in ihm wohl eine Art Doppelgänger seines Lieblingshelden Scipio Africanus, nur mit schwächeren Farben darstellte'; cf. Fraccaro 1911a, 304 and 1939, 25f (=1956, 320 and 414) on his role in the trial of L. Scipio at XXXVIII 58–59. Antias also adds him to the *legatio* to Prusias about Hannibal in 183 (Livy XXXIX 56.7, contrast Pol. XXIV 5.1).

19. Livy XXXVI 36.3 (after the dedication of the temple); cf. XXIX 14.14 (Megalesia instituted in 204), XXXIV 54.3 (first *ludi scaenici* in 194).

20. The *elder* Ti. Gracchus was the subject of much late-annalistic eulogizing (cf. p. 99 above), which Antias certainly exploited, if he did not invent it: see Fraccaro 1911a, 257–65 and 318–20 (=1956, 289–94 and 329f) on Livy XXXVIII 52.9–53.7, emphasizing the deliberate contrast with Gracchus' son. No doubt with the same aim, someone – Antias, perhaps? – took the pretty story of Tiberius' betrothal to Appius' daughter Claudia and attributed it to the elder Ti. Gracchus and Scipio Africanus' daughter Cornelia (Plut. *TG* 4.4, Livy XXXVIII 57.2–8).

21. Val. Max. II 4.5; cf. Warde Fowler 1920, 56f on the lateness of the story.

22. Censorinus *de die nat.* 17 (*ludi saeculares*); cf. Münzer 1891, 5–9, esp. 7f. Scipio: Asc. 69C, cf. Livy XXXIX 22.8 for votive games of L. Scipio in 186. Note Musti 1970, 86–90 on the controversy about the origins of the *ludi Romani*, tentatively identifying Antias as one of the protagonists.

The interest in *ludi saeculares* is in itself an argument for the forties B.C. as Antias' *floruit*: see Weinstock 1971, 191–7 on the *saeculum* due to end in 49 or 46 B.C.

and the celebration of the secular games of 249 B.C., is likely to have involved him in more polemic against the Claudii.[23]

One of the recurring motifs in the hostile version of Claudian history is the dependence of the arrogant patricians on their lictors. Here again there is a Valerian corollary: Publicola had the axes removed from the lictors' *fasces* and lowered them before the sovereign people.[24] In his account of the supposedly illegal triumph of Appius the consul of 143, the hostile author made great play with the numbers killed on each side in the campaign. We know that Antias was interested in the numerical requirements for a triumph, and wrote up at least one case where they were disputed.[25] In details and in major themes alike, the characteristics of Valerius Antias and of the anti-Claudian author coincide so often that it is hard to resist the conclusion that they are identical.

Cicero does not mention Antias.

In two passages he discusses the development of Roman historiography, deploring the jejune brevity of Fabius, Cato, Piso and the other second-century historians, giving Coelius Antipater some credit for a rough-hewn attempt at literary effect, and insisting on the need for an expert orator to write history worthy of the name.[26] The first passage, written in 55, has a dramatic date of 91 B.C., and is therefore unhelpful about the historians who wrote after Coelius.[27] The second, however, has a contemporary setting, evidently in 52.[28] In the intervening 40 years, Asellio and 'Clodius' (presumably Claudius Quadrigarius[29]) had marked a regression to the weak standards of those who wrote before Coelius; Licinius Macer had shown a certain acumen, but he had no Greek learning

23. See p. 90 above, for Livy's treatment of P. Claudius Pulcher and his sister. According to Censorinus (17.10), Livy followed Antias in dating the third Secular Games to the consulship of Pulcher and Iunius Pullus.
24. Cic. *rep.* II 55, Plut. *Popl.* 10.7, etc.
25. Livy XXXVII 60.6 (189 B.C.), cf. XXXVIII 47.5–6.
26. Cic. *de or.* II 51–65, *leg.* I 6–7.
27. Cic. *de or.* II 54–5: 'ceteri non exornatores rerum sed tantummodo narratores fuerunt' (probably referring to Fannius and Vennonius, cf. *leg.* I 6) . . . 'nemo enim studet eloquentiae nostrorum hominum'. Cic. *Att.* IV 13.2 for the date of composition.
28. After Clodius' murder (Cic. *leg.* II 42), but before Cicero went to Cilicia, since it is set in Arpinum with no hint of the civil war.
29. Denied by Badian (1966, 20), on the grounds that the style of Quadrigarius' surviving fragments is not *languidus*. But if the 'Clodius' of Plut. *Numa* 1 is rightly identified as Quadrigarius (see Frier 1975, 73), it is not easy to see who else Cicero could be referring to. Cn. Gellius may also have been mentioned at this point (Cic. *leg.* I 6), but the text is very uncertain.

and his speeches were inept;[30] Sisenna was the best so far, but his one Greek model was Clitarchus and he was inadequate as an orator. Of Antias, not a word.

The usual explanation of Cicero's silence is that Antias was not a senator, and Cicero therefore ignored his work, or was even unaware of it: 'the histories of prominent men like Macer or Sisenna would naturally come to his attention while the work of a literary recluse would be overlooked'.[31] But he cites Vennonius, who was no less obscure, and it is not likely that any substantial history of early Rome would have totally escaped his notice while he was working on the *de republica* and *de legibus*.[32] The knowledge of history was an important part of the senator's qualifications, as Cicero observes in this very dialogue, and an even more important part of the qualifications of the orator, who drew his *exempla* from it.[33] *Exempla* certainly abounded in Antias. It seems improbable that Cicero, who was more interested in history than most, and seriously considered the possibility of writing it himself, would not have found Antias' work if it had been available to him. With a total bulk of more than 75 books, it was not an easy thing to overlook if you were interested in the subject.

Besides, the whole burden of Cicero's complaint is that Roman historiography has been too bald, too dry, not sufficiently oratorical. Whatever Antias' faults, and they were legion, that could hardly have been said to him. He included many speeches, as his treatment of the 'trials of the Scipios' shows,[34] and the sheer length of his history suggests that he must have been an 'elaborator of his material', by this means among others, and not a mere *narrator*.[35] Cicero might not have liked his speeches (he did not like Macer's), but he was surely interested enough to read them.

To call Antias a literary recluse is, I think, to misjudge the impact of his work. It was, in its way, a work of art,[36] and in particular it

30. Cic. *leg.* I 7: 'in orationibus †multas† ineptus . . .'.

31. Ogilvie 1965, 13; cf. Badian 1966, 20f ('. . . not deemed worthy of inclusion, perhaps for social rather than literary reasons'), Rawson 1972, 42, etc.

32. Cic. *leg.* I 6, *Att.* XII 3.1 (Vennonius); *Att.* IV 14.1 (working on the *de rep.* in Atticus' library); cf. Rawson 1972, 35f.

33. Cic. *leg.* III 14; *de or.*, esp I 18, II 36. For this reason I am unconvinced by the suggestion that Cicero had not read much history before about 55 B.C. (Rawson 1972, 33f).

34. Fr. 45P (Livy XXXVIII 50–55, 58–60).

35. Cf. Cic. *de or.* II 54, n.27 above. Luce (1977, 184) believes that Antias' style would not have commended itself to Cicero, but gives no reasons.

36. Rightly insisted on by Fraccaro (1911a, 277–9 and 1939, 23f=1956, 302f and 412f); cf. Peter 1914, cccxxi–ii.

must have appealed to every lover of oratory, as it appealed to Livy:

> He [Livy] is perfectly willing to take from Antias the reports of speeches allegedly uttered by Terentius Varro, Fabius Cunctator, and Aemilius Paulus before the battle of Cannae . . . Polybius has no mention of their forebodings, and Livy is acquainted with his version. It is hard to avoid the conclusion that a love of oratory has contributed to Livy's decision to prefer the false account incorporating these utterances.[37]

The extent of Antias' influence on the subsequent historiographical tradition is enough to show how much of a stir his own history made. Educated Romans were connoisseurs of rhetoric (as well as enjoying fiction); they must have read Antias with interest and pleasure. Indeed, from the point of view of style and oratorical *ornatio*, Antias might even seem to have fulfilled the very qualities Cicero complained were lacking in the writing of Roman history.[38] When judged by criteria of historical reliability, of course, it was another story; but Cicero recognized the looser standards of the rhetorical historian, and would not on that account have judged Antias any more severely than he judged Clitarchus and Stratocles.[39] If Antias had published by 52, therefore, it remains inexplicable why Cicero does not mention him.

It is interesting to notice that Cicero's observations about the *rhetoricum genus* of writing history, and Atticus' laughing comment on the falsehood that gives the story more point, come in the *Brutus* (46 B.C.), which also contains the first evidence that Cicero had read Antias.

As the first of the early Romans whose exploits, recorded in the histories, imply some oratorical skill,[40] he names L. Brutus, M'. Valerius (brother of Publicola), and L. Valerius Potitus.[41] Brutus

37. Walsh 1961, 231.

38. He criticizes Macer for the absence of *eruditio Graeca*, and Sisenna for having only one Greek model (*leg.* I 7); his own projected history was going to πολλὰ συμμεῖξαι τῶν Ἑλληνικῶν (Plut. *Cic.* 41.1). Antias must have been hellenized enough, to judge by the Homeric duel of M. Valerius and Tarquin at Lake Regillus (Livy II 20.1–3, Ogilvie 1965, 286), and the appeal his Valerian speeches evidently had for Dionysius of Halicarnassus.

39. Cic. *Brut.* 42f, p. 31f above. I am therefore unconvinced by Syme's suggestion (1964, 47 and 154) that Cicero ignored Antias because he was not a 'real' historian.

40. Cic. *Brut.* 52, 'quantum ex monumentis suspicari licet'. *Monumenta* must mean literary works, presumably histories in which speeches were attributed to these characters (Jordan 1872, esp. 210ff).

41. *Ibid.* 53–4. Potitus appears also in *rep.* II 55, which I take to represent the pre-Antian tradition of the freedom-loving Valerii (cf. Cic. *Flacc.* 1, 25); it may have derived from Piso (cf. Boscherini 1975, 147–50).

and Potitus are predictable, as the champions of *libertas* against the Tarquins and the Decemvirs respectively; but M'. Valerius is cited for his persuasiveness in putting an end to the first plebeian secession, in flat contradiction of the ancient story of Menenius Agrippa and his fable about the belly and the limbs.[42] Since we know that Antias 'wrote up' M'. Valerius and his exploits (in a passage which Cicero demonstrably did not know in 55 B.C.[43]), the authorship of this variant can hardly be in doubt.[44] It *has* sometimes been doubted, but only on the *a priori* grounds that Cicero never read Antias at all.[45] That, as we have seen, is unlikely in itself; the natural inference is that in 52 B.C. he had not read Antias, but in 46 he had. Indeed, it has been very convincingly argued, on entirely independent grounds, that Antias' account of the regal period and the early Republic appeared precisely at this time, the chronological *termini* being 52 and 44 B.C.[46]

If that is the case, then Cicero became aware of Antias at exactly the same period that he became aware of the author of the 'hostile version' of Claudian history (pp. 111 above). Indeed, the very same passage in the *Brutus* provides the earliest evidence for both, since another of the 'presumed orators' of the early Republic is M'. Curius, cited for his speech against an illegally anti-plebeian Appius Caecus.[47] It seems a reasonable economy of hypothesis to identify the two as a single historian whose work was appearing for the first time in the early 40s B.C.

Velleius Paterculus, however, says that Antias wrote in the 80s or 70s (p. 113 above). On the one hand, we have an unequivocal statement by an ancient author; on the other, a body of circumstantial evidence which I think it is fair to describe as overwhelming.

There is no satisfactory escape from the dilemma, but my own view is that it is easier to impute an error to Velleius than to accept the consequences of his date. Even if we do not identify Valerius Antias as the author of the 'hostile version', the idea of his having published in the 70s and remained unknown to Cicero for 30 years

42. Cf. Ogilvie 1965, 312f on Livy II 32.8–12 (at 32.8 Menenius is called *facundus vir*). The age of the story is guaranteed by the obscurity of the Menenii in the middle and late Republic.
43. Asc. 13C (see p. 46 above); Cic. *Pis.* 52, cf. *har. resp.* 16.
44. So Jordan 1872, 198; Münzer 1891, 22 (cf. 55 on Antias' Valerii and secessions in general); Ogilvie 1965, 211.
45. E.g. Rawson 1971, 42 (tentatively suggesting Macer).
46. See Cloud 1977a, 207–13 on the trial of Horatius (between 63 – or possibly 52 – and 30); 1977b, 225f on the death of Romulus (between 52 and 44); 1977a, 211f on C. Iulius the Decemvir (between 52 and 44).
47. Cic. *Brut.* 55, cf. p. 89 above.

is most implausible; and if we *do* identify him with the anti-Claudian annalist, as the interrelation of the Claudian and Valerian legends seems to require, then it becomes practically impossible. With such a weapon available to be used against Clodius in 61 or 56, Cicero could surely not have failed to use it.

Suppose, for instance, that Antias' history stopped about the time of Sulla (his latest datable fragment is on 91 B.C.), after an announcement in his preface that he would bring the story down to his own time. That would at least account for Velleius' date.[48]

We need not imagine that Antias died before he finished, like Thucydides; there were patrician Claudii alive and influential in the 40s and 30s B.C. who might well have made it difficult for him to write about Clodius.[49] Perhaps he decided where to stop when Octavian married Clodius' daughter in 43.[50]

For Clodius – if we accept the late date of composition – must have been both the origin and the intended culmination of one of his main themes. Claudian violence and Claudian contempt for the gods could not but remind the reader of the master of the street-gangs of the 50s, who had begun his senatorial career with a scandalous case of sacrilege.[51] It may seem strange that such a rabid *popularis* should have given rise to a schematic picture of his family as arrogant patricians lording it over the *plebs*, but we must not forget that Clodius' enemies strongly denied that he was a real *popularis* at all.[52] Antias' popular Valerii were reconcilers of civil strife, not leaders of it:[53] men of passion and eloquence on their fellow-citizens' behalf, but always within the constitution. They

48. See Cloud 1977b (esp. 225) for a convincing explanation. Last datable fragment: 64P (Pliny *NH* XXXIV 14).

49. Cf. Wiseman 1970a, 207–13 on Clodius' son, a promising young man in 44 (Antony *ap.* Cic. *Att.* XIV 13a.2), and his nephews, of whom the elder became consul in 38 B.C. and triumphed in 32. Cf. Cloud 1977b, 226: 'the political situation between 44 and 41 was confused and potentially lethal to an unimportant person who might exhibit strong opinions or theatrical attitudes upon recent constitutional history'. Livy (pref. 5) knew of the pressures that affected the writer of recent history.

50. Suet. *Aug.* 62.1, Dio XLVI 56.3, Plut. *Ant.* 20.1. It is possible that Octavian's niece Marcella *maior* married Clodius' son about the same time: Wiseman 1970a, 215–7 (on Tac. *Ann.* IV 52, 66.1).

51. The Ciceronian evidence is endless; but on violence, cf. especially *dom.* 76 ('conscelerata illa vis'), *Vat.* 33 ('illa vis et furor'), and on Clodius as a *contemptor divum*, *dom.* 139, *har. resp.* 5, etc.

52. E.g. Cic. *Sest.* 104ff, *har. resp.* 42ff. Cf. Hillard 1976, 471–9 on Clodius' intermittent support from *optimates*.

53. Cf. Münzer 1891, 55 on their role in three successive secessions of the *plebs*.

were very different from Clodius, and the poor but honest Romans they were supposed to have championed were very different from the urban *plebs* of the 50s B.C.[54]

The hired claques and gangs of slaves which Clodius' supporters could be made out to be[55] have more in common with Appius Caecus' *forensis factio*, and the crowds of clients at the beck and call of the Claudii from Attus Clausus onwards, than with the freedom-loving citizens whom Antias' heroic Valerii defended from tyranny. For Cicero, Clodius himself was the tyrant,[56] and it is likely that Antias shared that view.[57]

Moreover, it applied to the whole family, not Clodius alone. Whatever the limitations imposed by their respective careers,[58] other things being equal his brothers Appius and Gaius – and his sisters too, for that matter – would stand by Clodius in a crisis.[59] In some political contexts, it made sense to speak of the *gens Claudia* as a unit.[60] It is not easy to get behind the impassioned rhetoric of Cicero's attacks and imagine how Clodius and the Claudii appeared to less committed Romans, but there are two passages – also by Cicero, but when he was being deliberately restrained – which can give us a more reliable insight.

The first is in the *pro Caelio*, where Clodius' sister is the main witness for the prosecution and Cicero wishes to suggest that her family, on her behalf, are out to ruin Caelius.[61] The prosecutors say they have witnesses who will testify against him:

54. Cf. Lintott 1968, 193f (cf. 179f, 196f) on the difference between urban and rural popular support. Clodius was never – as the Valerii supposedly were – a champion of agrarian legislation; however, M. Valerius Messalla Niger (*cos*. 61) was on the land commission in 59 (*ILS* 46).

55. E.g. Cic. *Sest*. 104–6; *dom*. 5–6, *har. resp*. 22, *Att*. IV 3.2, etc. On the 'slaves', see Treggiari 1969, 172–5 and 265f.

56. Cic. *dom*. 110, *Mil*. 80, 89, *Att*. VI 4.3; Dunkle 1967, 163.

57. Cf. p. 116 above for his approval of Scipio Nasica; and Wiseman 1979b, 49, for the possibility that Antias wrote up the execution of the would-be tyrant Manlius Capitolinus.

58. The extent of their political co-operation is well studied in detail by Hillard (1976, esp. chapters 3 and 6).

59. E.g. Cic. *Sest*. 77, *Att*. IV 2.3, 3.4, 11.2 (Appius in 57); Dio XXXIX 21.2 (Gaius in 56), *Att*. II 1.5, 12.2 (Clodia in 60 and 59). Also after Clodius' death: Asc. 34C (the young Appii in 52), Cic. *fam*. III 10.3 to Appius ('non tibi solum sed tuis omnibus . . .').

60. E.g. Cic. *Sest*. 81, *QF* II 12.2.

61. Cic. *Cael*. 20–22; for Clodia's motivation, see *Cael*. 1 (with the same distinction between *oppugnare* and *accusare*), 2, 19, 31f, 36, 55, 78. Cicero is deliberately tactful and names no names, in order not to affront the presiding *iudex quaestionis* (cf. *Cael*. 32); but as at *Cael*. 38 and 48–9, on Clodia, it is obvious whom he means.

> But you realize by now, gentlemen of the jury, the whole nature of this attack on my client, and when it is made it will be your duty to repulse it. For those who are attacking M. Caelius are not those who are prosecuting him. The shafts are hurled openly, but they are supplied in secret. I say this with no intention of bringing ill-will upon those to whom this should be even a matter of pride. *They* are performing their duty, defending their own, doing what gallant gentlemen normally do: when injured they resent it, when angered they strike out, when provoked they fight. But granted that such gentlemen have good cause to attack M. Caelius, it is *your* responsibility, as wise jurymen, not to consider it reason enough to satisfy other men's resentment instead of your own oath.
>
> You can see what a throng there is in the Forum, what sorts of people there are, with what a variety of interests. Out of all this crowd, how many do you think there are who, when they think something is required of them by men of power, influence and persuasion,[62] regularly offer their services of their own accord,[63] devote their energies to them, and promise them their testimony as witnesses? If it should happen that any of that sort push themselves forward into this trial, then by your wisdom, gentlemen of the jury, you must shut your ears to their avarice, and make it clear that you have given your attention equally to my client's innocence, your own sworn responsibility, and the position of all citizens against men whose power is dangerous.

That subtly-drawn picture of the *viri fortissimi* of the Claudian house tells us, I think, more about their real power and influence than pages of Cicero's usual ranting against Clodius as the *pestis rei publicae* – and the final phrase, on the *condicio omnium civium* when faced with *periculosae potentiae*, could have come from the speech of a fifth-century Valerius confronting an Appius Claudius.

The second passage is just a phrase, but a significant one. It comes in a letter to Q. Metellus Nepos, Clodius' cousin and Clodia's brother-in-law, who as consul in 57 supported Clodius by obstructing the attempts to get Cicero recalled from exile. Cicero, hearing that he has changed his mind, writes from Dyrrhachium to

62. '. . . potentibus, gratiosis, disertis'; cf. Vell. II 45.1 on Clodius as *disertus*, Cic. *Cael.* 19, 78 on Clodia's *gratia*.

63. Cf. Cic. *fam.* III 9.2 (to Ap. Claudius in 50 B.C.): 'quod te adeunt fere omnes, si quid velis'.

beg him not to be influenced by his Claudian relatives: 'please don't attack me just to satisfy the arrogance and cruelty of your kin'.[64] Since Cicero could not afford to risk offending Nepos by overstating the case, we may infer that Clodius and his family really did display in the 50s B.C. the characteristics which the hostile version attributed to the patrician Claudii of the early Republic.

The cruelty Cicero refers to was the particular case of his own exile, and the vindictive behaviour of Clodius and his relatives at the time;[65] the arrogance, however, was evidently a more general family characteristic. Clodius' elder brother Appius was still a byword for shameless effrontery long after his death,[66] and the activities of all the Claudii of that generation show with appalling clarity how casually and openly they assumed they could have their own way, regardless of legality or the opinion of their fellow-citizens.

Clodius' attempt in 61 to frustrate the voting on the bill to set up his trial was made with no attempt at concealment; he was equally open about his 'adoption' by the plebeian Fonteius in 59, not pretending that it was anything but a political gambit, or that he himself was anything but a patrician Claudius still; his squads of strong-arm men were organized in 58 at the *tribunal Aurelium* in the Forum, just about the most public place in the entire city; and in 57 the attacks on Cicero and his property were marked by the same contemptuous defiance, as Clodius ordered his *operae* to burn and pillage in broad daylight, 'with the whole of Rome looking on'.[67] Gaius Claudius was no less brazen in his attempt to bribe the jury at his extortion trial in 51, and his son Appius *minor* was so candid about the arrangements he and his father had made that he ended up facing two prosecutions himself.[68] On the female side, Clodia evidently employed two of her many hangers-on to punish a young

64. Cic. *fam.* V 4.2 ('propter adrogantem crudelitatem tuorum'), cf. Shackleton Bailey 1977, I 292.

65. Cic. *dom.* 58–60, 62 etc. cf. *Cael.* 50 (Clodia); Lintott 1968, 46ff for *crudelitas* in general.

66. Cic. *fam.* V 10.2 (Vatinius to Cicero, 44 B.C.): 'si me hercules Appi os haberem . . . tamen hoc sustinere non possem'. As Shackleton Bailey rightly says (1977, II 428), 'perhaps Appius' own personality helped to establish the tradition' (*sc.* of Claudian arrogance).

67. Cic. *Att.* I 14.5; *dom.* 35, 37; *red. Quir.* 13, *dom.* 54; *Att.* IV 3.2–3. Cf. also the Tigranes episode in 58 (Asc. 47C, Cic. *dom.* 66, Dio XXXVIII 30.1f, Plut. *Pomp.* 48.10), the revenge against Ptolemy of Cyprus for an insult ten years earlier (Dio XXXVIII 30.5), and the senatorial occasions when Clodius was in a minority of one (Cic. *red. Sen.* 26, Dio XXXIX 29).

68. Caelius *ap.* Cic. *fam.* VIII 8.2–3.

man who had offended her, by inflicting a homosexual assault on him.[69] As for Appius, his correspondence with Cicero in 51 and 50 reveals the same pattern of behaviour in detail: blatant disrespect, obsessive touchiness about supposed slights against himself, irritation at the most tactful letters of complaint, and a casual – and justified – assumption that when he wanted Cicero's help he could count on it automatically.[70]

The combination of *potentia*,[71] wealth,[72] and pride of birth[73] resulted in a recognizable common characteristic among the Claudii of Cicero's generation. Shamelessness, insolence, and a headstrong and precipitate mentality were some of the phrases contemporaries used to describe it.[74] We have no reason to suppose it was an inherited characteristic, but it is easy to see how an author writing in the late 50s or early 40s could plausibly make it one.[75]

—

If the *superbia Claudiana* of the hostile version can be accounted for by the behaviour of the patrician Claudii of the 50s B.C., and the *vis Claudiana* by the activities of Clodius in particular, perhaps some of the other aspects of the legend may be attributed to the same origin.

The consul who canvasses for his brother's election (p. 100 above) might be Appius in 54, when Gaius was hoping to stand;[76] the theatre-going sister of the sacrilegious Publius (p. 90 above) might

69. Cic. *Cael.* 71; *Cael.* 67 on Clodia *imperatrix* (cf. *dom.* 24, 'imperium Clodianum'), *Att.* II 23.3 for her political threats against Cicero, '*openly* flaunted'.
70. See esp. Cic. *Att.* V 16.4, 17.6 (*iniuria*), *fam.* III 6.3–4, 7.5. Cicero on Appius: 'natura es *φιλαίτιος*' (*fam.* III 7.6), 'genus sermonis minus liberale' (8.5), 'suspicio quaedam et dubitatio tua' (10.6), '*ὑπομεμψιμοίρους* litteras' (*Att.* VI 1.2). Appius on Cicero: 'stomachosiores litterae' (*fam.* III 11.5).
71. Clodius as *potentissimus homo*: Schol. Bob. 85St, cf. Cic. *dom.* 49 etc. Clodia as *mulier potens*: Cic. *Cael.* 62, 63. Appius' sources of political influence (listed at Cic. *fam.* II 13.2, III 10.9) are comparable with those cited in *Rhet. Her.* I 5.8 as evidence of *potentia.*
72. Appius' *opes*: Cic. *fam.* II 13.2, III 10.9. His *avaritia*: *fam.* VIII 12.1. Clodia's *opes*: *Cael.* 36, 38, 57, 67. Clodius: Plut. *Caes.* 9.2.
73. Appius: Cic. *fam.* III 7.5. Clodius: Cic. *har. resp.* 26 ('generis sui mentio'), cf. *dom.* 116.
74. Cic. *dom.* 4, 116, *har. resp.* 1 (Clodius' *impudentia*), *fam.* VIII 12.3 (Caelius on Appius and his agent as *insolentissimi homines*), *Cael.* 35 (Clodia's *mens effrenata atque praeceps*); cf. *Cael.* 38, 49, 53, 55 on Clodia as *procax*, *proterva*, *immoderata*, *temeraria*, Sall. *Hist.* V 12M on Clodius, 'ex insolentia avidus male faciendi'. Hillard (1976, 374–93) gives a good reconstruction of the characters of the Claudii.
75. Plutarch's description of Clodius at *Caes.* 9.2 reads very much like Dionysius on the early Claudii (esp. *αὐθάδης*).
76. Cic. *Scaur.* 33–5.

be Clodia, whose interest in the stage is hinted at by Cicero;[77] the brutal general with the rebellious army (p. 78 above) might be Appius in 51, whose forces mutinied as he was about to leave his province.[78] Similarly, the triumphal procession of Ap. Claudius the consul of 143, supposedly without authorization and in defiance of the tribunes' opposition (p. 102 above), could have been suggested by that of C. Pomptinus in 54, for which the enabling legislation was passed at an assembly convened before dawn by a friendly praetor; some of the tribunes opposed it as illegal, and there was bloodshed on the day of the procession itself, which could evidently only be held by force.[79] Notoriously, it was Appius as consul who made it possible.[80]

Claudian clients are one of the most conspicuous themes of the hostile version, and here too the men of the 50s B.C. may have suggested it. The Claudii had long had extensive *clientelae* abroad, especially in the Greek East,[81] but it was their urban clients, particularly freedmen,[82] who were most conspicuous. 'No other family appears in the annalistic tradition with so many homonymous hangers-on, presumably thought of as their freedmen':[83] perhaps the prototypes of M. Claudius the Decemvir's client, and Claudius Glicia the client of P. Claudius Pulcher, are to be sought in men like Damio, the freedman of Clodius who besieged Pompey's house in 58, or the P. Clodius who assisted the prosecution of Caelius.[84] Damio was Clodius' tribunician *apparitor*, and his behaviour is very reminiscent of that attributed to the lictors of the fifth-century Claudian consuls; the praetor who tried to protect Pompey's house

77. Cic. *Cael.* 64 ('plurimarum fabularum poetria'), *Sest.* 116 (*embolia*). Cf. Macr. *Sat.* II 6.6: Clodius wanted Laberius to write a mime for him.
78. Cic. *Att.* V 14.1, *fam.* XV 4.2.
79. Dio XXXIX 65.2, Cic. *Att.* IV 18.4, *QF* III 4.6. Cf. Schol. Bob. 149St on the opposition of Vatinius (and Caesar's other friends) to the *supplicatio* which would naturally lead to the triumph (cf. Cic. *fam.* II 15.1 'ea quae sequuntur', V 10.3, etc); the counting of enemy dead was evidently one of the criteria (cf. *fam.* VIII 11.2, if *hostibus* is read – but see Shackleton Bailey 1977, I 420), which makes another point of reference with the story of the *cos.* 143 (p. 101f above).
80. Cic. *Att.* IV 18.4, *QF* III 4.6; *fam.* III 10.3 for Pomptinus' sense of obligation in 50 ('qui a te tractatus est praestanti ac singulari fide, cuius tui benefici sum ego testis').
81. See Rawson 1973, *passim*; specific references to *inherited* influence at Cic. *fam.* XIII 64.2, *IG* III 439, *Inschr. von Pergamum* II 409, Suet. *Tib.* 6.2.
82. See Treggiari 1969, 172–5 on Clodius' followers. He tried to have all the freed Cypriot slaves called Clodii and thus attached explicitly to his own patronage (Dio XXXIX 23.1).
83. Rawson 1973, 220.
84. Asc. 46–7C, Cic. *Cael.* 27.

appealed to the tribunes, and the tribune who responded was physically attacked.[85]

Two of the most conspicuous clients in the hostile tradition, Cn. Flavius (p. 88 above) and M. Claudius Glicia, were supposedly *scribae* of their Claudian patrons. In the 50s, not only did Clodius send a client of his own to Cyprus as Cato's *scriba*,[86] but his closest confidant and most trusted lieutenant was the *scriba* Sex. Cloelius, whom he employed to draft his laws and administer the corn-dole, as well as to burn down public buildings.[87] In particular, there are tantalizing parallels between Sex. Cloelius on the one hand and Claudius Glicia on the other, both agents of sacrilegious Publii Pulchri: on 1 January 58 B.C., Cloelius anticipated his patron's restoration of the guilds by holding the banned *ludi Compitalicii*; in his capacity as *magister* of the guild and president of the games, he wore – to Cicero's eloquent disgust – the purple-bordered *toga praetexta*.[88] Claudius Glicia, it will be remembered, turned up at the games in his *toga praetexta* even though he had been compelled to abdicate from his dictatorship.[89] (His patron's sister was at the games too: Sex. Cloelius was widely believed to be on intimate terms with Clodia.[90]) It seems, moreover, that the right to wear the *toga praetexta* was among the preoccupations of Valerius Antias.[91]

It may be significant in this context that Antias had a detectable antipathy to Etruria in his history of early Rome, and associated the Etruscans with rebellious slaves.[92] Clodius had extensive properties in Etruria – according to Cicero, his estates stretched from the

85. His report is quoted by Asc. 47C: '. . . ab hoc apparitore P. Clodi vulneratus sum, et hominibus armatis praesidiis dispositis a re publica remotus Cn. Pompeius obsessusque est'. The Claudian client Servius Pola, twice employed to attack Caelius (Cie. *QF* II 12.2, *fam.* VIII 12.2–3) is described as 'homo taeter ac *ferus*': cf. p. 78 n.14 above on Appius the *cos.* 471.

86. Plut. *Cato min.* 34.3.

87. Asc. 33C, Cic. *dom.* 25, 47, 83, 129, *har. resp.* 11, *Sest.* 133; Shackleton Bailey 1960, 41f for the name. *Aedes nympharum* (etc) burnt: Cic. *Cael.* 78, *Mil.* 73; Cloelius also burnt down the *Curia* after Clodius' death (Asc. 7, 33C).

88. Cic. *Pis.* 8: 'tu [Piso] . . . Sex. Cloelium, qui numquam antea praetextatus fuisset, ludos facere et praetextatum volitare passus es'; Asc. 7C (cf. Festus 272L, Livy XXXIX 7.2, *CIL* IX 4208) on *magistri praetextati*. See Lintott 1968, 77–83 and Treggiari 1969, 168–77 on the *collegia* and *Compitalicia*; Warde Fowler 1920, 42f and 60f on the *toga praetexta* worn by the sacrificant, and on the worship of the *Lares* (including the *Lares Compitales*) by slaves in particular.

89. Livy *epit.* 19, p. 90 above.

90. Cic. *dom.* 25, 47, 83, *Cael.* 78.

91. See Livy XXXIV 7.2 (from L. Valerius' speech in the *lex Oppia* debate), and Festus 272L (a Valerius invoked at the end of the item).

92. See Musti 1970, 111 and 115 (on Dion. Hal. V 26.3, 51.3 etc); *ibid.* 80, 94f, 108f, 124 etc on Antias and Etruria in general.

Janiculum to the Alps! – and it is a constant charge in the speeches of 53 and 52 B.C. that he kept bands of armed slaves on them to terrorize his neighbours and take over their land.[93]

Another of Antias' interests may help to illuminate one more recurring theme. We know that he made much of Numa,[94] and reported at length the discovery and destruction of 'Numa's books' in 181 B.C. It is not quite clear from our sources whether or not he regarded the books as Pythagorean (as the earlier annalists had), nor whether he approved or disapproved of the decision to burn them;[95] what *is* clear is that in the late Republic Pythagoreanism had a reputation which Antias would probably not have wished to attach to the Sabine king. Cicero attacked Vatinius for it in 56:[96]

> You call yourself a Pythagorean, hiding your hideous and barbaric practices behind the name of a philosopher: what depravity of mind, what madness obsessed you so great that even though you have taken up foul and unheard-of rites, summoning the souls of the dead, honouring the *di manes* with the entrails of boys, yet you despised the auspices by which this city was founded?

According to Alexander 'Polyhistor', the most learned Greek scholar of the time, Pythagoras had been a pupil of 'Zaratos the Assyrian' (i.e. Zoroaster), and for the men of the late Republic his name was now inextricably linked with Chaldaean astrology and the Eastern wisdom of the Magi.[97]

93. Cic. *de aere alieno Milonis* quoted in Schol. Bob. 172St ('eosdem ad caedem civium de Apennino deduxisti'); *Mil.* 26 ('servi agrestes ac barbari'), 50, 55, 74, 87, 98. Even in 43, the Clodian estates made it impossible for Cicero to use the Via Aurelia (Cic. *Phil.* XII 23). Cf. Rawson 1977, 340–3 on Claudian connections with Etruria (some rather speculative).

94. Fr. 6P; Ogilvie 1965, 89, cf. Musti 1970, 74–7 (and all his ch. iv on the 'tendenza filosabina').

95. Pythagorean: Cassius Hemina (fr. 37P) and Piso (fr. 11P) *ap.* Pliny *NH* XIII 84–7; Antias *ap.* Plut. *Numa* 22.6f and Pliny *NH* XIII 87 (frr. 7–8P) called them 'Greek philosophy' only. Livy XL 29.8 ('adicit Antias Valerius Pythagoricos fuisse') is probably the result of a confusion with Piso: see Peter 1914, cxci, who points out that Livy would no longer have Antias' second volume or Piso's first available for consultation, and was presumably quoting from memory. The praetor responsible for the burning of the books (against the tribunes' opposition, Livy XL 29.12) was one of the Petillii who were given a bad press by Antias in his narrative of the trials of the Scipios (Livy XXXVIII 50.5, 56.2 etc).

96. Cic. *Vat.* 14, with Schol. Bob. 146St on the 'factio minus probabilis' to which Vatinius belonged.

97. Alex. Polyhistor (on whom see p. 160 below) *FGrH* 273F94; Diog. Laert. VIII

The Chaldaeans had been expelled from Rome on one occasion in the second century,[98] and a hundred years later those who professed their mysteries were still objects of suspicion. Cicero's friend P. Nigidius Figulus, the leading 'Pythagorean' of the time, may even have been prosecuted for his astrological forecasts, and the description of his group of friends as 'Nigidius' sacrilegious brotherhood' confirms the sense of opposition between this sort of communication with the gods and the traditional Roman *auspicia* which Cicero exploited in his attack on Vatinius.[99]

Nigidius was particularly interested in divination – by the stars, by dreams, by weather signs, by sacrificial entrails, and so on.[100] His system was based on the Pythagorean idea of the immortality of the soul: all the air is full of souls, or *daimones*, and it is they who send prophetic dreams, omens and other signs. The Chaldaeans knew how to contact the *daimones* directly, through their reflections in water (hydromancy), and even to bring souls from the underworld itself, by the use of blood (necromancy).[101] Varro attributed the former technique (rationalized, he thought, as the nymph Egeria) to Numa himself, and it may have been for this reason that Iulius Hyginus made the eponymous ancestor of the Sabines a Persian before he was a Spartan – for how else could Numa have known of it, before Pythagoras' time?[102] Varro was certainly not an enemy of the traditional Roman religion: his view was evidently that the old Roman practices were proved to be true now that the 'lost lore' was revealed on which he believed they were

---

1.3 on Pythagoras as the pupil of Chaldaeans and Magi; Varro *ap*. Aug. *CD* VII 35 (Pythagoras anticipated by Numa in the use of Persian divination), cf. Cic. *div*. I 2, 36, 93, Plut. *Mar*. 42.8, Val. Max. VIII 7.2 etc on the Chaldaei, Momigliano 1975, ch. 6 (esp. pp. 141–9) on Zoroaster and the Hellenistic Greeks.

98. Val. Max. I 3.3, Livy *epit. Oxy*. 54.

99. Cic. *Timaeus* 1 ('acer investigator et diligens earum rerum quae a natura involutae videntur'); Dio XLV 1.4 (prosecution?); ps.Cic. *in Sall*. 14 ('sodalicium sacrilegii Nigidiani'); Apul. *apol*. 42, Jer. *chron*. on 45 B.C.

100. His works included *de augurio privato* (Gell. *NA* VII 6.10), *de extis* (*ibid*. XVI 6.12), *de somniis* (Lyd. *de ostentis* 45 – including Etruscan thunder-lore), *de vento* (Suet. fr. 152R, on weather-forecasting), as well as the astrological *Sphaera Graecanica* (Pliny *NH* VI 218 etc).

101. Diog. Laert. VIII 1.32 (from Alexander Polyhistor); Strabo XVI 2.39 (C 762), etc.

102. Varro *ap*. Aug. *CD* VII 35, cf. Serv. *Georg*. I 19 for Varro's use of Nigidius; he also used his contemporary Castor Rhodius (Aug. *CD* XXI 8), who believed in 'anticipated' Pythagoreanism in early Rome. Hyginus *ap*. Serv. *Aen*. VIII 638 ('a Sabo qui de Perside Lacedaemonios transiens ad Italiam venit'); *ibid*. for the traditional version, in Cato and Gellius, that Sabus was a Spartan and the Sabines therefore appropriately frugal and strict (Dion. Hal. II 49.3).

based. But it was a learned specialist's concept, which could not be expected to appeal to the ordinary piety of the man in the street.[103]

Valerius Antias was not an intellectual. He rationalized Numa's use of water with a pretty story that Varro would certainly class as poets' theology, not philosophers'.[104] He calls the volumes from the tomb merely 'pontifical books', with no suggestion that they contained the secret reasons for the pontiffs' rites.[105] His family *sacra* were concerned with the gods of the underworld, but not in any way remotely like the necromantic practices of the Chaldaeans.[106]

Appius Claudius, on the other hand, *was* an intellectual.[107] Like Varro, he was interested in the origins of Roman institutions;[108] like Nigidius Figulus, he wrote a *liber auguralis* which treated Roman augury as one means of divination among many.[109] He had long had contacts with the half-hellenized kingdoms of the upper Euphrates, where Chaldaean divination flourished,[110] and he was evidently a friend of Antiochus the king of Commagene, whose grandiose hilltop shrine at Nemrud Dağ includes a monument bearing the regal horoscope.[111]

103. As Varro explicitly said, in his distinction between the gods of the philosopher and those of the people (Aug. *CD* IV 27). Cf. Apul. *apol.* 27 for popular suspicion of philosophers as impious *magi*.

104. Fr. 6P (Arnob. *adv. nat.* V 1), cf. Ovid *fasti* III 285ff, Plut. *Numa* 15.3–12 (μυθολογοῦσι γὰρ . . .).

105. Varro *ap.* Aug. *CD* VII 34: 'ubi sacrorum institutorum scriptae erant causae . . . cur quidque in sacris fuerit institutum'.

106. Val. Max. II 4.5 for the Valerii and the cult of Dis and Proserpina at 'Tarentum' (Münzer 1891, 5f). The other Tarentum was a Spartan colony, at which the 'Spartan Sabines' legend originated in the fourth century B.C. (Strabo V 4.12, C 250, cf. Cornell 1975, 3 n.4): Antias presumably accepted the Spartan origin of the Sabines, and would surely have been horrified to think that the Valerii and their fellow-countrymen were descended from a Persian.

107. Cic. *fam.* II 13.2, III 10.9 on his *ingenium* and the *studia* he shared with Cicero.

108. Cic. *Brut.* 267: 'et satis studiosus et valde cum doctus tum etiam exercitatus orator et cum auguralis tum omnis publici iuris *antiquitatisque* nostrae bene peritus'.

109. Cic. *fam.* III 4.1, 9.3, 11.4 (dedicated to Cicero, 51); cf. Serv. *Aen.* X 175 (Nigidius). Cf. Rawson 1977, 356f, who makes the attractive suggestion that Appius was influenced by Athenodorus of Tarsus (cf. Cic. *fam.* III 7.5, with Diog. Laert. VII 149 on divination).

110. See especially Plut. *Luc.* 21 (written up in Archias' Lucullus poem? Hillard 1976, 174–208); Rawson 1973, 231, cf. 235–7 on Clodius. Armenian, Commagenian and Chaldaean *haruspices*: Juv. *Sat.* VI 548–65.

111. Dörrie 1964, 201–7; Cic. *QF* II 11.3, Appius as consul in 54 canvassing support to get the Senate to honour Antiochus by the grant of the *toga praetexta* (cf. p. 127 above).

Appius believed in the efficacy of augury,[112] but not in a way that would reassure the conventionally pious Roman. He believed equally in the Pythagorean consultation of souls (*psychomanteia*), and the summoning from the underworld (*nekyomanteia*) that appeared so shocking in the 'Pythagorean' Vatinius.[113] It is likely enough that he set the Roman practices of divination against this background in his book on augury, justifying them in a way that Varro (and Cicero) might approve,[114] but the ordinary Roman would find profoundly distasteful.

With this in mind, we may look again at the 'Claudian sacrilege' theme of the hostile version. No doubt the Good Goddess scandal, and Clodius' supposed 'destruction of the *auspicia*' in his tribunate,[115] put the idea into the author's mind. But the particular concentration on the sacred chickens may be because of Appius. Two out of the three surviving fragments of Appius' book on augury are concerned with divination from chickens, and the explanation of the technical terms *tripudium* and *sollistimum*.[116] That could be coincidence, but it is noticeable that nothing of the sort appears in the surviving quotations from Appius' augural colleague and fellow-patrician M. Valerius Messalla Rufus.[117]

It is, I think, in the relations between Messalla Rufus and his cousin on one side, and Appius Claudius and his brothers on the other, that we must look for the reason why Valerius Antias included in his *History of Rome* such a venomous and sustained character-assassination of the Claudian house. Their rivalry is overshadowed by the greater political events of the 50s B.C., but there are sufficient indications in Cicero's correspondence to reveal the main outlines of it.

112. Cic. *div.* I 29f, 105, II 75.
113. Cic. *div.* I 132 (*psychomantia*), *TD* I 37 (νεκυομαντεῖα).
114. Did the supposedly Pythagorean nature of Ap. Claudius Caecus' gnomic *sententiae* originate in Appius' book? Cic. *TD* IV 4 (45 B.C.): 'mihi quidem etiam Appi Caeci carmen . . . Pythagoreum videtur'.
115. Cic. *red. Sen.* 11, *har. resp.* 58, *Sest.* 33, 56.
116. Festus 382, 386L (Funaioli 1907, 426–7); cf. Livy X 40.5, Cic. *div.* I 128, II 72, 77. The third (Festus 241L) is evidently an example of the Phrygian, Pisidian and Cilician art of bird-divination (Cic. *div.* I 2, 25, 92, 94).

Tripudium is also used of the Salian dance (Livy I 20.4); C. Claudius *pr.* 56 was a Salius (Cic. *Scaur.* 34), and it was said of Ap. Claudius *cos.* 143 that he 'pro gloria obtinuerit quod inter collegas [*sc.* Salios] optime saltitabat' (Macr. *Sat.* III 14.14 – from the hostile version?).
117. Funaioli 1907, 427–9 for the fragments of Messalla's *de auspiciis*. He also wrote a book on Roman families (Peter 1906, 65).

The ups and downs of their respective fortunes may be plotted in tabular form:[118]

	M. Valerius M.f.M'.n. Messalla 'Niger', M. Valerius (M.f.M.n.) Messalla 'Rufus'.	Ap. Claudius Pulcher, C. Claudius Pulcher, P. Clodius Pulcher.
62	Rufus praetor(?)	
61	Niger CONSUL	Publius accused of sacrilege: acquitted
60		
59		
58		Publius tribune
57		Appius praetor
56		Gaius praetor, Publius curule aedile
55	Niger CENSOR	
54	Rufus accused of bribery: trial postponed	Appius CONSUL
53	Rufus CONSUL	
52		Publius murdered
51	Rufus accused of bribery: acquitted	Gaius accused of extortion: condemned
	Rufus accused *de sodaliciis*: condemned	Gaius' son Appius *minor* accused of (a) violence, (b) extortion: acquitted?
50		Appius accused of bribery: acquitted
		Appius accused of treason: acquitted
		Appius CENSOR

In his consulship at the time of Clodius' trial, Messalla Niger took a strong moral line, much approved by Cicero, and was resolutely hostile to the accused;[119] he was a *pontifex*, and may

118. Rufus' praetorship inferred from Cic. *Sull.* 42 (he was standing for election in 63); his filiation from *ILLRP* 496, where the grandfather's initial is evidently needed to distinguish the cousins (Münzer 1955, 125).

119. Cic. *Att.* I 13.3 ('Messalla vehementer adhuc agit ⟨et⟩ severe'), 14.5 (Clodius' attacks on him). Cicero's approval: I 13.2, 14.6.

have remembered Clodius' attacks on the priesthoods in an earlier *cause célèbre*.[120] Three years later, with Clodius tribune and Cicero in exile, he was one of the very few who could be expected to support Quintus Cicero against Clodius' threats.[121] A laconic reference in 55 may suggest that Niger and his fellow-censor were being attacked by Appius and Clodius in the noisy atmosphere of the gladiatorial games.[122] One can imagine the sort of thing that was shouted: Niger had himself been disgraced by the censors in 70 B.C., and had the misfortune to bear a strong facial resemblance to a well-known mime actor.[123]

As for Messalla Rufus, Appius (though five years younger) had caught him up in the competition for high office. He beat him to the consulship in 54,[124] and was thus well placed to frustrate Rufus' attempt for the following year.[125] Appius and his consular colleague L. Ahenobarbus made a secret bargain, written and witnessed, with two of Messalla's competitors (C. Memmius and Cn. Domitius Calvinus), that in return for their help in getting them elected, Memmius and Calvinus would, on their election, provide three augurs to say that they had been present at the passing of an imaginary *lex curiata* giving Appius and Ahenobarbus the *imperium* necessary to go to their provinces; or, failing that, they would pay them four million sesterces.[126] Eventually Memmius, one of the partners in the deal, was persuaded to confess, much to the horror of Ahenobarbus, who was prostrated by the disgrace. Not so Appius, who had no reputation to lose.[127] But the disclosure must inevitably have made Messalla Rufus his bitter enemy.

When the elections were postponed yet again, and the tactical advantages for Messalla of an *interregnum* or even a dictatorship were being canvassed, Appius was scheming against it.[128] Messalla was charged with bribery; the prosecutor was Q. Pompeius Rufus,

120. Plut. *Cato min.* 19.3, cf. Macr. *Sat.* III 13.11.
121. Cic. *QF* I 3.9: 'Messallam tui studiosum esse arbitror'.
122. Cic. *Att.* IV 11.2 (from his villa): 'qua re ut homini curioso perscribe ad me quid primus dies, quid secundus, quid censores, quid Appius, quid illa populi Appuleia'. The other censor was P. Servilius Isauricus, whose son, praetor the following year, opposed Appius consistently: *Att.* IV 15.9 (on Messius), *QF* III 4.6 (on Pomptinus).
123. Val. Max. II 9.9, IX 14.5, Pliny *NH* VII 55.
124. Cic. *Att.* IV 7.1 for Rufus' intended candidature.
125. For which he was a strong candidate (Cic. *Att.* IV 16.6).
126. Cic. *Att.* IV 15.7, 17.2–3, *QF* II 15.4, 16.2, III 1.16 (specifying Messalla's exclusion), 2.3, 6.3.
127. Cic. *Att.* IV 17.2: 'hic Appius erat idem: nihil sane iacturae'.
128. Cic. *QF* III 7.3 (December 54): 'de dictatore tamen actum adhuc nihil est; Pompeius abest, Appius miscet'.

a close friend of Clodius,[129] and the defence counsel were to be two of Clodius' long-standing enemies, Cicero and Hortensius.[130] That prosecution came to nothing, and Messalla, meanwhile was eventually elected half-way through what should have been his year of office. But the bribery charge stuck (he had been, as Cicero put it at the time, 'generous to the populace'),[131] and Messalla was eventually brought to trial in 51. Hortensius got him off, to the incredulous disgust of all, but a second indictment followed under the *lex Licinia de sodaliciis*; he was condemned and went into exile.[132] Cicero was in Cilicia at the time, so we have no details of Messalla's fall; but considering his hostility to him in 54, it would be very surprising indeed if Appius, just back from Cilicia himself, did not join in the attack.

Clodius was dead, murdered by Milo's gladiators on the Appian Way. C. Claudius was in exile, having been found guilty of extortion in his praetorian province. While Appius flourished, however, Messalla Rufus' family must have felt themselves still unavenged. His record in Cilicia had laid him open to a charge of extortion,[133] but his enemies chose instead to prosecute him for bribery and treason.[134] Thanks to a concerted effort by his supporters (including Pompey), Appius' more scandalous misdeeds were hushed up,[135] and so effective an image of moral rectitude did he present that he was not only acquitted at both trials but immediately elected to the censorship!

His conduct in that office was remarkable. Seeing himself as scouring the state clean of unwholesome elements,[136] he expelled a large number of senators (including, in particular, those whose fathers had been freedmen),[137] denounced extravagant luxury, in the form of extensive estates and collections of sculpture and

129. Cic. *Att.* IV 17.5, cf. Asc. 50–51C (his sister was the woman Clodius had broken in on the Bona Dea to visit); cf. Cic. *fam.* VIII 1.4 (Caelius) – it was rumoured in 51 that he had assassinated Cicero.
130. Cic. *Att.* IV 17.5, *QF* III 7.3, cf. *Att.* I 16.2 on Hortensius' hatred of Clodius. Hortensius was Messalla's maternal uncle (Val. Max. V 9.2, cf. Plut. *Sulla* 35.6).
131. Cic. *Att.* IV 17.3: 'Messalla noster . . . liberalis in populo valde fuit. Nihil gratius'.
132. Cic. *fam.* VIII 2.2, 4.1 (Caelius), *Att.* V 12.2, *Brut.* 328.
133. Cic. *Att.* V 15.2, 16.2, 17.6, 20.1, 21.7 and 10, VI 1.2 and 6, 2.8, 3.5.
134. To Cicero's surprise (*fam.* III 11.2); but he had certainly infringed the *lex Cornelia de maiestate* (cf. *fam.* III 6.6, 10.6). Cic. *fam.* VIII 6.1–3 (Caelius), III 10.1–5, 11.1–2, 12.1 on the trials.
135. Cic. *fam.* VIII 6.3 (Caelius): 'consaepta omnia foeda et inhonesta sunt'.
136. Cic. *fam.* VIII 14.4 (Caelius); 'persuasum est ei censuram lomentum aut nitrum esse. Errare mihi videtur; nam sordis eluere vult, venas sibi omnis et viscera aperit'.
137. Dio XL 63.3–4, Hor. *Sat.* I 6.21.

pictures,[138] and exposed, with the greatest possible publicity, the sexual morals of young men like Curio and Caelius Rufus.[139] Appius himself was guilty of most of the vices he attacked;[140] the impudence of his hypocrisy – or, perhaps, the blind arrogance of his conviction that he was in the right – must have exacerbated the resentment of his enemies to a fury of indignation.

It can safely be assumed, from the nature of his work, that Valerius Antias was a client of the patrician Valerii. The fact that he bore their gentile name suggests, though one cannot be sure, that he was descended from a freedman of the family. It is tempting to speculate that he was one of the humbly-born senators Appius expelled, his interest in the *toga praetexta* reflecting the curule office he might otherwise have hoped to gain.[141] The evidence does not allow us to know; but if his work is rightly dated to the early 40s rather than the 70s B.C., then the fall of Messalla Rufus and the success of Appius Claudius provide an intelligible motive for one of its most conspicuous themes.

—

Antias had evidently reached the late fourth century by 46 B.C., and the middle of the third by 44.[142] The author of the rival version, who set himself to answer his slanders by the same technique, may have already begun before Antias had finished, though the apparent allusion to the Claudii Nerones may perhaps date him after 38.[143] On the other hand, his history was available in the 20s, to be used by Livy in book II and Dionysius in book V. Since he was a historian whose work had literary pretensions, with set speeches and dramatic scenes, we can hardly identify him with Atticus, Varro, Nepos or Iulius Hyginus.[144]

There is only one possible candidate: Q. Aelius Tubero.[145] He

138. Cic. *fam.* VIII 14.4 (Caelius), *Att.* VI 9.5.

139. Dio XL 63.5–64.1 (Curio), Cic. *fam.* VIII 12.1–3, 14.4 (Caelius); for their respective reputations, cf. Cic. *Att.* I 14.5 (*filiola Curionis*), *Rhet. Lat. Min.* 124H (*pulchellus Iason*).

140. Cic. *fam.* VIII 12.3, 14.4 (Caelius); confirmed, in the case of *signa et tabulae*, by Cic. *dom.* 111–2.

141. Pp. 127, 134 above; cf. Cic. *Verr.* V 36, *Cluent.* 154 etc. for entitlement to the *praetexta*.

142. Cic. *Brut.* 55, *ND* II 7.

143. See p. 112 above on Plut. *Popl.* 21.4. Cf. Cloud 1977b, 227, acutely citing Livy *pref.* 2 ('novi *semper* scriptores') as evidence for the late publication date of Antias and Tubero; I think he is wrong, however, to rule out the *Brutus* as a *terminus ante quem* for Antias' early-republican books.

144. Their annals were not on a big enough scale: see Peter 1906, 6–8 (Atticus), 24 (Varro), 25f (Nepos, cf. pp. 157ff below), 72f (Hyginus).

145. On whom see Ogilvie 1965, 16f. *Pace* Badian (1966, 22 and 36 n.120), Livy IV

was the father of Q. Aelius Tubero, consul in 11 B.C., and of Sex. Aelius Catus (consul A.D. 4), whose daughter was called Aelia Paetina. The *cognomina* show that the Tuberones regarded themselves as related to Sex. Aelius Paetus Catus and his brother P. (consuls in 201 and 198 B.C.), who are mentioned in the *Digest* as two early jurists writing on the Twelve Tables, *interpretatio* and *legis actio*.[146] Two generations after them comes Q. Aelius Tubero the Stoic philosopher, nephew of Scipio Aemilianus,[147] and two generations later again, the annalist L. Aelius Tubero who served as legate under Q. Cicero in 61.[148] Our Q. Tubero was presumably his son.

Not surprisingly, with a family history like that, he was noted for his learning in many fields. He started off as an orator, but after failing in his prosecution of Q. Ligarius before Caesar in 46, turned in disgust to the law. He studied under A. Ofilius, married a daughter of Ofilius' teacher Ser. Sulpicius Rufus (*cos.* 51), and became an expert in both public and private law, his works being noted for their old-fashioned style.[149] Cicero praised him in a lost work quoted by Gellius:[150] 'Q. Aelius Tubero has a legal knowledge as great as that of his ancestors, and *doctrina* far above them'. Gellius was surprised at this judgment, not believing that the jurist's learning was greater than that of his great-grandfather the Stoic philosopher, but Cicero was surely right. The breadth of Tubero's erudition was remarkable – an orator, a jurist like his distant forebears, something of a natural scientist,[151] and a historian who tried to write like Thucydides.[152] His learning explains why his friend Dionysius refers just to 'Aelius Tubero' as a source,[153] without distinguishing him from his father: in the schol-

---

23.1 rules out Cicero's friend L. Tubero as Livy's source; Ogilvie (1965, 571) rightly defends the MSS reading Q. Tubero (*pace* Werner 1968, 509–11). It is true that L. Tubero wrote *annales* (Cic. *QF* I 1.10, cf. *Lig.* 10 'homo cum ingenio tum etiam doctrina excellens'), but since Quintus was an historian too (Suet. *DJ* 83.1, Dion. Hal. *Thuc.* 25) there is no need for emendation.

146. Pomp. *Dig.* I 2.2.38.

147. See Cic. *Off.* III 63, *Brut.* 117, Tac. *Ann.* XVI 22, etc.

148. Cic. *QF* I 1.10; n.145 above.

149. Pomp. *Dig.* I 2.2.46; cited on senatorial procedure by Gell. *NA* I 22.7.

150. Cic. *de iure civili in artem redigundo* quoted by Gell. *NA* I 22.7.

151. Cf. Pliny *NH* XVIII 235, quoting him on astronomy.

152. Dion. Hal. *Thuc.* 25 (cf. *ibid.* 1: Dionysius dedicated the Thucydides essay to him); Ogilvie 1965, 17. See p. 112 above for Thucydidean influence on the 'favourable version'.

153. Dion. Hal. I 80.1: *ὡς δὲ Τουβέρων Αἴλιος δεινὸς ἀνὴρ καὶ περὶ τὴν συναγωγὴν τῆς ἱστορίας ἐπιμελὴς γράφει.*

arly world of the 30s and 20s, there was only one Aelius Tubero who mattered.

It might be thought that if Dionysius' source were also his patron, we should expect him to be more prominently cited. But Dionysius was not subservient; he disagreed with Tubero about Thucydides, and even says at one point in his essay that his patron will not like what he is going to say, but it is true all the same.[154] In his pursuit of *akribeia*, it is reasonable that Tubero's history should have been only one of many that he used; on the other hand, his closeness to Tubero may be one of the reasons why the pro-Claudian version is more prevalent in Dionysius than it is in Livy.

It is, I think, significant that at one of the few places where Livy does use the favourable version about the Claudii, in the appeal of C. Claudius to Appius the Decemvir in 449, Appius is described as a man whose *imago* would be most honoured by posterity as a legislator and the founder of Roman law. Again, when praetors are to be elected for juridical duties in 296, Appius Caecus is chosen, as being '*iuris* atque eloquentiae peritus'.[155] In the *Digest*, too, Pomponius begins his historical survey of republican jurisprudence with Appius the Decemvir, as the man responsible for the Twelve Tables, and then goes on to Appius Caecus, who is said to have had great legal knowledge, and to have written on *actiones* and *usurpationes*.[156] (In fact, the *legis actiones* were published by Cn. Flavius, and Appius was evidently not connected with that until the hostile version made Flavius his scribe, as part of the familiar picture of Claudian arrogance and *clientela*; the apologetic version no doubt accepted the supposed fact, as so often, but turned it to Appius' advantage, making him another heroic figure in the history of Roman law.) The works of Tubero will have been familiar to Pomponius, and the Twelve Tables and *legis actiones* were among the subjects dealt with by Tubero's jurist ancestors Sex. and P. Aelius Paetus.

The part supposedly played by the Claudii in the development of Roman law may have been one of the ways in which Tubero sought to rescue their reputation. Indeed, his scholarly nature and professional interest in the law may well have been one of the reasons why he decided to refute Antias at all; for even in the extant fragments it

154. Dion. Hal. *Thuc.* 55 *ad fin*.

155. Livy III 58.2, X 22.7; Caecus' eloquence was interpreted in a demagogic sense by the hostile version (p. 88f above), but legal expertise could hardly have been held against him.

156. Pomp. *Dig*. I 2.2.36.

is clear that Antias' invented episodes were full of legal absurdities and anachronisms.[157]

No doubt there were other reasons. A *nobilis* like Tubero could not have approved of Antias' irresponsible denigration of a great aristocratic house,[158] and the patrician Claudii – Nerones and Pulchri – now enjoyed the favour of Octavian,[159] whose progress in the 30s from brutal warlord to champion of Italy was more or less contemporary with the writing of Tubero's history. Above all, his refutation of Antias implied a defence of the patriciate, as his far-sighted and statesmanlike patrician Claudii strove to preserve decent standards in an age of chaos and concession. The Aelii were not one of the old patrician families, but they were granted patrician status either by Caesar, under the *lex Cassia*, or perhaps by Octavian, under the *lex Saenia* in 30 B.C.[160]

In comparison with Antias, the scholarly and old-fashioned Tubero appears at first sight to mark an improvement in the standards of historiography. But though his motives were no doubt sounder and more responsible than those of his predecessor, his methods were essentially the same. Cicero praised his *doctrina*, Dionysius called him a diligent collector of historical material;[161] what *doctrina* can mean in an historian we shall see in Part III *à propos* of Cornelius Nepos,[162] and though the material Tubero collected did include Licinius Macer's data on magistrates from the 'linen books',[163] the Claudian speeches Dionysius borrowed from him show that his treatment of it was inescapably rhetorical.

Antias' work was the more popular, but Tubero was at least a gentleman. His version of events no doubt appeared preferable to

157. See Fraccaro 1911a, 289–95 and 301–3 (=1956, 311–4 and 318–9), on the trials of the Scipios; Crawford 1973, 1–7 (esp. 3), on the Caudine Forks treaty; Cloud 1977a, 207f and 212, on the trial of Horatius for *perduellio*; cf. also Wiseman 1979b, 48 on the trial and execution of M. Manlius.
158. It may be significant that the wife of Ofilius, Tubero's teacher in jurisprudence, was called Clodia (Val. Max. VIII 13.6, Pliny *NH* VII 158), and the philosopher Tubero had evidently thought well of Ap. Caecus' *sententiae* (Cic. *TD* IV 4).
159. Cf. p.112 above on the Nerones; Livia was also descended from the Pulchri *via* her father Livius Drusus Claudianus (Suet. *Tib.* 3.1); Ap. Claudius *cos* 38 must have earned his consulship by fighting for Octavian.
160. Pomp. *Dig.* I 2.2.46 ('fuit autem patricius . . .'); Tac. *Ann.* XI 25 (*lex Cassia, lex Saenia*), Dio XLIII 47.3, XLVI 22.3 (Caesar); patricians were evidently also created in 33 (Dio XLIX 43.6).
161. Cic. *ap.* Gell. *NA* I 22.7; Dion. Hal. I 80.1 (n.153 above).
162. P. 164f. below. Cf. Serv. *Aen.* II 15: Tubero on the Trojan Horse as a siege-engine.
163. Livy IV 23.2, cf. X 9.10.

the Valerii and the Claudii themselves, at a time when noble families needed to stand together rather than fight each other. It can have been only a few years after the completion of Antias' history that a M. Valerius Messalla adopted the son of an Appius Claudius[164] – an alliance which might not have been possible had not Tubero's refutation of the anti-Claudian legend enabled the two families to put behind them the enmity that first gave rise to it.

Messalla Appianus, the heir of the two great houses, married Augustus' niece, but died in his consulship in 12 B.C. He left a son, whose daughter, Valeria Messallina, became the wife of a patrician Claudius – Ti. Claudius Nero Drusus, the future emperor.[165] He had just divorced Aelia Paetina, daughter or grand-daughter of Q. Tubero the historian;[166] indeed, he was an historian himself,[167] and must have known the legendary history of the two families as well as anybody, but it did not stop him marrying Messallina. If it had, he would have been lucky. As it was, in whatever corner of Tartarus is reserved for slanderers, Valerius Antias must have enjoyed seeing a fitting vengeance taken on the house of Appius.

164. See Syme 1955, 157 on the parentage of M. Valerius Messalla Barbatus Appianus (*CIL* I² p. 28 for his full name, and his death in office): the adoptive father was perhaps M. Messalla *cos.* 32, who must be the son of Messalla Rufus (cf. Crawford 1974, 457 on his coin-issue in Rufus' consulship); the natural father was no doubt Ap. Claudius *cos.* 38, nephew of Appius the censor (cf. Wiseman 1970a, 207–9; *ibid.* 213 n.34 on the adoptive son's *cognomen*).
165. Suet. *Claud.* 26.2: Messallina was the daughter of Claudius' *consobrinus* Messalla Barbatus; the latter must therefore have been the son of Appianus (from his name) and Marcella *minor*, the daughter of Claudius' grandmother Octavia; cf. *CIL* VI 4421, 4493, 4501 etc. for slaves and freedmen of Messalla in the *monumentum Marcellae*.
166. Suet. *Claud.* 26.2, Tac. *Ann.* XII 1.
167. Suet. *Claud.* 21.2, 42.2; Peter 1906, 92–4.

PART III

Catullus and Cornelius Nepos

Who am I giving this smart little book to,
new, and just polished up with dry pumice?

Cornelius, you; because you already
reckoned my scribblings really were something
when you, alone of Italians, boldly
unfolded all history in three volumes —
the effort, my God! and the erudition!
So have this little book, such as it may be.

Whatever its value, patroness Maiden,
let it survive more than one generation.

CATULLUS, *poem 1*

Chapter 9

POETRY AND HISTORY

When Virgil died, his will ordered that the *Aeneid* should be destroyed. Augustus forbade it, and a minor poet of the time congratulated him on taking thought for his country's *history*:[1]

tu, maxime Caesar,
non sinis et Latiae consulis historiae.

To us, that is odd: Virgil was not writing history as we understand it. But I hope it will now be clear to the reader that the Greeks and Romans understood it in a way very different from ourselves. The purpose of this final study is to illustrate another aspect of the difference, the common ground of poetry and history.

Our distinction between the works of Clio and the works of Calliope is, in fact, also an ancient one. The very reason we find it strange to call the *Aeneid* history is that our preconceptions about the proper functions of history and poetry are largely conditioned by what Thucydides, Aristotle and Polybius said on the subject.[2] But we have seen already that Thucydides, at least, was a very untypical historian (p. 41 above), and in trying to reconstruct what was *normally* taken for granted in the ancient world we must not be overawed by these great names, or forget that their observations were largely polemical: what they protested against is at least as important as what they practised themselves.

As regards Aristotle and Polybius, that point was brilliantly made by Professor Walbank in a paper published nearly 20 years ago, in which he demonstrated 'the fundamental affinity, going back to the earliest days, of both history and tragedy', an affinity

> insisted upon throughout almost the whole of the classical and later periods down to the Byzantine scholiasts. It was there by virtue of descent and of analogous literary techniques, it was encouraged by a common moral aim and

1. Donatus *vita Verg.* 38 (Sulpicius Carthaginiensis), ps.Probus *vita Verg.* (Servius Varus). Cf. Serv. *Aen.* I 382 on Lucan.
2. Thuc. I 21.1, cf. 22.4; Arist. *Poetics* 9, 23 (1451a36–b32, 1459a17–b7); Pol. II 56.7–12.

> by the sharpness of Greek emotional sensibility, and it was taught in the rhetorical schools to generations of Greek students.[3]

What is true of history and tragedy is all the more true of history and epic.

Thucydides, defending his introductory account of early Greek history, contrasts it equally with that of the poets, whose version was too 'decorative' (*ἐπι τὸ μεῖζον κοσμοῦντες*), and that of the prose *logographoi*, who were too concerned with pleasing their audience (*ἐπὶ τὸ προσαγωγότερον τῇ ἀκροάσει ἢ ἀληθέστερον*); and the same collocation of prose and poetry may be implicit where he justifies the absence of the mythical element (*τὸ μυθῶδες*) in the main body of his history, contrasting his 'possession for ever' with a *prize performance* for immediate effect.[4] Poets and rhapsodes competed for prizes,[5] not (so far as we know) prose writers. The effect of the 'star' Homeric rhapsode Ion on his audience, acutely cited by Walbank as analogous to that of the historians objected to by Polybius,[6] reminds us that the 'sharpness of Greek emotional sensibility' to which he refers was played on by epic as much as by tragic poetry, and that each had something in common with the writing of historical work for recitation.[7]

As for the 'common moral aim' of providing examples to follow and avoid, that also was shared by history as much with epic as with tragedy. At least as early as the fifth century B.C. Homer was

3. Walbank 1960, *passim* (quotation from p. 223); cf. also Walbank 1972, 32–40.

4. Thuc. I 21.1 (cf. p. 4 above on *κοσμεῖν*), 22.4.

5. Aristotle (*Poetics* 145 1b37) uses the same word *ἀγώνισμα* of tragic competitions; it could, however, also be used of forensic oratory (p. 27 above), and that is what Pliny, at least, understood Thucydides to mean (Pliny *ep.* V 8.11). Macleod (1978, 68 n.17) suggests that Thucydides was thinking of displays of epideictic oratory.

Early epic bards' contests: Hesiod *WD* 650–3 (Chalcis), Hymn. Hom. *Apollo* 149f, cf. 173 and Thuc. III 104.5 (Delos); superseded by those of rhapsodes: Hdt V 67.1 (Sicyon), Plate *Ion* 530a–b (Athens, Epidaurus), cf. Plut. *Per.* 13.11. From Theognis (993ff) to Theocritus (cf. Schol. Theocr. p.2 Wendel on the supposed origin of bucolic singing-matches), it was natural for poetic recitation to be thought of as competitive. Herodotus is described as an *ἀγωνιστής* by Lucian in the story of his self-advertisement at the Olympic games (*Herodotus* 1), but the word cannot be meant literally: it is clear from the context that he had no competitors. See now Momigliano 1978, 62–6.

6. Plato *Ion* 535c, Walbank 1960, 230f. Cf. Dion. Hal. *Thuc.* 15 on the portrayal of horror and pathos *ὥστε μηδεμίαν ὑπερβολὴν μήτε ἱστοριογράφοις μήτε ποιηταῖς καταλιπεῖν* – by Thucydides!

7. Thucydides uses the word *ἀκρόασις* in both passages; cf. also his contemporary Cratippus (*ap.* Dion. Hal. *Thuc.* 16) on the necessity of avoiding anything offensive *τοῖς ἀκούουσιν*.

being used as the repertory of ethical teaching,[8] and the idea that the bards were the teachers and philosophers of the heroic age must originate from the use of extant epic poets for the purpose.[9] The exemplary function of the myths of Hades, mentioned by Diodorus, was perhaps exercised less on the tragic stage than by the *nekuia* of *Odyssey* X, and whatever underworld scenes there were in the epic treatment of Orpheus, Heracles and Theseus.[10]

The audience's pleasure at the *logographoi* of Thucydides' day (Herodotus among them) was fundamentally the same as that of Odysseus and the Phaeacians at the performance of the bard Demodocus:[11] it included the *frisson* of pity and terror and the recognition of good and bad moral examples, but above all it was the enjoyment of good stories. The subject matter of bard and historian was the same – *κλέα ἀνδρῶν*, the famous deeds of men, whether at Thebes or Troy or Salamis.[12]

It is sometimes argued that Herodotus distinguished legend from history in much the same way that we do, on the strength of his description of Polycrates' thalassocracy as the first 'of what is called the time of men', as opposed to that of Minos 'and any other who may have controlled the sea before Polycrates'.[13] But all Herodotus means is that Polycrates was (as he says) 'the first *we know of*'; the distinction he makes is between men of whom his informants had first-hand information and those of whom they did not. There is no suggestion that the latter – characters like Minos who belong before living memory – are any less 'historical' than the former, only that Herodotus cannot vouch personally for the reliability of the stories about them.[14] Despite what is often

8. Aristophanes *Frogs* 1030–6, Xen. *Symp*. 3.5, 4.6, cf. Antisthenes frr. 51–62 Caizzi; subsequently in Hor. *epist*. I 2.1–4, Strabo I 2.3 (C 15–17), Dio Chrys. *orat*. 53, etc.

9. Schol. *Od*. III 267, Athenaeus I 14a–d, Strabo I 1.10 (C 7).

10. Diod. Sic. I 2.2; Walbank 1960, 229, cf. Wardman 1976, 69f. One might add Tartarus and the Isles of the Blessed in the Hesiodic tradition, the White Island in the cyclic poets, etc. Cf. p. 38 above on the exemplary purpose of history.

11. Hom. *Od*. VIII 367f. For Herodotus, cf. Lucian *Herodotus* 1, 7, Plut. *Mor*. 862B.

12. Hom. *Od*. VIII 73 (Demodocus), *Iliad* IX 189 (Achilles); Hdt I pref., *ὡς μήτε . . . ἔργα μεγάλα . . . ἀκλεα γένηται* (Strasburger 1972, 12–14); Clio's name was derived from *κλέος* (Diod. Sic. IV 7.4). Herodotus was called *Ὁμηρικώτατος* (ps. Longinus *de subl*. 13.3), probably with reference to his style: cf. Dion. Hal. *Thuc*. 23 and Strabo I 2.6 on Hecataeus and other early logographers, with Strasburger 1972, 20–30 on Homer as a quasi-historian.

13. Hdt III 122.2: *τῆς ἀνθρωπηίης λεγομένης γενεῆς*. Cf. Finley 1975, 18.

14. On the mutually exclusive nature of *μῦθος* and personal enquiry, see Wardman 1960, 404 (on Herodotus) and 411f – though he does not draw what seems to me the

said,[15] Herodotus is no more 'scientific' about Minos than Thucydides was, who called him the first thalassocrat 'whom we know of by report'. The old stories might be rationalized, but they were not rejected as mere legends.[16] A much more revealing Herodotean passage is II 145.4, on the dates of the generations of Semele and Dionysus, Heracles and Alcmene, Pan and Penelope. They belonged in the same time-span as the historian himself, and not in any separate 'time of gods'.

It is true that the Stoic Cleanthes in the third century B.C. found verse a better medium than prose for writing about the gods, but that does not mean that the subject matter of poets and prose-writers was divided into mutually exclusive compartments, even on the criterion of divine involvement.[17] Greek epic poets hardly ever dealt with contemporary themes,[18] and may well have felt their material restricted in practice to stories in which the gods might come in naturally, leaving those entirely on the human plane – and especially events within living memory – to historians writing in prose; but the converse certainly did not hold good. Prose writers often rationalized the divine stories into quasi-human form, but evidently felt no inhibitions about treating them in the first place. The distinction is not between history and poetry *per se*, but between contemporary history, in the Thucydidean manner, and everything else. For Thucydides (I 1), the only real history was what surviving witnesses could be cross-examined about, and within that definition of the 'recoverable past' there was no room for the poet. But the past beyond human memory – Minos as opposed to Polycrates – belonged to poet and prose-writer alike, even when the gods came into it.

At the other end of the Greek historiographical tradition from

---

likely conclusion, that *μῦθος* might be *defined* as that which lies beyond living memory. Certainly it is too simple to assume that Greek historians meant by *mythos* more or less what we mean by 'myth' (e.g. Wardman 1960, 405 on stories that raised problems 'as to when the heroic period began to shade into the merely historical'); for Hecataeus, at least, *μῦθος* and *λόγος* were evidently interchangeable (*FGrH* 1Fla–b).

15. E.g. How and Wells 1912, I 32 and 295.

16. Thuc. I 4.1, *ὧν ἀκοῇ ἴσμεν* (cf. Isocr. *Panath.* 43, 205 on Minos as a historical character); cf. p. 49 above for rationalization.

17. *Stoic. vet. frag.* I 486 (quoted by Philodemus): I owe this reference to Prof. A. A. Long. In the third book of the *Republic*, Plato has both prose and verse *μυθολογοῦντες* in mind (380c1, 390a1–2, 39[illegible]a–b).

18. The exceptions are Agis of Argos and Choerilus of Samos, who were condemned on all sides as the worst poets ever: Q. Curtius VIII 5.8, cf. Arr. *Anab.* IV 9.9 (Agis); Hor. *epist.* II 1.232–41, *AP* 357 and scholiasts (Choerilus); Brink 1971, 365–6.

Herodotus, Lucian too is sometimes quoted as proving that different rules applied to history and to poetry.[19] They did, but the difference was only one of degree. The 'poetic' features Lucian deplores, namely *mythos* and *encomion*, are both specified elsewhere in his essay as appropriate to history, in small doses[20] – and the history Lucian is talking about is contemporary and political, Rome's wars against Vologeses and the Parthians. What his evidence really shows is the way the common ground of poetry and history had by his time extended even into the territory marked out by Thucydides and Polybius.[21]

Isocrates is a safer witness for the orthodox view. For him, the Trojan War and the Persian Wars are both *mythoi*, of equal historical validity. For a myth with divine protagonists, like that of Demeter and Kore, he does *argue* the case that the events really happened; otherwise, as with the Athenians' battle with the Amazons, the historicity of the stories is taken for granted.[22] That this attitude was the normal one is surely proved by the paintings of the Stoa Poikile – Amazons, Persians and contemporary Peloponnesians all equally 'historical' as enemies of Athens – or by the treasury of Athena's temple at Lindos (Rhodes), which contained mementos of Heracles and Menelaus, Artaxerxes and Amasis, without distinction of historicity.[23]

In some cases, not only the subject matter but also the manner of treatment was the same for the poet as for the historian.[24] The cyclic poets chronicled the Trojan War and its aftermath by 'filling in' before and after the *Iliad* and *Odyssey*, just as the continuators of Thucydides began their histories from the point, insignificant in itself, where Thucydides left off. Aristotle, in his attempt to distinguish the subject matter of epic and history, honourably concedes

19. Lucian *Historia* 8, cf. Finley 1975, 12.
20. *Ibid.* 9 (praise), 60 (myth); cf. Plut. *Mor.* 855D for their appropriateness in digressions, on which see Wardman 1960, 406–8. In the same work (*ibid.* 45), Lucian recognized the need for poetic sublimity at the appropriate places in a work of history; and it came naturally to him (*ibid.* 57) to cite poetic narrative for his examples.
21. Even a Thucydidean historian naturally brings mythological ethnography into his geographical excurses: cf. Syme 1964, 152f and 193–5 on Sall. *BJ* 17, *Hist.* III 61–80M.
22. Isocr. *Paneg.* 158, cf. 68–71, *Archidamus* 42, *Areop.* 75, etc.; *Paneg.* 28–33 (cf. Wardman 1960, 412) on Kore, Paus. I 15.1 for the Stoa Poikile. Cf. Plato *Euthyphro* 6b–c for poets' stories about the gods as literally true.
23. Blinkenberg 1941, 161–82. Casson (1974, 233–5) gives an entertaining list of tourist attractions which shows the same lack of differentation between (in our terms) the mythical and the historical.
24. Cf. p. 50 n.49 above (on Virgil).

this point – though it proves, in fact, that his distinction was an unreal one.[25] The treatment of the undifferentiated continuum from (in our terms) heroic legend to genuine history was equally the province of the *epopoios* and the *logopoios*,[26] in Aristotle's day (and long after) as it had been in Thucydides'.

Eratosthenes insisted that since the poet *invents*, his work has value only as entertainment and not as instruction.[27] That opinion was rejected by Strabo, who defined poetry as a mixture of *historia*, *diathesis* ('composition') and *mythos*:

> the aim of *historia* is truth . . . the aim of *diathesis* is vividness, as when Homer brings on battle scenes; the aim of *mythos* is pleasure and astonishment. But to invent everything is not persuasive, and not Homeric.

As he says elsewhere, the same applies to prose writers like Herodotus, Ctesias, Hellanicus, Theopompus and the historians of Alexander in India, who 'deliberately weave in myths, not in ignorance of the facts but by inventing impossibilities for the sake of astonishment and pleasure'.[28] We know (by the tripartite definition and the reference to *adynata*) that Strabo's position here was the orthodox one, that of the grammarians whose effect on the literary education of generations of Greek writers Walbank so cogently pointed out: they divided narrative into just these three categories, and extended the range of *historia* at the expense of *mythos* to cover practically all the legendary stories that were not physically impossible.[29] So if he avoided this narrowly-defined *mythos* – or at least signalled it clearly, like Theopompus – the prose writer was as entitled to invent material as the poet was. To invent *everything* is not persuasive; but the aims of truth and vividness allowed the historian too to be, as Aristotle said of poets, the inventor (ποιητής) of his plot – provided always that it was treated 'according to probability'.[30]

25. Arist. *Poet.* 1459a17ff, esp. 29 (σχεδὸν δὲ οἱ πολλοὶ τῶν ποιητῶν τοῦτο δρῶσι); cf. Gomme 1954, 1–4.
26. Pearson 1939, ch. i; cf. Walbank 1960, 221f and Strasburger 1972 (esp. 14ff).
27. Eratosthenes *ap.* Strabo I 1.10, 2.3, 2.12, 2.17 (C [illegible], 15f, 22, 24): Pfeiffer 1968, 166f.
28. Strabo I 2.17 and 35 (C 24, 43): in the latter passage Theopompus is commended for pointing out what was *mythos*.
29. Walbank 1960, 225–8: the more usual name for διάθεσις was πλάσμα (Sext. Emp. *adv. gramm.* I 263) – the same word Eratosthenes had used of Homer's 'inventions' (Strabo I 2.3, C 16 *ad fin.*). On *adynata*, cf. pp. 49 above, 159 below.
30. On the εἰκός criterion, see Wardman 1960, 409–11 and p. 49 above; the

Perhaps the most extreme example of 'creative historiography' (to borrow Pearson's excellent phrase) is the construction of a fictitious heroic past for Messenia by Myron of Priene and Rhianus the Cretan – one a prose writer and the other an epic poet, but each equally an 'authority' for Messenian history.[31] In a similar way, the legends of Daedalus and Cocalus, Demeter and Kore, Heracles and Eryx (and the cattle of Geryon) had been created by sixth- and fifth-century writers to provide a 'historical' justification for the Greek colonists of Sicily and Italy.[32] This corpus of material was exploited and greatly expanded by Timaeus, an historian praised for his inventiveness;[33] his account of the early 'history' of the Greek West included a great deal of legendary material, even including metamorphoses, and Professor Pearson has recently pointed out how very similar it was to the work of the Hellenistic poets.[34]

—

If the connection of historiography with the recherché subtlety of Hellenistic poetic techniques seems paradoxical, that is the fault of too 'Thucydidean' a perspective on our part. Rhianus, for instance, has well over 100 pages of commentary devoted to him in Jacoby's *Fragments of the Greek Historians*, yet he is also a prime example of that delicate 'arte allusiva' by which the poets of that time exploited their erudition, particularly in Homeric studies.[35] Duris of Samos is another example: well described by Ferrero as 'tra poetica ed istoria', he was both an historian and a Homeric scholar whose sensibilities anticipate those of Callimachus.[36] Novelty was what the Hellenistic poets sought at all costs, either in subject matter or in the treatment of traditional material, and that, as Josephus complained, was equally the besetting obsession of the

best-known example is probably Herodotus' version of the stories of Io, Europa, Medea and Helen at I 1–5.

31. Paus. IV 6.1–4; Jacoby *FGrH* nos. 106 and 265; Pearson 1962, 397–426, esp. 410ff (425 on 'creative history-writing').

32. Pearson 1975, 185–92; a particularly clear example is the Eryx story as a justification for Dorieus' expedition (Paus. III 16.4).

33. Ps. Longinus *de subl.* 4.1 (cf. 1.2); Cicero (*de or.* II 58) calls Timaeus 'rerum copia et sententiarum varietate abundantissimus', and Polybius (XII 4a.1–d.8) is contemptuous of his credulous acceptance of myth. Cf. Gelzer 1935, 271f=1964, 222f.

34. Pearson 1975, *passim*, esp. 175f, 185, 194f; cf. Murray 1972, 203f for the use of Herodotus by Hellenistic poets.

35. Jacoby 1943, 87–200; Giangrande 1970a, *passim* and 1977, 273–9; cf. Pfeiffer 1968, 148f.

36. Ferrero 1963, esp. pp. 86f, 94 (on Proclus *Comm. Tim.* I 90 Diehl). Schol. Gen. *Iliad* XXI 499 for his *προβλήματα Ὁμηρικά*.

Greek historiographical tradition.[37] The culmination, perhaps, of this determination to be different was the perversely heterodox 'pre-history' of Dionysius Scytobrachion in the second century B.C.,[38] but it was certainly not restricted to such baroque figures. Greek accounts of the foundation of Rome provide an important and characteristic example:[39]

> one could write on the subject in an original manner, disentangling the difficulties in most satisfactory fashion, yet without coming into any conflict with accepted mythology.

The poet asserts his originality by the unorthodox use of Homeric phraseology, or by treating heroic subject-matter in a profoundly unheroic manner;[40] the historian asserts his by interpreting a familiar episode – Theseus and Ariadne, for example – in a way which respects the canonical 'plot' but puts it in a new context and re-interprets the motivation of the characters.[41] The technique is the same, and we are tempted to treat the man who does it in prose differently from the man who does it in verse only because Thucydides and Polybius professed a different sort of history. One of the re-interpreters of early Athenian pseudo-history was Cleidemus, whose *akribeia* was noted by Plutarch in the context of Theseus' battle with the Amazons; Polybius, quite rightly from his point of view, deplored that sort of 'precision' as nothing more than circumstantial detail introduced to make pseudo-historical fiction plausible, but his rigorous attitude merely confirms how widespread the technique was.[42]

In specifying the type of history *he* professes, Polybius contrasts it with 'genealogies, myths, the planting of colonies, the foundation of cities and their ties of kinship', but admits that they are a kind of history too, though not appealing to the same sort of serious-

37. Call. *Aitia* I 1.25–8, *Anth. Pal.* XII 43.1–2; Jos. *contra Ap.* I 25–6. Cf. Thuc. III 38.5 on the Athenians as 'slaves to every new paradox'; not that Thucydides himself was free from this vice, refusing as he did to accept what his contemporaries took for granted as the cause of the Peloponnesian War (cf. Aristophanes *Ach.* 530ff, *Peace* 606ff), and mentioning it only in passing (I 42.2, 67.4, 139.1, 144.2). On novelty, see Vitr. *de arch.* V pref. 1: 'historiae per se tenent lectores; habent enim novarum rerum varias expectationes' (see p. 30 above on variety and *delectatio*).
38. See Pearson 1939, 110–5.
39. Bickerman 1952, 67; see now Cornell 1975, 25–7.
40. E.g. (respectively) Giangrande 1967, *passim* and 1970b, 262–77; Otis 1963, 8–12; Lyne 1978, 181–2.
41. Plut. *Thes.* 15–22; Pearson 1942, 149–53. Cf. pp. 26, 64f above on the influence of the rhetorical schools.
42. Plut. *Thes.* 27.3; cf. Pol. III 33.17 on *οἱ ἀξιοπίστως ψευδομένοι τῶν συγγραφέων*.

minded reader as his own.[43] Those who *did* like such material were as likely to enjoy it in verse as in prose: the history of 'foundation' literature, for example, goes from Semonides and Panyassis through Hellanicus and Ion of Chios to Callimachus and Apollonius Rhodius,[44] and the rest of the subject matter Polybius specifies was to be found both in early epics and in the logographers, as well as the Alexandrians who rediscovered and exploited them.[45]

This amalgam of genealogy, mythology and geography appealed, according to Polybius, both to the man who likes a story (*ὁ φιλήκοος*) and to the 'extravagantly curious' (*ὁ πολυπράγμων καὶ περιττός*). 'Extravagant' is perhaps an inexact translation of *perittos*, which had connotations of refined elaboration as well as excess.[46] It was the quality one associated with Euphorion (as in Theodoridas' epitaph);[47] unsympathetic critics called it mere wordiness,[48] but the accumulation of carefully chosen detail was just what was required by an important category of readers – such amateurs of *historia fabularis* as the emperor Tiberius, an admirer of Euphorion, Rhianus and Parthenius who precisely exemplifies Polybius' second category.[49]

Euphorion the poet was writing 'history' in the same sense as the prose chronicler Philochorus, with whom he shares the status of an authority on the 'expedition' of Dionysus against Athens;[50] his technique is essentially that same *akribeia* we have seen in Cleidemus, whose original treatment of the Theseus story is indeed described by Plutarch as *perittos*.[51] The word perfectly expresses

43. Pol. IX 1.4, 2.1 Cf. Murray 1972, 212f on the indistinguishability of Greek historiography, ethnography and geography.

44. Cf. Jacoby 1947, 4f; von der Mühll 1963, 201; Strasburger 1972, 37 n.121.

45. See especially Pearson 1939, 8–10; also 1942, 136–44 on Ister.

46. Pol. IX 1.4. Zimmermann (1934, 180) translates *τὸ περιττόν* as 'die hohe künstlerische Form'; *ibid.* 184f for the connotations of the word, and cf. (e.g.) Dion. Hal. *Thuc.* 23, 50 etc for its application to historiography.

47. Anth. Pal. VII 406.1: *Εὐφορίων ὁ περισσὸν ἐπιστάμενός τι ποιῆσαι*. Cf. van Groningen 1953, 26 (*ibid.* 21ff on Euphorion in general).

48. E.g. Lucian *Historia* 57 on Euphorion, Callimachus and Parthenius compared unfavourably with Homer (in a historiographical context); cf. also Plut. *Mor.* 513A–B for Antimachus as *περιττὸς καὶ ἀδολέσχης*.

49. Suet. *Tib.* 70.2–3: *fabularis* translates *μυθώδης*, but 'fabularis historia' is in no way an oxymoron. For Tiberius' refined taste, see Stewart 1977 (esp. 85–7) and Horsfall 1977, 180.

50. Barigazzi 1963, 422; *ibid.* 420f on Euphorion's geographical fragments, another point of contact with the prose historiographers.

51. Plut. *Thes.* 19.8 *ἰδίως δέ πως καὶ περιττῶς*, cf. 27.3 (n.42 above); for the collocation of the two ideas in other contexts, cf. Arist. *Top.* 141b13, Isocr. 15.264,

the exquisite sophisticated erudition of Alexandrian literary taste, and it is no surprise to find the learned Parthenius sending his collection of love stories to Cornelius Gallus for that admirer of Euphorion to work up into epic or elegy, and apologizing for their unelaborated state by observing that they lacked the quality of which Gallus was master – *τὸ περιττόν*.[52]

Parthenius' outline plots provide, in fact, the culminating proof of the equivalence of poetry and prose for the connoisseur of history as it was normally understood. Most of them carry a note indicating where Parthenius found the story concerned,[53] and their tabulation reveals 22 prose sources, 15 in verse, and two unidentifiable:

PROSE	*nos.*
Andriscus *Naxiaca* (*FGrH* 500)	9, 19
Aristocritus *peri Miletou* (*FGrH* 493)	11
Aristodemus of Nysa *historiae*	8
Aristotle	14
Asclepiades of Myrlea *Bithyniaca* (*FGrH* 697)	36
Cephalon *Troica* (*FGrH* 45)	4, 34
Hegesippus *Palleniaca* (*FGrH* 391)	6, 16
Hellanicus *Troica* (*FGrH* 4)	34
authors of *Milesiaca* (*FGrH* 496)	14
Neanthes (*FGrH* 84)	33
Phaenias of Eresus	7
Phylarchus (*FGrH* 81)	15, 25, 31
Theagenes (*FGrH* 774)	6
Theophrastus	9, 18
Timaeus *Sicelica* (*FGrH* 566)	29
Xanthus *Lydiaca* (*FGrH* 765)	33
TOTAL	22

VERSE	*nos.*
Apollonius Rhodius *Argonautica*	28
Apollonius Rhodius *Caunou ktisis*	1, 11

Plut. *Cic.* 8.5 etc; Tarutius' detailed horoscope of Romulus is described by Plutarch (*Rom.* 12.3–6) as *ξένον καὶ περιττὸν*.

52. Parth. *narr. am.* pref. 2, cf. Virg. *Ecl.* 10.50. Note the description of his sketches as *ὑπομνήματα* (*commentarii*), as if they were the unelaborated drafts for historical narratives (cf. p. 6 above).

53. Nos. 10, 12, 17, 20, 21, 23, 24, 30, 32 and 35 are unattributed.

Euphorion *Apollodorus*	28
Euphorion *Thrax*	13, 26
Hermesianax *Leontium*	5, 22
Licymnius of Chios	22
Moero *arae*	27
Nicaenetus *Lyrcus*	1
Nicander *peri poieton* (*FGrH* 271–2)	4
Philetas *Hermes*	2
Simmias of Rhodes	33
Sophocles *Euryalus*	3
TOTAL 15	

UNKNOWN	*nos.*
'Dectadas'	13
Diodorus of Elaea	15
TOTAL 2	

Virgil studied Greek with Parthenius, and must have shared his literary attitudes. At about the time his friend Gallus was working on Parthenius' stories, he was supposedly beginning an epic on the Alban kings, which would have filled in an awkward gap in Roman 'history' just as Myron and Rhianus did for Messenian.[54] Apollo diverted him from that,[55] but the epic he *did* write naturally incorporated a vast amount of that mythological, geographical and genealogical material which had been the province of historians from the very beginning.[56] In that sense, it was indeed his country's history that Augustus saved from the fire.

54. Macr. *Sat.* V 17.18; Serv. *Ecl.* 6.3, cf. Prop. III 3.3f (the job still needed to be done).
55. Virg. *Ecl.* 6.3–5, on which see Clausen 1976b, 245f (it was an appropriately Callimachean Apollo).
56. See for instance Horsfall 1973, *passim.*

Chapter 10

THE INTELLECTUAL BACKGROUND

Like Polybius a century earlier, though at a humbler social level, Parthenius too came to Rome against his will, as a result of his country's conquest.[1]

The third Macedonian War, which led to Polybius' exile, was a turning point in the hellenization of Roman culture: the effect on the Romans, for instance, of the teaching of the Stoic scholar Crates of Mallos on his diplomatic mission in 168 B.C., and of the lectures of Carneades during the philosophers' embassy to Rome in 155, is explicitly attested,[2] while men like Panaetius and Polybius himself exercised a less dramatic but longer-lasting influence on the attitudes of educated Romans by their association with members of the Roman ruling class.[3] All that is well known; what is less often remembered is the even greater effect a century later of the Mithridatic wars.

In Polybius' time, Rome learnt to accept Greek culture; in Parthenius', she became a part of it[4] – for the very good reason that practically all the rival centres of literary and artistic patronage had disappeared. In 20 years, from the mid-70s to the mid-50s B.C., *direct* Roman rule was established over Cyrene, Bithynia, Cilicia,

1. Suidas *s.v. Parthenios*; for the date (66 B.C.?) and circumstances, cf. Wiseman 1974a, 47–50. Polybius: Pol. XXXI 23, XXXII 3.14, Plut. *Cato maior* 9.2–3; Paus. VII 10.11 (167 B.C.).

2. Suet. *gramm.* 2; Plut. *Cato maior* 22 etc. For Crates, see Pfeiffer 1968, 235–46.

3. Panaetius: Cic. *fin.* IV 23 (Scipio, Laelius, Q. Tubero), *Brut.* 101 (C. Fannius) and 113f (P. Rutilius), *de or.* I 75 (Q. Scaevola), *rep.* I 34 (Scipio, Laelius), *Mur.* 66 (Scipio); Walbank 1965a, 1–2, Astin 1967, 294ff (the exact date of Panaetius' arrival in Rome is not known, but was before 140 B.C.). For a brilliant sketch of Polybius, Posidonius and the Romans, see Momigliano 1975, ch. 2.

4. The contrast is too schematic, but not (I hope) wholly misleading. I am suggesting a slight modification of Professor Momigliano's view: 'since the third century B.C. there had been a Latin Hellenism, never identical with the Greek, but never separable from it' (Momigliano 1975, 11). I think the evidence shows that in the late Republic there was a moment when the Greeks tried to make the 'Latin Hellenism' identical with their own, and at least succeeded in making it very different from what it had been in the third century B.C.

Pontus, Syria and Cyprus. The courts of kings were gone: Pella in 168, Pergamum in 133, now Antioch and Nicomedia as well, and though Alexandria remained, it was only on Roman sufferance. (Ptolemy Alexander had willed his kingdom to Rome; the bequest was not taken up, but Auletes' precarious succession had to be secured by the garrison Gabinius installed in 55 B.C.[5]) This change in Roman policy from inactive hegemony to aggression and annexation in the Greek East is of critical importance for the history of Greco-Roman culture. However restricted the real power of the Hellenistic monarchs had been under Roman hegemony in the second century B.C.,[6] they had still been patrons though they could not be conquerors; perhaps some of them were the more ready to add lustre to their courts by subsidizing philosophers and literary men now that other means of conspicuous display were not available. By the middle of the first century, on the other hand, their place was occupied by proconsuls who were there one year and gone the next: for all practical purposes, the centre of patronage was inevitably Rome.[7]

For Greek intellectuals, then, the Rome of the first century B.C. could no longer be what it had been a hundred years earlier – merely a field to conquer from a secure base outside. Now it was the centre of things, and had to be absorbed into the Greek tradition.

The effect can be clearly seen, for instance in the work of the Alexandrian scholar Philoxenus, who worked in Rome and wrote a treatise on the Roman language as a dialect of Greek;[8] or in that of Simylos and Butas, Greek elegiac poets who used Roman legends and Roman traditions in the Callimachean manner;[9] or in that of

5. Cic. *leg. agr.* I 1, II 41f, with Badian 1967, 178–92; cf. also Shatzman 1971, 363–9. Gabinius' garrison: Caes. *BC* III 4.4, Dio XLII 5.4, Val. Max. IV 1.15.

6. Their impotence may, in fact, have been less than is normally thought: see Sherwin-White 1977, 62–4.

7. Cf. Jocelyn 1977, 350–2 (on philosophers) for Roman patronage as parallel to that of Hellenistic kings. On the need for patrons, cf. Juv. *Sat.* VII 1–7 (where *Clio* is the Muse who starves).

8. Suidas *s.v. Philoxenos*; quotations in Funaioli 1907, 443–6. See Gabba 1963, 188–94, Pfeiffer 1968, 273f, Fraser 1972, II 690. Cf. also Fraser 1972, I 474f, 519, 809f on the migration of Alexandrian intellectuals to Rome, Suidas *s.v. Timagenes* for one of the first of them (brought back by Gabinius in 55).

As Gabba points out (1963, 191ff), the idea that Evander brought letters in general (and Aeolic Greek in particular) to Rome goes back as far as Fabius Pictor (fr. 1P). But only now do we find Greek scholars working out the implications in detail: cf. (e.g.) Varro *LL* V 88 and Gell. *NA* XVI 12.5 on Hypsicrates.

9. Plut. *Rom.* 17.6, 21.8, Arnobius *adv. nat.* V 18; Momigliano 1969, 482f. For Butas, cf. also Wiseman 1974a, 136f; for Simylos' unorthodox treatment of Tar-

Dionysius of Halicarnassus, determined to prove the Greek-ness of the Romans not only in their legendary origins but in the very nature of their laws and customs.[10] It may be significant that the critical period of the Mithridatic wars lies between the work of Lucilius, bilingual and thoroughly hellenized but using his Greek in an entirely *un*-Greek literary form, and that of Varro, whose satires were Menippean; and between the patrons of Archias at the turn of the century, flattered at having their *res gestae* praised in Greek epic,[11] and those of Parthenius and Philodemus, who had to cope with Hellenistic learning and philosophy on the Greeks' own terms.[12]

In this context it is easy to appreciate the *novelty* of the Callimachean school of Latin epic and elegy founded by Parthenius and his patron and pupil Cinna:[13] the writers were 'poetae *novi*' and *οἱ νεωτέροι*, their works were '*nova* carmina'.[14] Their ideals and techniques – of which Catullus clearly approved[15] – provoked resistance from more old-fashioned readers, even profoundly committed philhellenes like Cicero.[16] *A fortiori*, the Roman reading

---

peia, cf. Cornell 1975, 16–27, esp. 25f – an excellent discussion of Greek versions of Roman history. For Greek antiquarians in the Varronian tradition, compare Nicostratus' *de senatu habendo* (Festus 470L); the *αἴτια Ῥωμαϊκά* of Castor of Rhodes (Plut. *Mor.* 266E, 282A: cf. p. 129 n.102 above) were evidently an attempt to interpret Roman customs in Pythagorean terms.

10. Dion. Hal. I 90.2, VII 70.2 – promise fulfilled at II 7–29? See Balsdon 1971, 18–27 (esp. 24f), Musti 1970, 11–14, 18–20. The idea of Rome as a Greek *foundation* goes back at least to Heraclides Ponticus (Plut. *Cam.* 22.2), but Dionysius had to re-establish the point against hostile Greek accounts that insisted on the barbarism of the Romans' origins (I 4.2): cf. Gabba 1974b, 633 and 636, Jocelyn 1971, 52–60.

11. Cic. *Arch.* 5f, 19–21. This sort of patronage remained important (Cic. *Arch.* 28, *Att.* I 16.15 for Archias in the 60s), and offers another example of the common ground of 'historical' prose and verse: cf. *Arch.* 24 on Theophanes of Mytilene.

12. Cicero's travesty of L. Piso's philosophical understanding at *Pis.* 69 should not be taken literally; perhaps the contents of the Herculaneum library are better evidence. On the westward migration of Greek libraries as well as Greek scholars, see Earl 1972, 850f and 855, Marshall 1976, 257f; on Philodemus, see Grube 1965, 193–206, Murray 1965, 161–82 (esp. 177ff on Piso); on philosophers as a partial exception to the 'drift to Rome', see Jocelyn 1977, 335ff (cf. 345–8: they had less need of patronage).

13. See Clausen 1964, 181–96, Wiseman 1974a, 47–56.

14. Cic. *orator* 161, *Att.* VII 2.1, Virg. *Ecl.* 3.86.

15. Cat. 95, cf. 22 (Callimachean allusion at 22.3?), 36, 116.2 etc.

16. Untypical philhellenism: Cic. *Att.* I 15.1, *QF* I 2.28, *Flacc.* 9; Plut. *Cic.* 5.2, Dio XLVI 18.1. Criticism of *cantores Euphorionis*: Cic. *TD* III 45. Follows Plato rather than Callimachus (and the *poetae novi*) in approving of Antimachus: Cic. *Brut.* 191, Gigante 1954, 72f.

public in general needed a course of re-education to be able to take part in the 'international' literary culture to which the Roman tradition was now being forcibly assimilated.[17]

One man evidently conscious of this need was Cornelius Nepos. In the preface to his *Lives of the Generals of Foreign Nations* (addressed to Atticus, that most bi-cultural of all Romans), he argues against the prejudice of 'those unfamiliar with Greek literature' who think nothing proper except what their own traditions allow – a remarkably un-Roman plea for tolerance regardless of *mos maiorum*. The *Lives* are written, he says elsewhere, for the benefit of these *rudes Graecarum literarum*: they were a sort of crash course to help the ordinary reader in a literary world where ignorance of things Greek was no longer tolerable.[18]

Much more significant than this popularizing work as an indication of Nepos' conception of Greco-Roman culture is his major work of history, the *Chronica*. As the title implies, Nepos' work invited comparison with that of the Athenian Apollodorus, whose chronicle listed historical events in order from the Trojan War to his own time.[19] But Apollodorus wrote in Pergamum at the court of King Attalus, to whom the work was dedicated – only two generations before Nepos, but in a different world.[20] The work had to be done again, because it did not include Roman material.[21] Nepos remedied the omission, bringing the events of the Roman tradition into the mainstream of 'world history' as created by the Greeks. Thus Homer was synchronized with the reign of the Silvii in Alba (about 160 years before Rome was founded), Archilochus with that of Tullus Hostilius, the birth of Alexander with the consulship

17. Cf. Cic. *Arch*. 23, pointing out to the *iudices* that 'Graeca leguntur in omnibus fere gentibus, Latina suis finibus, exiguis sane, continentur'. For the limits of Roman mastery of Greek, see Jocelyn 1977, 353–8 and Horsfall 1977, 180.

18. Nepos *vitae* pref. 2–3, XVI 1.1. Note also fr. 17P on historiography: 'non ignorare debes unum hoc genus Latinarum litterarum adhuc non modo non respondere Graeciae sed omnino rude atque inchoatum morte Ciceronis relictum'.

19. *Chronica* (cf. Frier 1975, 92 on Greek titles of Roman works): Gell. *NA* XVII 4.4 (Apollodorus), 21.3 (Nepos); Apollodorus' work is also named at ps.Lucian *macrob*. 22, and frequently in Diogenes Laertius and Stephanus of Byzantium (*FGrH* 244 F1–42). See Jacoby 1902 *passim*, and 1926, 716–812; also Pfeiffer 1968, 253–66.

20. Ps.Scymnus *periegesis* 16–18, 46–9 (*FGrH* 244T2); Rawson 1976, 692–3 on the absence of Pergamene literary influence on second-century Roman historians.

21. Except in so far as the Romans affected the existing Hellenistic world picture: e.g. *FGrH* 244F22–5 (Gallic campaigns), 57 (Carneades' visit). It seems that Apollodorus deliberately omitted the foundation of Rome: Jacoby 1902, 26–8 (cf. Gabba 1976, 91).

of M. Fabius Ambustus and T. Quinctius Capitolinus, and so on.[22]

The subject matter of Apollodorus' chronicle is categorized for us by an admiring reader in much the same terms as Polybius' definition of serious history (*πραγματικὴ ἱστορία*) – battles, expeditions, the activities of nations and monarchs, etc.[23] But the similarity is entirely illusory: the fragments show that Apollodorus' conception of history was the amalgam of mythology, geography and history (in our sense) that had been orthodox ever since Hecataeus and Hellanicus, with the characteristically Hellenistic addition of data on philosophers and literary figures.[24] The mythological element is restricted by the fact that he started from the fall of Troy, no doubt owing to the difficulty of putting the earlier material in strict chronological order (much of it found its way into another major work, the commentary on Homer's *Catalogue of Ships*); Nepos, however, evidently found no difficulty in including even the reign of Saturn in his chronological framework.[25]

Nepos' more famous contemporary Varro, in his work *de gente populi Romani*, divided the past into three periods: the obscure (*ἄδηλον*), from the origins of man to the 'first flood', which cannot be reckoned in years; the mythical (*μυθικόν*), from the flood to the first Olympiad, so called because of the nature of the stories set in that period; and the historical (*ἱστορικόν*), the events of which are contained in 'true histories'.[26] The distinction between mythical and historical stories, which seems at first sight so close to our own, is really due more to Varro's philosophical scruples than to his standards as an historian.[27] The legendary stories to which he denied the status of true history were those involving the gods: Augustine's account in book XVIII of the *City of God* reveals Varro

22. Nepos fr. 2P (Gell. *NA* XVII 21.3), 4P (*ibid.* 21.8), 6P (Solinus 40.4). For this interpretation of Nepos, cf. Alfonsi 1942–3, esp. 333f, and Gigante 1967, 125–7; *contra*, Wardman 1976, 79.

23. Ps.Scymnus 26–31, cf. Pol. IX 1.4.

24. Disproportionately prominent in the surviving fragments because of Diogenes Laertius' systematic citation of the material on philosophers. But dramatists (F35, 48), epic and elegiac poets (F63, 74), historians (F49) and medical writers (F73) were also included.

25. Minucius Felix *Octavius* 21.4 (fr. 1P) – not actually naming the work.

26. Censorinus *de die nat.* 21.1 (Varro fr. 3P): 'primum ab hominum principio ad cataclysmum priorem, quod propter ignorantiam vocatur adelon; secundum a cataclysmo priore ad olympiadem primam, quod, quia multa in eo *fabulosa* referuntur, mythicon nominatur; tertium a prima olympiade ad nos, quod dicitur historicon, quia res in eo gestae *veris historiis* continentur'.

27. For Varro as 'philosopher and historian', cf. App. *BC* IV 47, Plut. *Rom.* 12.3, Cic. *Phil.* II 105 etc.

as a Euhemerist, rationalizing away the legends which offended a philosopher's view of the divine nature – for the gods of the philosopher, as he explains in the *res divinae*, are not the gods of the poet.[28] But even Varro's second period can be measured in time, if only uncertainly,[29] and there is no reason to suppose that he doubted the events on the human plane that were supposed to have taken place within it.[30] Here again, where modern standards of historical reliability appear to be applied in the ancient world, the evidence on closer inspection turns out to reveal a quite different set of criteria. Essentially, Varro's attitude is the same as that of the Hellenistic historians who refused to credit *adynata*, but accepted any traditional story that was not *a priori* impossible (pp. 49, 148 above). So too with Nepos, whose placing of the *Saturnia regna* in 'historical time' is no different from Varro's synchronism of the Trojan War with the reign of Latinus the son of Faunus.[31]

The geographical content is even more striking than the mythological. Apollodorus, whether or not he himself wrote a *Geography*,[32] was certainly looked on by geographical writers as one of themselves.[33] Even in the fragments securely attributed to the *Chronica*, we find the names of towns and settlements as far apart as Phoenicia and Spain which he found it appropriate to register.[34] Nepos almost certainly did the same, though the evidence has been obscured by Hermann Peter's gratuitous listing of his geographical fragments under the *Exempla*.[35] A man so familiar with the Greek historical tradition,[36] who followed his source even to the extent of

28. Aug. *CD* XVIII 2ff, esp. 10 (Varro fr. 7bP) 'haec Varro non credit, ne deorum naturae seu moribus credat incongrua', and 12–13, 16 (frr. 13, 14, 17P) on the distinction between poets' *fabulae* and *historica veritas*. *Res divinae*: Varro *ap*. Aug. *CD* VI 5; Funaioli 1907, 233–49, cf. Peter 1906, xxxv. On Euhemerism in the second century B.C., see Rawson 1976, 692–6; on the origins of rationalism, cf. Trenkner 1958, 4.

29. Censorinus *loc. cit.*: 'secundum non plane quidem scitur, sed tamen ad mille circiter et sescentos annos esse creditur'. Cf. Hdt. II 145.4 (p. 146 above).

30. E.g. fr. 10P (Aug. *CD* XVIII 10) on the reigns of Cecrops and Cranaus.

31. Varro fr. 17P (Aug. *CD* XVIII 16).

32. Strabo (XIV 5.22, C 677) accepted it as genuine; not so Jacoby (1926, 799ff).

33. Cf. n.20 above. The iambic metre, which Apollodorus used in order to make memorizing easier, was adopted by geographers in both Greek (ps.Scymnus, Dionysius) and Latin (Avienus *ora maritima*), a remarkable tribute to his influence; see Jacoby 1902, 60–74, esp. 70f. Nepos, however, evidently kept to prose.

34. F13 (Spain), 19 (Phoenicia).

35. Peter 1906, 30–2, frr. 6–16. In his introduction (p. liii), Peter recognizes the parallel with Apollodorus, and admits 'magnus profecto in chronicis patebat campus rerum varietati'.

36. Such familiarity is best illustrated by Cicero (cf. n.16 above) and Lucceius (p. 30 above). The history Cicero hoped Lucceius would write (Cic. *fam.* V 12. 4–5) was

using the same title for his own work, will surely have included geographical material where appropriate just as Apollodorus did – and the appropriate contexts included those foundation-stories and genealogical aetiologies which Polybius avoided but most Greek historians took for granted as their normal material.[37]

In the Rome of Nepos' day, the Greek scholar who exemplified the historiographical tradition most conspicuously, even to the extent of being called 'History' himself (though 'Polyhistor' is the nickname he was normally known by), did so in a sequence of works of which the fragments are very largely geographical.[38] Cornelius Alexander's books, primarily on the peoples of Asia Minor and the East with whom the Romans were coming into closer touch through the campaigns against Mithridates,[39] were evidently distinguished by real and objective sociological observation (if we may judge by his work on the Jews), but within the familiar context of mythological geography and aetiological genealogy.[40]

This is particularly clear in the wretchedly few – and uncertainly attributed – remnants of his five books *On Rome*, which provide legendary explanations for the river-names Tiber and Anio, genealogies for the Marruvii and the Roman patricians, and a Greek etymology for the Oromobii of Comum and Bergamum.[41] He is well described by Jacoby as a polymath in the Callimachean style: though Parthenius is not known to have used him (one wonders about professional jealousy between them), the very titles

---

full of precisely the kind of *θεατρικαί τινες περιπέτειαι* which had been part of the Greek historiographical tradition from the Ionian logographers (Dion. Hal. *Thuc.* 5) to Phylarchus and the 'tragic historians' whom Polybius attacked (Pol. II 56, cf. Plut. *Them.* 32.4).

37. See p. 150f above. Nepos fr. 14P (Pliny *NH* VI 5), on the origin of the Veneti, is a good example.

38. Suet. *gramm.* 20 (*FGrH* 273). Cf. Suidas s.v. *Alexandros Milesios* (prisoner of war, bought by a Cornelius Lentulus as *παιδαγωγός*, and freed), Serv. *Aen.* X 388 ('quem Lucius Sulla civitate donavit'); Jacoby 1943, 248f for the suggestion that he was manumitted by Sulla after the proscription of his master.

39. Jacoby 1943, 256. Momigliano (1975, 121) believes that 'he was encouraged by his Roman patrons to put together information about the new countries opened up to Roman conquest and influence'; cf. Murray 1972, 204–10 on an analogous third-century phenomenon, Hellenistic ethnographers 'who interpreted for the new rulers of the world the alien cultures which now belonged to them'.

40. Jacoby 1943, 252f; *FGrH* 273F19 on the Jews. He is cited by Pliny (*NH* I 3) on *situs*, *gentes* etc.

41. Ps.Plut. *Mor.* 315e–f (F20, Anio and *εὐγενέστατοι*), Serv. *Aen.* VIII 330 (F110, Tiber), X 388 (F111, Marruvii: 'haec fabula in Latinis nusquam invenitur auctoribus'), Pliny *NH* III 124 (F104, Oromobii – improving on Cato). *περὶ Ῥώμης*: Suidas (F70).

of his works betray his affinity with the sources of Parthenius listed at the end of the last chapter. It is entirely appropriate that his pupil and imitator Iulius Hyginus should have written a commentary on the *propempticon Pollionis* of Parthenius' patron, the poet Cinna – a work full of learned geographical mythology.[42]

Like his master, Hyginus wrote at length.[43] His *diligentia* in amassing material is praised by Columella (who observes, however, that his account of the origin of bees is too *fabulosum* to be of much help to the practical landowner),[44] and Servius describes his work *On the Cities of Italy* as 'very full' – full, that is, of the sort of mythological detail that would appeal to Polybius' πολυπράγμων καὶ περιττός type of reader (p. 151 above).[45] Nepos, on the other hand, was concise ('all history in three volumes'); but that reflects merely a different type of book, not a different attitude to historiography. The *Chronica* presumably gave names and dates without very much elaboration, exploiting the same sort of material as Hyginus and Alexander but in a systematically chronological context. In the reign of Tiberius, for instance, the citizens of Interamna Nahars in Umbria believed that their town was founded in what we should call 673 B.C.,[46] information that could have come either baldly from a work like the *Chronica* or in detailed narrative from a work like *de Italicis urbibus*. Certain similarities are demonstrable between Nepos and Hyginus,[47] and it is likely that both of them aspired to the kind of learning exemplified by Cornelius Alexander 'Polyhistor'.

—

Nepos was not merely a hellenized Roman. He was also a *Transpadanus*.[48] His surviving geographical fragments – unlike

42. Suet. *gramm.* 20 ('studiose et audiit et imitatus est'); Charisius I 134K for the *propempticon*, with a quotation (on Athens) which gives an idea of its nature; cf. Wiseman 1974a, 48. Titles (cf. p. 152f above): *Aigyptiaka, peri Bithynias* etc.

43. Cf. Suidas on Alexander: συνέγραψε βίβλους ἀριθμοῦ κρείττους.

44. Col. IX 2.1f. As he says in the same passage, 'Hyginus veterum auctorum placita secretis dispersa monumentis industrie collegit . . .'; cf. Jacoby 1943, 252f on Cornelius Alexander as a collector of details.

45. Serv. *Aen.* VII 678 ('de urbibus Italicis Hyginus plenissime scripsit et Cato in originibus'), cf. VIII 638 for an example.

46. *CIL* XI 4170 (A.D. 32): 'post Interamnam conditam DCCIIII' – two forty-year generations after the foundation of Rome, by Varro's reckoning? Cf. Harris 1977, 15f for other 'municipal eras' (none so early – not even Patavium, with its Trojan foundation-legend).

47. Both wrote *exempla* (Gell. *NA* VI 18.11, X 18.5, p. 38 above); both were in touch with contemporary poets (Nepos and Catullus, Hyginus' commentary on Cinna and *de poetis*) – cf. n.52 below.

48. *Padi accola* (Pliny *NH* III 127), 'Insubrian' (Pliny *ep.* IV 28.1 with Cic. *fam.* XV

Alexander's in this respect – seem to betray a special interest in northern Europe and the Celtic world, from Spain to the Scythian lands to the north of the Pontus and the Caspian.[49] It was from Q. Metellus Celer, proconsul of Gaul in 62 B.C., that he heard the story of the Indian merchants who had arrived in Germany after having supposedly been swept round the Northern Ocean by a storm (the German chief gave them to Metellus as a present); by misreporting a similar tale about the sailing of the Southern Ocean from Alexandria to Gades, he put himself clearly in the tradition of Homer and the earliest geographers, who believed that the world was surrounded by water.[50] He also believed that Histria was named after the river Ister, flowing from the Danube into the Adriatic, a notion that presumably derived from those (like Apollonius and Callimachus) who brought the Argonauts back from the Pontus that way.[51] It is no surprise to discover that Nepos defined *litterati* – among whom he presumably included himself – as 'interpreters of the *poets*'.[52]

Like other Transpadane authors, Nepos was careful to record that the Veneti were originally Eneti from Paphlagonia, who had migrated under Antenor after the fall of Troy.[53] Though the fragments do not happen to confirm it, it is very likely that he also exploited those two other rich sources of 'western' legend, the fall of Phaethon and Hercules' labour with the cattle of Geryon,[54] both

---

16.1) – so perhaps from Mediolanum (cf. Pliny *NH* III 124). Did Livy use Nepos for his excursus on the Gauls? It contains three synchronisms (V.33.5, 34.1 and 8, cf.Ogilvie 1965, 702) of just the kind the *Chronica* offered (e.g. fr.9P, Pliny *NH* III 125).

49. Spain: fr. 8P. Gaul: frr. 9–11P. Pontus and Caspian: frr. 12, 15P. The only others (frr. 13, 16P) refer to Carthage, which he discussed in the *de inlustribus viris* (Serv. *Aen*. I 368). Jacoby 1943, 250f on Alexander's lack of interest in the West and North. For the Hellenistic foundation-stories of the Cisalpine centres, and their irrelevance to the historical reality, see Mansuelli 1970–1, 25f.

50. Pomp. Mela III 5.44, 9.90, cf. Pliny *NH* II 169–70 (frr. 6–7P); for Eudoxus of Cyzicus, see Cary and Warmington 1963, 123–8 and 269f n.47. In his first passage (on the Indians), Mela says specifically: 'praeter physicos Homerumque universum orbem mari circumfusum esse disserit Cornelius Nepos'; cf. also Strabo I 2.8 (C 20), *καὶ οἱ πρῶτοι δὲ ἱστορικοὶ καὶ φυσικοὶ μυθογράφοι*.

51. Pliny *NH* III 127 (fr. 10P); cf. Strabo I 2.39 (C 46), citing Callimachus *Aetia* fr. 11 Pf on the foundation of Pola; also Lycophron 1022, Hyginus *fab*. 23.5, etc. The idea goes back at least to Theopompus (*FGrH* 115F129).

52. Suet. *gramm*. 4 (fr. 18P); cf. Columella IX 2.2 on Hyginus' *poetica licentia*.

53. Pliny *NH* VI 5 (fr. 14P), cf. Livy I 1.1–3, Virg. Aen. I 242–9.

54. On which see, in general, Diggle 1970, 3–32, 180–220, and Robertson 1969, 207–21. The two stories were possibly connected at an early stage in the tradition: Huxley 1969, 105 on the *Herakleia* of Pisandros of Rhodes, which mentioned Phaethon's mother Clymene.

of which provide important evidence for the continuing creative vitality of Greek aetiological pseudo-history in the Hellenistic period and down into Nepos' own time.

Among the 'many poets and historians' who, according to Diodorus,[55] told the story of Phaethon's fall into the Eridanus, with the metamorphosis of the weeping Heliades, his sisters, into poplars and of their golden tears into drops of amber, there were some who enriched the tale by attaching to it the previously independent legend of Cycnus. Cycnus was king of the Ligurians, 'the other side of Eridanus, beyond the Celtic land', and had from Apollo the gift of musical singing; when he died, he was changed by Apollo into a swan.[56] The swans of Eridanus were part of the Phaethon story, taking off in alarm when the chariot crashed and singing the sad tale, with the help of Zephyrus, from Cayster to the Danube.[57] The Alexandrian elegist Phanocles, in his account of the beautiful boys of legend, made Cycnus the lover of Phaethon, metamorphosed – like the Heliades – in compassion for his grief, and later versions kept the connection, even though they disapproved of the pederastic motivation (rather weakly making Cycnus a relative of Phaethon's mother) and added a further metamorphosis by catasterizing Cycnus into a constellation.[58] All these elements are alluded to by Virgil and Ovid in a way which shows that the story of Cycnus, obscure to us, was familiar in all its details to the hellenized Romans of the first century B.C.[59]

As for Hercules' journey with the cattle of Geryon, one of the aetiological stories attached to it was the origin of the Gauls, whose eponym Galates was supposedly fathered by the hero on the

55. Diod. Sic. V 23.2, cf. Pol. II 16.6 and 13ff, Plut. *Mor.* 557D on the aetiological justification for the story, which perhaps goes back to Aeschylus (Diggle 1970, 28). See Walbank 1957, 178f for a convenient summary account of the Eridanus, identified as the Padus by Pherecydes in the sixth century B.C. (Hyginus *fab.* 154.2). On the 'amber routes' from Jutland and the Baltic which gave rise to the story of the Heliades, see Cary and Warmington 1963, 52–4, 143–5, and Piggott 1965, 120, 137f.

56. Paus. I 30.3; Lucian's account (*Electrum* 4) perhaps implies that all his people were equally beloved of Apollo, and granted the same metamorphosis.

57. Philostratus *imag.* I 11.3, cf. Himerius *or.* (ed. Colonna) 47.4, 48.7 and 36; Virg. *Aen.* XI 457 on the supposedly musical swans of the Padus delta, a legend wittily mocked by Lucian (*Electrum* 4).

58. Phanocles fr. 6 Powell (ἔρωτες ἢ καλοί), Serv. *Aen.* X 189; Ovid *Met.* II 367f, Hyginus *fab.* 154.5; Claudian *de sext. cons. Honor.* 173, Nonnus *Dion.* XXXVIII 424–31.

59. Virg. *Aen.* X 188–93, Ovid *Met.* II 367–80. The story contains all the elements the *neoteroi* found most attractive: tragic love, aetiology and metamorphosis (cf. Wiseman 1974a, 54–6).

daughter of the Celtic king.[60] Timaeus and Callimachus – evidently followed by Timagenes of Alexandria – preferred the Sicilian version that Galates, with his brothers Celtus and Illyrius, were the sons of Polyphemus and Galatea.[61] Despite their authority, Parthenius returned to Hercules, but with a new story that offered greater aetiological possibilities in the age of Caesar's campaigns: Geryon's cattle were hidden by a girl called Celtine, daughter of Bretannus, and she would not return them to Hercules unless he slept with her; he did so, and she bore Celtus, 'after whom the Celts are named'.[62] As it turned out, the prestige of Caesar's own *Commentaries*, with their endorsement of the Britons' claim to autochthony,[63] prevented Parthenius' 'Bretannus' from being exploited, but the very fact of his invention shows that the traditional techniques of Greek *doctrina* were still alive and well in Nepos' time.

In his life of the elder Cato, Nepos passes an interesting judgment on the last two books of the *Origines*, which contained among other things an account of the wars in Spain:[64]

> In the same work he gave an account of noteworthy occurrences and sights in Italy and the Spains; and in it he showed great industry and carefulness, but no learning.

What Nepos felt the lack of in Cato's work was perhaps not so much the detailed material on Spanish geography and customs accumulated by Polybius, Artemidorus and Posidonius (the impressive results of which we now read in Diodorus and Strabo[65]) as the mythographical expertise of Asclepiades of Myrlea, who taught τὰ γραμματικά in southern Spain for a time and wrote a *periegesis* of the Spanish peoples in which the wanderings not only of Hercules but also of Teucer, Odysseus and Amphilochus were exploited – along with later Greek migrations – to provide a hellenocentric 'history' of the area.[66] Like *akribeia* (p. 151 above), *doctrina* should

60. Diod. Sic. V 24, not naming either the girl or her father; but since she was τῷ μεγέθει τοῦ σώματος ὑπερφυής, perhaps her father was the giant Celtus (Dion. Hal. XIV 1.3).
61. Timaeus *FGrH* 566T69, Call. fr. 378–9Pf, Timagenes *FGrH* 88F2; for Celtus and Illyrius see App. *Ill*. 2. Cf. Bickerman 1952, 68f on the historical context of the story.
62. Parth. *narr. am.* 30: no source quoted, so probably Parthenius' own invention, as perhaps Hercules' son Nemausus was too (Steph. Byz. *s.v.*).
63. Caes. *BG* V 12.1f, cf. Diod. Sic. V 21.2 and 5; Bickerman 1952, 75f.
64. Nep. *Cato* 3.4 (trans. J.C. Rolfe): 'multa industria et diligentia comparet, nulla doctrina'. Cf. Momigliano 1975, 65 on Cato and the Celtic peoples.
65. Diod. Sic. V 33–38, Strabo III *passim*; Momigliano 1975, 67ff.
66. Strabo III 4.3 (C 157), cf. 4.19 (C 166) on the inferiority of Roman historians to Greek in the 'filling in of gaps' left by previous accounts; the other side of that coin is

not be confused with what we – or Thucydides or Polybius – would regard as the proper virtues of the historian.

According to one version, Celtus and Iberus were brothers, sons of Hercules by a daughter of Atlas.[67] The Celtic and Spanish peoples were not sharply distinguished from each other, and the Pyrenees were not regarded as a natural frontier until well into the first century B.C., with the regularization of the Roman provincial boundaries.[68] It seems likely that Nepos' dissatisfaction with Cato's treatment of Spain is all of a piece with his interest in the 'legendary geography' of northern Europe,[69] and that his historical work was an attempt to systematize into the Greek world-picture not only Rome and her domestic legends but also the Transpadanes' trans-Alpine neighbours, and the whole of Rome's empire in the 'barbarian' west and north.

It is in this context, perhaps, that we should remember young Veranius, coming back from his tour of provincial duty under Piso in Spain.[70] Catullus looks forward to his disquisition on the *loca facta nationes* of the Iberi, and comments that that is his friend's habitual style (an argument, incidentally, in favour of the identification of Veranius with the Augustan antiquarian Veranius Flaccus, an expert on pontifical law who might well have been interested in more general historical erudition in his youth[71]). Catullus himself has quite a few pieces of recondite information about Spain and Spanish customs, including the notorious washing of teeth in urine, and other details evidently reported by Posidonius.[72] He also alludes to the metamorphosis of the Heliades,

---

Juvenal's 'quidquid Graecia mendax / audet in historia' (*Sat.* X 174f, cf. p. 48f above). For Asclepiades, cf. Pfeiffer 1968, 273; for the earlier mythological tradition on southern Spain, including the Gorgons and the battle of the Giants, see Schulten 1922, 31–6.

67. Dion. Hal. XIV 1.3, cf. Strabo III 2.13 (C 150) etc on the story of the Hesperides, set in Spain by 'poets after Homer'.

68. Not till Pompey in 71? See Ebel 1975, esp. 367–9; Strabo III 4.19 (C 166) on the boundaries. Note that Aeschylus had placed the Eridanus among the Iberians, and identified it with the Rhône (Pliny *NH* XXXVII 31).

69. N.49 above.

70. Cat. 9.6–8. Piso had a Greek in his train as well ('Socration', Cat. 47.1); not that that is any reason to believe in the oft-repeated notion that – despite what Catullus clearly implies – Piso was the proconsul of Macedonia (cf. Wiseman 1969a, 38–40: ignored by Della Corte 1976, 202f).

71. Cf. Syme 1957, 123 n.5; Aug. *ap.* Suet. *Aug.* 86.3; Funaioli 1907, 429-33 for his fragments (in Festus and Macrobius).

72. Cat. 37.20, 39.17–21; Diod. Sic. V 33.5, Strabo III 4.16 (C 164). *Cuniculosa Celtiberia*: Cat. 37.18, Strabo III 2.6 (C 144f); cf. also Cat. 29.19 (*aurifer Tagus*), 64.227 (*ferrugo Hibera*).

to an otherwise unattested detail in the story of Cycnus,[73] to the legendary origin of Verona[74] and of the Transpadane Etruscans,[75] and it may not be pure chance that he specifically endorses Nepos' Homeric view of Oceanus, 'mari totum qui amplectitur orbem'.[76] Catullus, unlike Cato, was not short of *doctrina*;[77] he and Nepos were equally at home in the literary world of Asclepiades and Parthenius.

73. Cat. 64.290f; 67.32, where Voss's *Cycneae* is normally read for the unintelligible *chinea* of the MSS (see Albertini 1973, 11–20 for exhaustive bibliography).
74. Cat. 67.34, where 'Brixia Veronae *mater* amata meae' may be meant literally: were Brixia and Verona eponymous heroines? Cf. Lanoios, Praenestus, Labicus – and Rhome.
75. Cat. 31.13 (*Lydiae undae*); cf. Justin XX 5.9 on the Etruscan Raetus, eponym of the Raeti above lake Garda, Livy V 33.7–11 on the Transpadane Etruscans in general, and Hdt I 94.2–7, Dion. Hal. I 27 etc on the Etruscans' supposed Lydian origin. The literary tradition on the extent of the Transpadane Etruscans' territory does not tally with the archaeological evidence (Albertini 1973, 21ff, esp. 23 and 35), no doubt because of the influence of 'Etruscanizing' historians, on whom see Musti 1970, *passim* (esp. 149–51); the opposing 'Sabinizing' tendency may conceivably account for the mysterious Sabini of *CIL* V 4893 (Albertini 1973, 50–57).
76. Cat. 64.30, evidently quoting a Greek line variously attributed to Euphorion and Neoptolemus of Paros (see Euphorion fr. 122 Powell); cf. n.50 above. *Mare Oceanum* and the Hyperboreans also appear at Cat. 115.6; the Sacae of 11.6, who were Scythians (Hdt VII 64.2, Choerilus *ap*. Strabo VII 3.9), may also be relevant to Nepos' interests.
77. *Doctus Catullus*: Lygd. [Tib.] III 6.41, Ovid *am*. III 9.62, Martial I 61.1 etc. One example of his Hellenistic erudition – conspicuous because uncharacteristically ill digested – is at 68.109–116, from a *Herakleia* (Euphorion is convincingly suggested by Mr. C. Tuplin in a forthcoming article). Normally Catullus' *eruditio* is *tacita*, as in Quintilian's definition of *urbanitas* (VI 3.17). The chronological indication Catullus adds to his source's material on the Pheneate *barathrum* ('tempore quo . . .', 68.113) may well have come from a work like Nepos' *Chronica*.

Chapter 11

THE DEDICATION POEM

Cui dono lepidum novum libellum
arida modo pumice expolitum?
Corneli, tibi: namque tu solebas
meas esse aliquid putare nugas,
iam tum, cum ausus es unus Italorum
omne aevum tribus explicare cartis,
doctis, Iuppiter, et laboriosis;
quare habe tibi quicquid hoc libelli.
Qualecumque quod ⟨*est*⟩, *patrona virgo,*
plus uno maneat perenne saeclo!

2 arido *V*   5 tamen . . . est *V*   8 tibi habe *V*   9 est *add. Bergk*   10 perire *0*

See the Bibliography for recent discussions: Copley (1951), Ferrero (1955), Pasoli (1959), Bolisani (1959–60), Zicàri (1965), Elder (1966), Gigante (1967), Cairns (1969), Levine (1969), Latta (1972), Németh (1972), Singleton (1972), Goold (1974), Piernavieja (1974), Carilli (1975), Clausen (1976), Buchheit (1977).

According to Servius, who was presumably thinking of this poem, Catullus made *pumex* feminine.[1] All the authoritative Catullan manuscripts have *arido* (masc.) in line 2, and that was the reading of grammarians from Caesius Bassus in the first century A.D. to Isidore in the seventh.[2] But *arida* is the more difficult reading: it is easier to believe that *arido* replaced it at an early stage in the transmission than that Servius' idea came from nowhere.[3] Ever since Ennius, Roman poets had sometimes used unorthodox genders for Latin nouns in order to draw attention to Greek models,[4]

1. Serv. *Aen.* XII 587: '*in pumice* autem iste masculino genere posuit, et hunc sequimur . . . licet Catullus dixerit feminino'.
2. *Gramm. Lat.* VI 148, 261, 401K; Isid. *Etym.* VI 12.3.
3. 'An unfocussed fiat of the wayward Servius', as Professor Goold puts it with characteristic *brio* (Goold 1974b, 253). But that is to sweep away the problem, not to answer it.
4. Gell. *NA* XIII 21.14 on Enn. *Ann.* 454V: '*aere fulva* dixit, non *fulvo*, non ob id solum, quod Homerus *ἠέρα βαθεῖαν* dicit . . .' (*Iliad* XX 446, XXI 6f). Nonius 311L: *lapides* feminine at Enn. *Ann.* 533V 'ad Homeri similitudinem' (*Iliad* XII 287, *Od.* XIX 494). Cf. also Virg. *Aen.* II 554/Hom. *Iliad* VII 104, XIV 787 (*finis*); Virg. *Ecl.* 5.38/Theocr. 1.133 (*narcissus*); Lucr. IV 926/Hom. *Od.* V 488 (*cinis*); Enn. *Ann.*

and we happen to be told explicitly – by Servius again, though in a different context – that Catullus too used this device.[5] Since the Greek for pumice is *κίσηρις* (fem.), it is reasonable to infer that *arida pumice* is an example of the technique.

Catullus' reason for using it here may be detected if we compare poem 4. In that poem, the yacht is made to tell its story rather like a garrulous old man reminiscing: the very first thing it says is expressed in a Greek construction (4.2, 'ait fuisse navium celerrimus'), and the name-forms *Cycladas*, *Propontida* and *Amastri* reinforce the idea that the talking boat talks with a Greek accent.[6] Why? Because, as the reader immediately discovers, it comes from Greek-speaking Pontus. Greek name-forms are similarly used in poem 36, where travel from the Greek world is implied in the prayer;[7] in poem 31, Catullus on his return from Bithynia bids the 'Lydian' waters *χαίρειν* in both senses of the word;[8] his imagined journey to the East is illustrated by three consecutive Graecisms in a single line;[9] and Arrius, en route to Syria in poem 84, is mocked for his pronunciation in a bilingual pun.[10] The Greek world is even more omnipresent in poems 63, 64 and 66,[11] where Greek name-forms are correspondingly frequent (*Cybeles*, *Minoidi*, *Tethyi* etc); the atmosphere in poems 64 and 68b is further hellenized by quotation from Greek poets[12] and by the use of Latin words in a way unintelligible except to Greek-speakers.[13] With these parallels

---

282, 315V (*pulvis/κόνις*?); Virg. *Ecl.* 6.63, Lucr. IV 51 (*cortex/βύβλος*?); see Klotz 1931, from whom these examples are taken.

5. Serv. *Aen.* V 610: 'notandum sane etiam de Iride arcum genere masculino dicere Vergilium; Catullus et alii genere feminino ponunt, *referentes ad originem*, sicut "haec cattus" et "haec gallus" legimus'. Catullus also has *finis* (64.217), and both he and Calvus have *cinis* (68.90, 101.4, cf. Non. 291L), in the feminine: see n.4 above.

6. The metrical licence at 4.9 and 4.18 may be in imitation of Greek models; and despite the scepticism of Fordyce, I think the adjectival use of the adverb at 4.10 ('iste post phaselus') is a Graecism too, with *iste* representing the Greek definite article.

7. 36.13f (*Ancona*, *Amathunta*): see Wiseman 1969a, 42–5. On the phenomenon in general, see Ross 1969, 101f.

8. 31.12 ('salve . . . atque gaude'): see Cairns 1974, 11f.

9. 11.3 (*ut*=*ὡς*, *longe resonans*=*πολύφλοισβος*, *Eous*=*ἠῷος*): see Lyne 1975, 30f.

10. 84.12: see Harrison 1915, 198 (*contra* Fordyce 1961, 377) on *Ionios/χιονέους*.

11. Cf. also poem 62, the Greek background of which is shown by lines 1 and 7: *duobus* at 62.65 may be an imitation of the Greek dative.

12. E.g. 64.30 (p. 166 n.76 above), 64.96 (Theocr. 15.100), 64.111 (Cic. *Att.* VIII 5.1); 68.109ff (p. 166 n.77 above).

13. E.g. 64.18 (*nutrix/τίτθη*), 64.89 (*flumina/ῥέεθρα*), 64.367 (*vincla/κρήδεμνα*); 68.112 (*audit/ἀκούει*), where the next word *falsiparens* translates *ψευδοπάτωρ* (Call. *Hymn* 6.98). Cf. also Ross 1969, 67f on postponed particles: eight times in 64, twice in 68b.

in mind, we can hardly doubt that *arida* at 1.2 is an unobtrusive announcement of Catullus' mastery of Greek, with the implication that his work is written for readers literate in both languages.

It is now generally and (I think) rightly accepted that poem 1 is in some way programmatic, and that lines 1–2 refer as much to the content of the book as to its external appearance:[14] *novitas* and *lepor* also apply to the character of Catullus' work,[15] 'polish' and the use of the pumice-stone were familiar metaphors for literary craftsmanship.[16] In this context the word *lepidus* may have had a particular significance for the Greek-speaking reader, if he associated it with the Callimachean catch-word λέπτος.[17]

The literal meaning of the two words is not the same, but it is clear that the connotations of *lepidus* were opposite to those of *amplus*, *gravis* and *crassus* – 'solid' or even 'fat', as opposed to the slender grace of λεπτότης – and therefore that the Greek word's significance overlapped substantially with that of the Latin.[18] Many more absurd etymologies of Latin words were accepted by the Romans of Catullus' generation, as we know from Varro; the 'parasitic vowel in Greek loan-words' was a familiar feature of Latin, deplored by the patrician playwright C. Caesar Vopiscus in the early first century B.C. and exploited by Catullus himself for metrical convenience, so the extra syllable of *lepidus* would cause no problem;[19] and the change from τ to *d* may not have appeared as a change at all to scholars familiar with the early Latin transliterations *Alexanter* and *Cassantra*.[20] If our earlier inference is sound,

14. Thus Copley (1951), Ferrero (1955), Elder (1966), Gigante (1967), Cairns (1969), Levine (1969), Latta (1972), Németh (1972), though crudely, Singleton (1972), Carilli (1975) and Buchheit (1977); only Zicàri (1965) follows Kroll and Fordyce in restricting the description (arbitrarily, I think) to the physical appearance of the *volumen*.

15. *Novitas*: cf. Virg. *Ecl.* 3.86 (p. 156 above), Prop. I 16.41 etc; see Nisbet and Hubbard 1970, 308. *Lepor*: Cat. 6.17, 16.7, cf. 50.7.

16. *Pumex*: Prop. III 1.8 (cf. below). *Polire*: *Culex* 10, Cic. *de or.* I 63, *Acad.* I 2, *Brut.* 76, etc.

17. See Latta 1972, 204 and 210–3. Callimachus: *Aetia* I 24 (of his own Muse), *Epigr.* 27.3Pf (of Aratus), etc.

18. *Rhet. Her.* IV 32 for the contrast with *gravitas* etc; Hor. *epist.* II 1.76f for 'crasse . . . illepideve' (cf. Call. fr. 398Pf παχὺ γράμμα, alluded to at Cat. 95.10).

19. Lindsay 1894, 70f; *Gramm. Lat.* VI 8K (Vopiscus insisting on *Tecmessa* as a tri-syllable), Cat. 63.60 (*guminasiis*). Other notable examples of epenthesis include μούσμων/*musimo* (Strabo V 2.7, Lucil. 256M) and γιγγλισμός/*gingiliphus* (Petr. *Sat.* 73.4).

20. Lindsay 1894, 73, 81. The phenomenon was known to Quintilian (I 4.16: extant examples at *CIL* I² 553, 557, 566), and Verrius Flaccus evidently derived 'Tusculum' from δύσκολον (Festus 486L).

the work of Philoxenus betrays a new conception in Catullus' generation of the relationship of Latin to Greek;[21] a reader up-to-date with cultural innovations, given the hint by *arida* in line 2 to think in Greek, would no doubt take *both* the adjectives in the opening line of Catullus' work as indications of his position in the literary world.

The poets of the following generation preferred *tenuis* as a translation of the Callimachean λέπτος, but their association of the idea with literary polish was identical to that of Catullus (e.g. Propertius' 'exactus tenui pumice versus eat'), and since files as well as pumice-stones were used for polishing, the *labor limae* made proverbial by Horace is precisely what Catullus had in mind.[22] *Expolire* is the verb Catullus uses, the prefix suggesting, like Horace's phrase, the labour required to achieve the result. So Callimachus and Asclepiades had used πόνος,[23] Philetas and Meleager μόχθος,[24] to describe books of poetry in prologue- or epilogue-poems designed for a particular volume in the same way as Catullus 1. Meleager's poem, for instance, was the 'signature' (σφραγίς) to his *Garland*, addressed to the Diocles to whom the opening poem had dedicated the anthology – in phraseology borrowed by Catullus in these very lines.[25]

Catullus' dedicatee was Nepos, who had seen some value in his work and perhaps expressed it in the *Chronica*.[26] I hope the last chapter has shown that his approval of Catullus is not surprising, and that the poet's praise of the *Chronica* at lines 5–7 (where 'omne *aevum*' clearly refers to Nepos' title) is not a forced compliment,[27]

21. See above, p. 155. One man known to have had an interest in etymology both Greek and Latin may have been Catullus' friend and fellow-poet Cornificius (Funaioli 1907, 474–9, with Rawson 1978, 192–4).
22. Prop. III 1.8, cf. Cairns 1969, 155 and Fantham 1972, 173 n.35; Cic. *Acad*. I 2 ('limantur a me politius'), Hor. *AP*. 291. For the related image from sculpture (Call. fr. 398Pf οὐ τορόν, Hor. *AP* 441 etc), see Ferrero 1963, 70 and 88, Ronconi 1967, 1161.
23. Call. *Epigr*. 6.1Pf (cf. *Aetia* I 17 τέχνῃ), Asclepiades *Anth. Pal*. VII 1.1; the verbal form also in Meleager *Anth. Pal*. IV 1.4. Cf. Ronconi 1967, 1156.
24. Philetas fr. 10 Powell (verbal form πολλὰ μογήσας), Meleager *Anth. Pal*. XII 257.3; cf. Cairns 1969, 154.
25. *Anth*. Pal. IV 1.1: *Μοῦσα φίλα, τίνι τάνδε φέρεις πάγκαρπον ἀοιδάν*; (and see n.23); cf. Carilli 1975, 927.
26. As suggested by Bergk 1857, 581; followed by Gigante (1967, 125) and Goold (1974b, 257). Like Apollodorus (p. 158 above), Nepos included dates significant in literary history: does Vell. Pat. II 36.2 derive from him? (I do not understand Németh's idea [1972, 27] that Nepos was ironic or 'scornful' about Catullus' work: cf. Granarolo 1973–4, 58, n.16.)
27. Copley 1951, 203–5.

nor a paradoxical oddity,[28] nor a parody of pompousness,[29] nor an attempt to share reflected glory,[30] nor in any way ironical.[31] History and poetry had never been mutually incompatible (except in the austere Thucydidean conception, of history as necessarily political and contemporary, which we sometimes mistakenly assume to be the norm); their traditional common ground was never more diligently tilled than in the Hellenistic literary world of which Rome was now a major part, and even in that world there was never a historian more likely than Nepos to treat his material in a manner sympathetic to a *doctus poeta*.[32]

It has often been noticed that the virtues Catullus attributes to Nepos' work are just those which the sensitive and literate reader has been invited to see in his own *libellus*: innovation, conciseness, erudition and *labor*.[33] Professor Gigante, whose treatment of the problem seems to me much the best, even goes so far as to say that 'in un certo senso, il poeta saluta in Cornelio uno storico neoterico'[34] – a judgment with which I quarrel only in so far as the term 'neoteric' is too loosely applied even to poets.[35] In the sense that Nepos and Catullus shared the same hellenized literary outlook, it is surely beyond dispute.

—

There are, I think, two further ways in which Catullus 1 is programmatic, at least to the extent of giving the reader an idea of what sort of poetry he is to expect in the *libellus*. First, the easy naturalness of the style: 'careful artistry is combined with an impression of

28. Latta 1972, 207.
29. Elder 1966, 144 and 146.
30. Buchheit 1977, 70f.
31. Goold 1974b, 261 and 263, Németh 1972, 27; cf. Quinn 1972, 19 ('a hint of irony').
32. Cf. p. 162 above. Cicero, on the other hand, had no time for *nugae* in poetry (*Parad*. 3.26), nor for the *lyrici* (*ap*. Sen. *ep*. 49.5): in this, as in his attitude to historiography (cf. Rawson 1972, esp. 42f), his standards differ significantly from Nepos'.
33. E.g. Ferrero 1955, 52 n.21; Gigante 1967, 125f; Ronconi 1967, 1158–61, Cairns 1969, 153f; Carilli 1975, 927; Buchheit 1977, 68–70. On conciseness as a virtue (implicit in *libellum* and in *omne aevum tribus . . . cartis*), see now the important discussion in Woodman 1975, 279f and 282–7, esp. 279 n.6 (on historiography and Alexandrian poetry) and 286 n.4 (on Nepos); also Ronconi 1967, 1157 on Cat. 95 and Antipater *Anth. Pal.* VII 713.
34. Gigante 1967, 125; cf. Alfonsi 1942–3, 331. Ferrero (1955, 53f) had already seen the significance of the dedication in putting Catullus' work 'nel quadro della cultura e delle correnti letterarie del tempo'. See also Cairns 1969, 154 on Nepos' 'neoteric historical work', an idea treated with irony by Goold (1974b, 254) and dismissed as absurd by Clausen (1976a, 37 n.1).
35. Cf. Wiseman 1974a, 51f.

live informal immediacy'.[36] The indicative *cui dono* sets the tone at the outset, [37] and the colloquial *esse aliquid* and *nugae*, the exclamation *Iuppiter!* and the characteristic idiom of *quicquid hoc libelli* all foreshadow the style of the 1–60 polymetric poems and show that Catullus is going to wear his learning lightly.[38] Second, the poem's symmetrical construction: the *tibi . . . tibi* and *namque . . . quare* mark off, I think, the six lines on the dedicatee from the first two and the last two on the *libellus* itself, in a manner entirely characteristic of Catullus' regular techniques.[39] Before we can be sure of that, however, we must face the textual problem of lines 8–9.

Most editors take *qualecumque* with *quicquid hoc libelli*, thus allowing both an awkward asyndeton and an unparalleled heavy stop after the fourth syllable. Munro objected to this in 1878, followed immediately by Palmer and Vahlen, and Elder, Clausen and Goold rightly punctuate after *libelli* and take *qualecumque* with *quod*.[40] Goold further objects to the reading '⟨o⟩ patrona virgo', since he holds that *o* is not used by Catullus with an adjective before the noun.[41]

So far so good: but Bergk – followed by Munro and Goold – also objected to *patrona virgo*. Why? Meleager addressed a singular Muse, and Rhianus explicitly said that to call on one was to call on all nine.[42] The Muses appear anonymously as *doctae virgines* at 65.2 and simply as *deae* at 68.41. The Muse as a patroness of poets was an idea commonplace in Rome since before Catullus was

36. Williams 1968, 41; cf. Piernavieja 1974, 412–4.
37. See Pasoli 1959, 435f on the 'vivace pennellata' of the phrase.
38. See especially Copley 1951, 202 and 206, Zicàri 1965, 232f and 239f. I think Elder (1966, 144) and Latta (1972, 206) exaggerate the solemnity of lines 5–7; what contrast there is with the rest of the poem is surely the result of Catullus' use of the 'prayer-style' (cf. Levine 1969, 213ff). For the idiom in 1.8, cf. 3.2, 6.4f, 6.15, 9.10, etc.

On poem 1 as introductory to the 1–60 collection, see Latta 1972, 219 and Clausen 1976a, 39; on the *doctrina* of the 1–60 poems, see Cairns 1974, 8–12.
39. On which see Wiseman 1974a, ch.3.
40. Munro 1878, 1f, comparing Tac. *Ann*. XIV 55 'quidquid illud *et* qualecumque tribuisset'; Palmer 1879, 298, Vahlen 1879, 3; Elder 1966, 143; Clausen 1976a, 37; Goold 1974b, 254 and 259f. The postponed connecting relative is no problem (cf. 68.131 for a much more drastic example); and though there is no precise parallel for its positioning inside a subordinate clause, the word-order is perfectly intelligible, and much less contorted than that of (e.g.) 44.9 or 66.18.
41. Goold 1974b, 254f, with 1969, 197–9 on 31.12 etc. The extra solemnity of the vocative with *o* is not in itself an objection (cf. 36.11): see Zicàri 1965, 236 and Latta 1972, 208.
42. See n.25 above; Rhianus *ap*. Schol. Ap. Rhod. III 1 (quoted by Kroll).

born.[43] There are no good arguments against the manuscript reading, and two damning ones against Bergk's proposal *patroni ut ergo*: first the phrase itself, postpositional *ergo* being conspicuously archaic and practically never separated from its noun;[44] and second the implication that Catullus had, or needed, a patron. The parallel with Martial, on which both Munro and Goold rely heavily, is fallacious: because Martial was Catullus' 'arch-imitator', it does not follow that their social positions were in any way comparable.[45] Palmer put it unanswerably a century ago:[46]

> Martial and Statius were flatterers, and lived under a despotism and in an age of flattery, but Catullus was the reverse of a flatterer, and lived in a free state amid an outspoken public. Cornelius Nepos was a man on his own level, and Catullus dedicated his 'lepidus novus libellus' to him, not as a patron, but as a friend.

All line 9 requires, then, is the insertion of a monosyllable. If *o* is unsatisfactory, *est* is surely not: parallel passages abound, perhaps influenced by this very poem,[47] and though the verb is indeed 'not obligatory',[48] the syntax is clearer with it in. Bergk should take the credit for inserting *est*, however wrong the rest of his version is;[49] but the true reading of line 9 is, I believe, due to G. W. Williams, who offered it to his Balliol undergraduates in 1958, and has kindly allowed one of them to make it public here.

The structure of the poem, then, is quite clearly 2+6+2.[50] (Two

43. Suet. *gramm.* 6 (Aurelius Opillius), cf. also ps.Sulpicia *PLM* V 94.11. The 'Romanness' of the concept is comparable with the legal phrase *habe tibi* in the previous line.

44. *TLL* V 2 (1953) 759: 'vox antiqua iam ante Plaut. exoleta; legitur in titulis, in formulis sacris (sic omnes loci Catonis) et apud priscae Latinitatis imitatores'. See Clausen 1976a, 38 n.2, who rightly says 'the evidence against Bergk is clear and damning'. The Munro/Goold version of Bergk's reading ('qualecumque quidem patroni ut ergo', without ⟨*est*⟩ or punctuation) has the further disadvantage of a drastically postponed *ut*: cf. Goold 1974b, 260.

45. Munro 1878, 4–5; Goold 1974b, 253 etc. Bolisani (1959–60, 5) assumes that Nepos was Catullus' teacher; cf. Della Corte 1976, 46 and 54 on Catullus as a 'disciple' of Hortensius!

46. Palmer 1879, 299.

47. E.g. Martial III 1.1 ('hoc tibi quidquid id est . . .'), Stat. *Silv.* II pref. *ad fin.* ('haec qualiacumque sunt . . .'), Censorinus *de die nat.* 1.5 ('quodcumque hoc libri est . . .').

48. Goold 1974b, 258, citing Virg. *Aen.* I 78 and Prop. III 21.16 (Munro offered Mart. VII 26.3); at Lucr. II 16, however (cf. Goold 1974b, 259), 'hoc aevi quodcumquest' provides a good parallel for *est* in Catullus' line 9.

49. 'Qualecumque quidem est, patroni ut ergo': Bergk 1857, 581.

50. *Pace* Zicàri 1965, 237 (2+5+3) and Elder 1966, 144f (4+3+3); Latta (1972,

details help to strengthen the case, if it needs it: the 'rhyme-scheme' of the verse-endings, detected by Bardon and Piernavieja, and the characteristic use of a two line relative clause to end a hendecasyllable poem.[51]) Having explained why Nepos is to have his book, Catullus returns in his last two lines to the subject of the first two, the book itself – and he returns in the same allusive manner he had used at the beginning, boldly putting himself in the Callimachean tradition by asking of his patron Muse what Callimachus had asked of the Graces.[52]

---

207 and 209) presupposes the structure argued here, but his acceptance of a semicolon after *qualecumque* makes it less clear; Pasoli (1959, 435) is inexplicit.

51. Bardon 1970, 30; Piernavieja 1974, 412, 416. Relative clauses: 7.11f, 13.13f, 15.18f.

52. Call. *Aetia* I fr. 7.14Pf; so Zicàri 1965, 239, Cairns 1969, 156, Carilli 1975, 927.

Chapter 12

THE COLLECTION

There is no escaping the question, what the work *was* that the dedication poem introduced. The Callimachean echoes must mean that the *libellus*, as the diminutive form implies, was not a big book[1] – particularly if Roman readers were to pick up the connotation of *lepidus* as λέπτος. As we have seen, the first poem is characteristic of the 1–60 collection, but its informality makes it hard to believe that it was ever meant to introduce the whole corpus as we have it, including the ambitious and highly-wrought poems 63, 64 and 68b. The simplest hypothesis is that the *libellus* dedicated to Nepos was a volume of about 850 lines containing what we call poems 1–60.

However, the very fact that Catullus draws such conspicuous parallels between Nepos' work and his own may help us to see a further subtlety. Kenneth Quinn has brilliantly suggested that *tribus cartis* in line 6 may be another parallel: 'size is in that case one of the things that Cornelius' History and Catullus' Collected Poems have in common – both three volumes'.[2] As he points out, the collection as it stands falls into three conveniently *volumen*-sized sections: 1–60 (848 lines), 61–4 (795 lines) and the elegiac poems 65–116 (646 lines).[3] Though proof is out of the question, there are, I think, good reasons for accepting this idea.

1. Athen. III 72A: *Καλλίμαχος ὁ γραμματικὸς τὸ μέγα βιβλίον ἴσον ἔλεγεν εἶναι τῷ μεγάλῳ κακῷ* (Call. fr. 465Pf), no doubt with the same ambiguity between physical size and 'slenderness' of content as in Cat. 1.1–2 (cf. 95.9–10). Cf. Granarolo 1973–4, 57 for the possibility (remote, I think) that Catullus did *not* follow Callimachus' line on this.
2. Quinn 1972, 19.
3. *Ibid.* 12, 16. In *Catullan Questions*, I assumed a break between 68 and 69 – wrongly, I now think; the present discussion therefore supersedes Wiseman 1969a, 29–31. The same assumption by Ross (1969, 1, 6 and *passim*) is more important, in that it involves his controversial separation, as stemming from separate traditions, of the 'neoteric distichs' (65–68) and the 'epigrams' proper (69–116). On this point I share the reservations of Quinn in his admirably balanced review (1971, 83f); but even accepting Ross's view for the sake of argument, we should still not have to abandon the idea of a *volumen* containing both types of elegiac poem, since Ross himself admits 'neoteric experiments' among the 69–116 epigrams: Ross 1969, 24, 48, 58, 63, 103, 105, 110f, 131, 137 (on poems 69, 78, 80, 86, 88, 95, 99, 100, 116).

One of the very few overtly programmatic statements in Catullus is 65.12, addressed to his brother: 'I shall always sing songs that are sad because of your death'. Since 65 is the first poem in the metre of *flebilis Elegeia*, it is natural to take this as an announcement of the metrical change in the collection.[4] Is it, in fact, the introductory poem to a *volumen* of elegiacs? That was clearly not its original function, since presumably it was written to go with poem 66, the Callimachus translation, as a present to Hortalus. But the Muses in lines 2–3 might well have suggested to Catullus a 'programmatic' use of the poem in his collection, possibly even with lines 9–14 written in to make it more explicit.[5]

What makes this idea attractive is the reference to *carmina Battiadae* both in poem 65 and in the final elegiac poem, 116.[6] As Macleod has recently shown, poem 116 contains many features appropriate to a dedication,[7] and the last poem in a *volumen* was regularly as programmatic as the first.[8] The content of poem 116, juxtaposing erudition and vituperation, shows Catullus 'as a Callimachean poet driven into vulgar invective by the anger and frustration Gellius has caused in him'[9] – which would be an appropriate way of closing a *libellus* that contained the Callimachus translation (66) and a poem as highly wrought as 68b, followed by the scurrilous invective of the epigrams.

Assuming three parts to the collection, we find the Muses clearly

4. Schaefer 1966, 46–8; Wiseman 1969a, 14f and 17f. *Flebilis Elegeia*: Ovid *am*. III 9.3, cf. *her*. 15.7, Hor. *Odes* I 33.3.

5. Naturally this can only be a guess, but I see no reason to rule out this sort of rewriting on *a priori* grounds: see the sensible remarks of Quinn 1973, 387.

The same hypothesis may explain the problem of poem 51: it *is* tempting to take it as the 'original' Lesbia-poem, and even to end it at *lumina nocte* in the form Lesbia first read it, but the idea of a loose Sapphic stanza beginning 'otium Catulle . . .' getting *accidentally* attached to it is surely too high a price to pay for the idea. Suppose, however, that Catullus wanted to use it for a different purpose in his collection, e.g. to mark a transition from *otium* to *negotia*, poem 50 to poem 52: the addition of the last stanza would achieve that, and turn the innocent Sappho translation into the bitter poem we now have. That too is a guess, and there are arguments that could be brought against it (cf. Kenney 1976, 29); but it would be arbitrary to dismiss the very possibility out of hand.

6. 65.16, 116.2 (cf. Schmidt 1973, 233, Forsyth 1977, 352f). For the Callimachean subtlety and erudition of 65, cf. Wiseman 1969a, 18–20 on the allusion in line 14; and it is possible that the closing simile is meant to remind the reader of Callimachus' *Acontius and Cydippe* (so Daly 1952, 98f).

7. Macleod 1973, 304–9, esp. 308. I am glad to retract my suggestion (Wiseman 1969a, 27) that 116 may be a later addition: Macleod (*ibid*. 307) has solved the difficulties which forced me to this view.

8. E.g. Meleager (cf. p. 170 above), and the end of Callimachus' *Aetia*.

9. Macleod 1973, 309, cf. 305f.

present at the beginning of the first (1.9) and of the third (65.2–3). But they are also there at the beginning of the second, in poem 61, where Hymenaeus' descent from Urania (another Callimachean reference) and his home on Helicon near the Muses' spring of Aganippe are emphasized at the beginning and end of the *ὕμνος κλητικός* with which the poem opens.[10] Here too, moreover, the opening and closing passages of the putative *libellus* (61–4) make a distinct artistic pattern. Hymenaeus is summoned from his legendary haunts in Boeotia to come to a Roman marriage – a conventional enough idea, but the presence of the god at the wedding of Manlius and Vibia[11] (who are named as the purpose of his journey at line 16) contrasts sharply with the epilogue of poem 64, on the refusal of the gods to appear on earth in modern times when *pietas* is held in contempt. If 61–4 do form a *volumen* on their own,[12] then the gods' relationship with men might be seen as one of its unifying themes.

On the other hand, the instinct to put all the 'long poems' (61–8) together as a coherent unit can apparently be justified by appeal to a more conspicuous unifying theme, that of marriage. 'The ideas set out in the *epithalamia* are developed through the ambiguous auguries of the Parcae in 64, the plea for fidelity in 66 and the unfaithful reality of 67, into the quasi-marital celebration in 68b of the poet's own love, adulterous and doomed'.[13] Certainly the ideas on marriage, fidelity and adultery planted by Catullus in the reader's mind by the earlier poems are made to bear a rich poetic harvest in 68b, where Catullus' application of them to his own

10. 61.2, 27–30; Fedeli 1972, ch.2. Compare Posidippus' summons of the Muses (*λιμπάνετε σκοπιάς, Ἑλικωνίδες*, etc): Lloyd-Jones 1963, 80 (text) and 83–6. Callimachus: *Aetia* I fr. 2a.42–3Pf (in the *addenda* of Pfeiffer's second volume), cf. lines 16 and 30 for 'Aonian Aganippe'.

11. For the name, cf. Syme *ap*. Neudling 1955, 185, rightly accepted by Della Corte (1976, 87f).

12. Here again, the fact that an elegant copy of 61 was no doubt sent to Manlius, like the possibility (for which there is no evidence) that 63 and 64 may once have been circulated as independent poems, does not affect the issue of how Catullus saw fit to include them in a 'collected poems' edition. The poems were individual works of art, but so was the collection they made together, and it was the poet's juxtaposition of them that made it so.

13. Wiseman 1969a, 20–5 (quotation from p.24); the development of the theme from 61 to 62 (where the girls are given a good case to plead *against* marriage), and within 64 from the first joy of Peleus' marriage to the gloomy foreboding at the end, is also to be noted. Sandy (1971, 185–95) and Forsyth (1970, 66–9) would include 63 in the theme as well; and I suspect 68a may be relevant, if the addressee is the bridegroom of poem 61 (Wiseman 1974a, 103). But Schmidt (1973, 236) sees a difference between the treatment of the theme in 61–64 and that in 65–68.

situation is most movingly developed.[14] But the theme does not end with 68b: the very first Lesbia-poem in the epigrams sequence is on the possibility of her *marrying* Catullus (70.1), and the ideas of *fides* and *foedus* which are so important in the 69–116 poems have already been used as part of the marriage theme in poem 64.[15] So the existence of the marriage theme does not necessarily prove that poems 61–8, as opposed to poems 61–4, form a unit complete in itself.

What it *does* prove, I think, is that the collection as we have it was designed as a whole; that Quinn's three *libelli*, each introduced by the Muses and with a Callimachean allusion,[16] were the component parts of a greater unity. The closing poem of the first part, combining the themes of 1–60 as the very last poem combines those of 65–116,[17] also looks ahead to the treatment of them in mythological dress in the long poems – as the reader will realize in retrospect when he reaches Ariadne's speech in poem 64.[18] The number of such cross-references between the long poems and the 1–60 and 69–116 sequences is striking.[19] Some are no doubt haphazard, but it would be absurd to insist that they all must be; the natural inference is that Catullus was inviting his readers to compare his treatment of mythological themes with that of his personal experience (or what passes for it in the short poems), which in turn implies that the reader is expected to have all three parts of the work to hand.

I conclude, then, that the apparent contradiction involved in Quinn's hypothesis, that poem 1 introduces a single *volumen* but refers to three, is not really a contradiction at all. What Nepos held in his hand was a 'λέπτος libellus' of short poems in various metres, our 1–60 sequence; but at the same time he was given allusively to

14. Cf. Wiseman 1974a, 72f and 114–7.

15. 64.132f, 144, 174, 182 (*perfidus*, *fidelis*, *fides*), cf. 76.3, 87.3 (also 91.1, 102.1); 64.335, 373 (*foedus*), cf. 87.3, 109.6.

16. 1.1 and 10 (pp. 169, 174 above); 61.1f and 27–30 (n.10 above); 65.16 (n.6 above); cf. Gigante 1954, 72 on Catullus as 'l'autentico Callimaco romano'. The Callimacheanism of Catullus and his contemporaries is well discussed by Lyne (1978, 180–4).

17. Cf. Wiseman 1969a, 16 on poem 60: love, bitterness and erudition (note the Graecism in line 1, the first known use of λέαινα as a Latin word).

18. 64.154–6. As Ross points out (1969, 29f), poems 60 and 64 are also linked by their allusion to Ennius' *Medea* (64.1–8).

19. E.g. 61.199–201/7.2–8; 64.1f and 7/4.3f; 64.29f/88.5f; 64.96/36.12–14; 64.100/81.4; 64.132–5 (cf. 56–9)/30.1–5; 64.139–42/70.1–4; 64.142/30.10; 64.191/76.18; 64.218/101.5; 68.46/78b.4; 68.92/101.6; 68.148/107.6; 68.158/77.4; 68.159/58.3. Cf. Wiseman 1977, 177f.

understand that Catullus' work, like his own, was in three books. What we can never know is whether Nepos' 'presentation copy' was just the 1–60 *libellus* or a *capsula* containing all three.[20] But I think we may be sure that the 'collected works' which Catullus' *scribae* wrote out for him, and which he wanted the Roman reading public to find in the shelves of the booksellers,[21] were in three rolls, to be read in order. Four generations later, when the *codex* technique enabled the contents of more than roll to be contained in one book, the *liber Catulli Veronensis* could be made in the form we have it now.[22]

—

It would be pleasant to be able to leave it at that. But so deeply rooted are the beliefs that (a) Catullus did not live to arrange his own poems for publication, and (b) the collection as we have it is the work of a posthumous editor, that some account must be taken of them. Let us look briefly at each of these ideas in turn.

(a) We do not know when Catullus died. All his dateable poems belong to 56–54 B.C.; Jerome gives his age at death as 30, which may well be a correct transcription from Suetonius, though the dates given (87–57) are impossible. It is often assumed that he lived from 84 to 54 – partly on a very weak argument from the names of the consuls of 87 and 84 B.C.,[23] mainly (I suspect) because that is the smallest alteration possible to account for the dateable poems. But to argue from that to the idea that the poems of 54 B.C. were written very soon before his death is simply circular.

> Now it is possible that, despite his youth, he knew he was going to die and therefore made an almost complete collection of his poems. But is it not more likely that he left behind a few published *libelli* and some odd poems which a compiler subsequently put together in the unique *liber* we have?[24]

20. Cf. Crinagoras *Anth. Pal.* IX 239: five rolls of Anacreon in one box.
21. Cat. 14.17f, *librariorum scrinia.*
22. So Quinn 1972, 13. For the transfer of boxed *volumina* to *codex* form, cf. Haslam 1976 (on the MSS of Demosthenes).
23. Munro 1878, 73. The names are: Cn. Octavius Cn.f.Cn.n., L. Cornelius L.f.L.n. Cinna (87); Cn. Papirius Cn.f.C.n. Carbo II, Cornelius L.f.L.n. Cinna IIII (84). The order of names (Degrassi 1947, 482 for the evidence) militates against the easy confusion of the two dates because of Cinna's consulships; besides, Jerome's other blunders, on the dates of Lucilius, Messalla Corvinus and Livy, admit of no such simple explanation, and were no doubt due only to the fact that, as he admits ('tumultuarium opus', in his preface), Jerome wrote in a hurry.
24. Wilkinson 1974, 85; the same argument in Goold 1974a, 8f. Both accept 54 as

This apparently attractive argument is also based on a fallacy, the confusion of 'collected poems' and 'complete poems'. There is not the slightest reason to assume that Catullus had to know that he was going to die before he could think of putting his poems together in a collection.[25] It would not, after all, prevent him from writing further poetry afterwards – for instance the Theocritean *φαρμακεύτρια* mentioned by Pliny or the Priapean poems quoted by the grammarians.[26]

Since we are dealing only with probabilities, let me offer (purely *exempli gratia*) an alternative order of events. Some time in 54, after the Lesbia affair had more or less blown itself out, Catullus heard the news of his brother's death and retired to his home at Verona.[27] He had already written a substantial collection of poems long and short, and at this milestone in his life he thought of collecting them into a corpus with a certain thematic unity. The brother's death was to be a *Leitmotiv* in the elegiac collection; what little writing he did, in response to requests from friends, was composed with this in mind (65, 68a), and a poem written (101) or rewritten (68.91–100)[28] was enough to create the new theme. He then returned to Rome, published his collection, wrote more poetry which is lost to us, and died there at some unspecified time before 32 B.C.[29] I repeat – one cannot be too careful – that this is not offered as what *must* have happened, but as what *may* have happened. It is consistent with the data that we have.

(b) As for the 'posthumous editor' so dear to Catullan scholars,[30] his shadowy existence derives merely from the 'multiplication of hypotheses beyond necessity', and should therefore be cut short with Ockham's Razor. Other things being equal, a collection of poems by Catullus, especially one beginning with a dedication-

---

the date of death: 'it is generally thought. . .' (Wilkinson), 'the consensus of opinion . . .' (Goold).

25. Though poem 38 is no longer cited as an intimation of mortality, poem 52 seems to have taken its place (Della Corte 1976, 245).

26. Pliny *NH* XXVIII 19; Nonius 200L, *Gramm. Lat.* VI 151, 260, 406K.

27. Cf. Wiseman 1969a, 37: the themes of the brother's death and the trip to Bithynia are kept so conspicuously separate in the collection that there is *no* reason to date the former event to 57 B.C.; and the comparative scarcity of references to it surely suggests that it took place quite soon before the collection was made.

28. Cf. Wiseman 1974a, 73–6.

29. The place is given by Jerome, the *terminus ante quem* by Nepos (*Att.* 12.4, cf. 19.1); Ovid (*am.* III 9.61) implies that he died young.

30. Della Corte (1951, 15–20 and 1976, 43f) even believes that the posthumous editor was Nepos himself: cf. Fronto *ad M. Caes.* I 7.4.

poem, ought to be Catullus' work:[31] the onus of proof is on those who declare it to be impossible. It is hard to find any statement *why* it should be impossible, beyond appeals to the placing of poem 51 after poem 11;[32] but that may not be inexplicable if we bear in mind the difference between the purpose of a poem as first written and the use made of it as a unit in the collection.[33]

It is sometimes said in more general terms that the order of poems is simply 'chaotic'[34] – a subjective judgment certainly worth no more in itself than the opinion of those, from Wilamowitz downwards, who have been conscious of deliberate and artistic arrangement.[35] More often scholars try to have it both ways, the odd 'purposed sequences' they can detect being attributed to hypothetical earlier Catullan collections, or to the hand of a posthumous editor to whom 'an occasional artfulness of arrangement may be owing' – even though, *ex hypothesi*, he was incapable of producing a collection that was an artistic whole.[36] The orthodox view is that the edition was put together in the second or third century A.D.;[37] but it has been rightly said of this idea that it is

> a strangely late date for a collected edition of so important a poet. Had Virgil read the epyllion only in a 'monobiblos', or did Martial know Catullus only from a collection of polymetric pieces?[38]

31. Rightly emphasized by Schmidt (1973, 238–42).
32. E.g. Tyrrell 1895, 91. Most recently in Wilkinson 1974, 84, Goold 1974a, 9; Clausen 1976a, 40; Kenney 1976, 29. For Lyne, it is axiomatic that 'our collection could not possibly have been produced by Catullus himself' (1978, 185 n.64, following Wheeler 1934, 22ff. and 39f).
33. See Quinn 1972, 56–60 (esp. 59), and n.5 above. Schmidt (1973, 226) supposes a 'chiastic' positioning of the first Lesbia-poem in the last quarter of the 1–60 sequence, and the last in the first.
34. E.g. Schmidt 1914, 278. *Contra* Weinreich 1959, 90: 'Chaos? Kosmos!'.
35. Wilamowitz 1913, 292, without argument; Quinn 1972, 9–20, cf. Williams 1968, 469f. Attempts at detailed explanation by Heck (1950), Weinreich (1960, 163–70), Tränkle (1967, 100–3), Wiseman (1969a, 1–31), Schmidt (1973), Offermann (1977). The fact that these analyses differ between themselves does not, of course, mean that none of them can be right: the point is that patterns *can* be detected, and therefore the anonymous editor is not the only possible explanation (Granarolo 1973–4, 59–62).
36. Quotation from Clausen (1976a, 40): that so good a scholar can hold this view is a tribute to the tenacity of the *communis opinio*, but not (alas) to its truth. Others admit much more blatant self-contradictions: cf. Wiseman 1976, 271, on the views of B. Coppel. 'Purposed sequences': Wheeler 1934, 26–9, following Ellis 1878, xlvi–1.
37. Wheeler 1934, 32; accepted by (e.g.) Wilkinson 1974, 84.
38. Ross 1969, 8 n.8.

So far as I know, that objection has never been answered.

There is, in short, no reason to conjure Anonymus Postumus up from limbo, and every reason to believe that what presents itself as Catullus' book is in fact Catullus' work. For why should we expect his design to be immediately apparent to us? Just because he was capable of writing individual poems of such direct simplicity that they still speak to us face to face after two millennia, it does not follow that he was always simple, much less that his tastes and attitudes necessarily coincide with ours.

Catullus and his friends wrote for a small and intelligent audience, and we must work hard to reconstruct the intellectual climate they inhabited and the standards of sensibility they took for granted. Otherwise we have no chance of properly understanding either the arrangement of his collected works or the full meaning of the poem in which he introduced them to his friend and fellow-Transpadane Cornelius Nepos. No doubt Nepos understood both perfectly well, for though he was a historian and Catullus a poet, in the literary world of Hellenistic Rome that distinction did not mean as much as it does to us. One was a great artist, the other not, but their intellectual heritage was the same.

BIBLIOGRAPHY

NOTE: Places of publication are given only for works published outside the United Kingdom.

ALBERTINI, A., *Brixiana: note di storia ed epigrafia* (Brescia, 1973) (Supplemento ai Commentari del' Ateneo di Brescia).

ALFÖLDI, A., *Early Rome and the Latins* (Ann Arbor, n.d. [1965]) (Jerome Lectures, seventh series).

ALFONSI, L., 'Sulla Cronaca di Cornelio Nepote', *Rendiconti dell' Istituto Lombardo*, LXXVI (1942–3), 331–40.

ANDERSON, W. D., *Ethos and Education in Greek Music* (Cambridge, Mass., 1966).

ASTIN, A. E., *Scipio Aemilianus* (1967).

BADIAN, E., review of Taylor, *Voting Districts*, *J. of Roman Studies*, LII (1962), 200–10.

—'The early historians', in T. A. Dorey (ed.), *Latin Historians* (Studies in Latin Literature and its Influence, 1966), 1–38.

—'The testament of Ptolemy Alexander', *Rheinisches Museum*, CX (1967), 178–91.

—*Publicans and Sinners: Private Enterprise in the Service of the Roman Republic* (Dunedin, 1972).

BALSDON, J. P. V. D., 'Some questions about historical writing in the second century B.C.', *Classical Q.*, III (1953), 158–64.

— 'Dionysius on Romulus: a political pamphlet?', *J. of Roman Studies*, LXI (1971), 18–27.

BARDON, H., *Propositions sur Catulle* (Bruxelles, 1970) (Collection Latomus, vol. 118).

BARIGAZZI, A.,'Il Dionysos di Euforione', in *Miscellanea di studi alessandrini in memoria di A. Rostagni* (Torino, 1963), 416–54.

BAUMAN, R. A., 'Criminal prosecutions by the aediles', *Latomus*, XXXIII (1974), 245–64.

BERGK, Th., 'Philologische Thesen', *Philologus*, XII (1857), 578–81.

BERNSTEIN, A. H., *Tiberius Sempronius Gracchus: Tradition and Apostasy* (New York, 1978).

BICKERMAN, E. J., 'Origines gentium', *Classical Philology*, XLVII (1952), 65–81.

BLINCKENBERG, C., *Lindos, Fouilles de l'acropole ii: Inscriptions* (Copenhagen, 1941).

BOLISANI, E., 'Catullo e Cornelio Nepote', *Atti Istituto Veneto*, CXVIII (1959–60), 1–9.

Bömer, F., 'Kybele in Rom: die Geschichte ihres Kults als politisches Phänomen', *Römische Mitteilungen des Deutschen Archäologischen Instituts*, LXXI (1964), 130–51.

Bonner, S. F., *Roman Declamation* (1949).

—*Education in Ancient Rome* (1977).

Borza, E. N., 'Cleitarchus and Diodorus' account of Alexander', *Procs of the African Classical Ass*, XI (1968), 25–45.

Boscherini, S., 'Una fonte annalistica su Valerio Publicola', in *Atti del convegno: gli storiografi latini tramandati in frammenti* (Studi Urbinati di storia, filosofia e letteratura XLIX: Urbino, 1975), 141–50.

Brink, C. O., *Horace on Poetry ii: the Ars Poetica* (1971).

Bruce, I. A. F., *An Historical Commentary on the 'Hellenica Oxyrhynchia'*, (1967) (Cambridge Classical Studies).

Buchheit, V., 'Würdigung des Dichterfreundes und Dichterpatrons bei Catull und Vergil', *Philologus*, CXXI (1977), 66–82.

Cairns, F., 'Catullus I', *Mnemosyne*, XXII (1969), 153–8.

—'*Venusta Sirmio*: Catullus 31', in T. Woodman and D. West (eds.), *Quality and Pleasure in Latin Poetry* (1974), 1–17.

Carilli, M., 'Le *nugae* di Catullo e l'epigramma greco', Annali della Scuola normale di Pisa, V (1975), 925–53.

Cary, M. and Warmington, E. H., *The Ancient Explorers* (2nd edn, Penguin Books, 1963).

Casson, L., *Travel in the Ancient World* (1974).

Clarke, M. L., *Rhetoric at Rome* (1953).

Clausen, W., 'Callimachus and Latin Poetry', *Greek, Roman and Byzantine Studies*, V (1964), 181–96.

—'Catulli Veronensis liber', *Classical Philology*, LXXI (1976), 37–43. [Cited as 1976a]

—'*Cynthius*', *American J. of Philology*, XCVII (1976), 245–7. [Cited as 1976b]

Cloud, J. D., 'Livy's source for the trial of Horatius', *Liverpool Classical Monthly*, II (1977), 205–13. [Cited as 1977a]

—'The date of Valerius Antias', *ibid*., 225–7. [Cited as 1977b]

Coarelli, F., 'Il tempio di Bellona', *Bullettino della Commissione Archeologica Comunale in Roma*, LXXX (1965–7), 37–72.

—*Guida archeologica di Roma* (Firenze, 1974).

Coffey, M., *Roman Satire* (1976).

Collingwood, R. G., *The Idea of History* (1946).

Copley, F. O., 'Catullus, c.I', *Trans. of the American Philological Ass.*, LXXXII (1951), 200–6.

Cornell, T. J., 'Notes on the sources for Campanian history in the fifth century B.C.', *Museum Helveticum*, XXXI (1974), 193–208.

—'Aeneas and the twins: the development of the Roman foundation legend', *Procs. of the Cambridge Philological Soc.*, XXI (1975), 1–32.

Cozza, L., 'Pianta marmorea severiana: nuove ricomposizioni di frammenti', in *Studi di topografia romana* (Quaderni dell' istituto di topografia antica vol. V: Roma, 1968), 9–22.

CRAWFORD, M. H., 'Foedus and sponsio', *Papers of the British School at Rome*, XLI (1973), 1–7.

—*Roman Republican Coinage* (1974).

—'The early Roman economy, 753–280 B.C.', in *Mélanges offerts à Jacques Heurgon: l'Italie préromaine et la Rome républicaine* (Collection de l'école française de Rome vol. 27: Rome, 1976), 197–207.

DALY, L. W., 'Callimachus and Catullus', *Classical Philology*, XLVII (1952), 97–9.

D'ANNA, G., 'Didone e Anna in Varrone e in Virgilio', *Rendiconti dell'Accademia dei Lincei*, XXX (1975), 3–34.

DEGRASSI, A., 'Fasti et elogia', *Inscriptiones Italiae* XIII.1 (Roma, 1947), XXIII.2 (Roma, 1967), XIII.3 (Roma, 1937).

DELLA CORTE, F., *Due studi catulliani* (Genova, 1951).

—*Personaggi catulliani* (2nd edn, Firenze, 1976).

DEVEREUX, G., 'The Self-blinding of Oidipous in Sophokles *Oidipous Tyrannos*', *J. of Hellenic Studies*, XCIII (1973), 36–49.

DIGGLE, J., *Euripides Phaethon* (1970) (Cambridge Classical Texts and Commentaries vol.12).

DORRIE, H., *Der Königskult des Antiochos von Kommagene im Lichte neuer Inschriften-Funde* (Göttingen, 1964) (Abh. d. Akad. d. Wiss. Göttingen, Philol.-hist. Klasse, 3rd series, vol. 60).

DRUMMOND, A., 'Some observations on the order of consuls' names', *Athenaeum* LVI (1978), 80–108.

DUNKLE, J. R., 'The Greek tyrant and Roman political invective of the late Republic', *Trans. of the American Philological Ass.*, XCVIII (1967), 151–71.

EARL, D., 'Prologue-form in ancient historiography', in H. Temporini (ed.), *Aufstieg und Niedergang der römischen Welt*, vol. i.2 (Berlin, 1972), 842–56.

EBEL, C., 'Pompey's organization of Transalpina', *Phoenix*, XXIX (1975), 358–73.

ELDER, J. P., 'Catullus 1, his poetic creed, and Nepos', *Harvard Studies in Classical Philology*, LXXI (1966), 143–9.

ELLIS, R., *Catulli Veronensis Liber* (1878).

FANTHAM, E., *Comparative Studies in Republican Latin Imagery* (Toronto, 1972) (Phoenix Supplementary vol. 10).

FEDELI, P., *Il carme 61 di Catullo* (Freiburg, 1972) ('Seges' vol. 16).

FERRERO, L., *Un' introduzione a Catullo* (Torino, 1955) (Univ. di Torino pubblicazioni della facoltà di lettere e filosofia, vol. vii.2).

—'Tra poetica ed istorica: Duride di Samo', in *Miscellanea di studi alessandrini in memoria di A. Rostagni* (Torino, 1963), 68–100.

FINLEY, M. I., *Aspects of Antiquity: Discoveries and Controversies* (1968).

—*The Use and Abuse of History* (1975).

FORDYCE, C. J., *Catullus: a Commentary* (1961).

FORSYTH, P. Y., 'The marriage theme in Catullus 63', *Classical J.*, LXVI (1970), 66–9.

—'Comments on Catullus 116', *Classical Q.*, XXVII (1977), 352–3.
FRACCARO, P., 'I processi degli Scipioni', *Studi storici per l'antichità classica*, IV (1911), 217–414. [Cited as 1911a]
—'Ricerche storiche e letterarie sulla censura del 184/183 (M.Porcio Catone L.Valerio Flacco)', *Studi storici per lantichità classica*, IV (1911), 1–137. [Cited as 1911b]
—'Ancora sui processi degli Scipioni', *Athenaeum*, XXVII (1939), 3–26.
—*Opuscula* vol. i (Scritti di carattere generale: studi Catoniani: i processi degli Scipioni) (Pavia, 1956).
FRASER, P. M., *Ptolemaic Alexandria* (1972).
FRIER, B. W., 'Licinius Macer and the *consules suffecti* of 444 B.C.', *Trans. of the American Philological Ass.*, CV (1975), 79–97.
FUNAIOLI, H., *Grammaticae Romanae Fragmenta* (Stuttgart, 1907) (Bibliotheca Teubneriana).
GABBA, E., 'Il Latino come dialetto greco', in *Miscellanea di studi alessandrini in memoria di A. Rostagni* (Torino, 1963), 188–94.
—'Considerazioni sulla tradizione letteraria sulle origini della Repubblica', in *Les origines de la république romaine* (Fondation Hardt Entretiens XIII: Geneva, 1967), 133–74.
—'Motivazioni economiche nell'opposizione alla legge agraria di Tib. Sempronio Gracco', in J. A. S. Evans (ed.), *Polis and Imperium: Studies in Honour of Edward Togo Salmon* (Toronto, 1974), 129–38. [Cited as 1974a]
—'Storiografia greca e imperialismo romano', *Rivista storica italiana*, LXXXVI (1974), 625–42. [Cited as 1974b]
—'Sulla valorizzazione politica della leggenda delle origini troiane di Roma fra III e IIVI secolo a.C.', in M. Sordi (ed.), *I canali della propaganda nel mondo antico* (Contributi dell' Istituto di storia antica vol. iv: Milano, 1976), 84–101.
GAY, P., *Style in History* (1975).
GELZER, M., 'Römische Politik bei Fabius Pictor', *Hermes*, LXVIII (1933), 129–66.
—'Der Anfang römischer Geschichtschreibung', *Hermes*, LXIX (1934), 46–55.
—'Die Glaubwürdigkeit der bei Livius überlieferten Senatsbeschlüsse über römische Truppenaufgebote', *Hermes*, LXX (1935), 269–300.
—review of Klotz, *Livius und seine Vorgänger*, *Gnomon*, XVIII (1942), 220–30.
—*Kleine Schriften*, vol. iii (Wiesbaden, 1964).
GENTILI, B., 'Storiografia greca e storiografia romana arcaica', in *Atti del convegno: gli storiografi latini tramandati in frammenti* (Studi Urbineti di storia, filosofia e letteratura XLIX: Urbino, 1975), 13–38.
GIANGRANDE, G., ' "Arte allusiva" and Alexandrian epic poetry', *Classical Q.*, XVII (1967), 85–97.
—'Hellenistic poetry and Homer', *L'Antiquité Classique*, XXXIX (1970), 46–77. [Cited as 1970a]
—'Der stilistische Gebrauch der Dorismen in Epos', *Hermes*, XCVIII (1970), 257–77. [Cited as 1970b]

—'Aspects of Apollonius Rhodius' language', in F. Cairns (ed.), *Papers of the Liverpool Latin Seminar* 1976 ('Arca' ii: Liverpool, 1977), 271–91.

GIGANTE, M., 'Catullo, Cicerone e Antimaco', *Rivista di filologia classica*, XXXII (1954), 67–74.

—'Catullo, Cornelio e Cicerone', *Giornale italiano di filologia*, XX (1967), 123–9.

GJERSTAD, E., 'Porsenna and Rome', in *Opuscula Romana* VII (Acta Instituti Romani Regni Sueciae vol. XXX: Lund, 1969), 149–61.

GOMME, A. W., *The Greek Attitude to Poetry and History*, (Berkeley, Cal., 1954) (Sather Classical Lectures vol. 27).

GOOLD, G. P., 'Catullus 3.16', *Phoenix*, XXIII (1969), 186–203.

—*Interpreting Catullus* (Inaugural Lecture) (1974). [Cited as 1974a]

—'O Patrona Virgo', in J. A. S. Evans (ed.), *Polis and Imperium: Studies in Honour of Edward Togo Salmon* (Toronto, 1974), 253–64. [Cited as 1974b]

GRANAROLO, J., 'Catulle 1948–1973', *Lustrum*, XVII (1973–4), 27–70.

GRIFFIN, J., 'Augustan Poetry and the life of luxury', *J. of Roman Studies*, LXVI (1976), 87–105.

GRONINGEN, B. A. VAN, *La poésie verbale grecque: essai de mise au point* (Amsterdam, 1953) (Mededelingen der Koninklijke Nederlandse Akademie van Wetenschappen, new series 16.4).

GRUBE G. M. A., *The Greek and Roman Critics* (1965).

HANNING, R. W., *The Vision of History in Early Britain: from Gildas to Geoffrey of Monmouth* (New York and London, 1966).

HARRIS, W. V., 'The Era of Patavium', *Zeitschrift für Papyrologie und Epigraphik*, XXVII (1977), 283–93.

HARRISON, E., 'Catullus, LXXXIV', *Classical Review*, XXIX (1915), 198–9.

HASLAM, M. W., 'A problem in the history of the transmission of texts exemplified in Demosthenes', *Liverpool Classical Monthly*, I (1976), 9–10.

HECK, B., *Die Anordnung der Gedichte des C. Valerius Catullus* (dissertation) (Tübingen, 1950).

HENDERSON, I., 'Ancient Greek music', in E. Wellesz (ed.), *Ancient and Oriental Music* (New Oxford History of Music vol. i: Oxford, 1957), 336–403.

HEURGON, J., 'Cincius et le loi du *clavis annalis*', *Athenaeum*, XLII (1964), 432–7.

—*The Rise of Rome to 264 B.C.* (trans. J. Willis), (1973).

HILLARD, T. W., 'The Claudii Pulchri 76–48 B.C.: Studies in their political cohesion' (Ph.D. thesis, Macquarie University, N.S.W., 1976).

HOMEYER, H., *Die antiken Berichte über den Tod Ciceros und ihre Quellen* (Baden-Baden, 1964) (Deutsche Beiträge zur Altertumswissenschaft, vol. 18).

HORSFALL, N., 'Corythus: the return of Aeneas in Virgil and his sources', *J. of Roman Studies*, LXIII (1973), 68–79.
—review of Wardman, *Rome's Debt to Greece*, *J. of Roman Studies*, LXVII (1977), 179–80.
HOW, W. W. and WELLS, J., *A Commentary on Herodotus* (1912).
HUXLEY, G. L., *Greek Epic Poetry from Eumelus to Panyassis* (1969).
JACOBY, F., *Apollodors Chronik* (Berlin, 1902) (Philologischen Untersuchungen, vol. 16).
—*Die Fragmente der Griechischen Historiker*, vol. iiC, (Berlin, 1926); vol. iiiA2 (Leiden, 1943).
—'Some remarks on Ion of Chios', *Classical Q.*, XLI (1947), 1–17.
JOCELYN, H., 'Urbs augurio augusto condita', *Procs. of the Cambridge Philological Soc.*, XVII (1971), 44–74.
—'Greek poetry in Cicero's prose writing', *Yale Classical Studies*, XXIII (1973), 61–111.
—'The ruling class of the Roman Republic and Greek philosophers', *Bulletin of the John Rylands Library*, LIX (1977), 323–66.
JORDAN, H., 'Die Einleitung des Ciceronischen Brutus', *Hermes*, VI (1872), 196–213.
KENNEY, E. J., review of Quinn, *Catullus, an Interpretation*, *Classical Review*, XXVI (1976), 28–30.
KLINGNER, F., *Römische Geisteswelt* (5th edn, München, 1965).
KLOTZ. A., 'Zu Catull', *Rheinisches Museum*, LXXX (1931), 342–56.
KROLL, W., *Catull* (Stuttgart, 1929) (Griechische und Lateinische Schriftstellerausgaben mit Anmerkungen).
LATTA, B., 'Zu Catulls Carmen 1', *Museum Helveticum*, XXIX (1972), 201–13.
LEUZE, O., 'Metellus caecatus', *Philologus*, LXIV (1905), 95–115.
LEVICK, B., *Tiberius the Politician* (1976) (Aspects of Greek and Roman Life).
LEVINE P., 'Catullus c.1: a prayerful dedication', *California Studies in Classical Antiquity*, II (1969), 209–15.
LINDSAY, W. M., *The Latin Language* (1894).
LLOYD-JONES, H., 'The seal of Posidippus', *J. of Hellenic Studies*, LXXXIII (1963), 75–99.
LUCE, T. J., *Livy: The Composition of his History* (Princeton, 1977).
LYNE, R. O. A. M., *Selections from Catullus: Handbook* (1975) (Cambridge Latin Texts).
—'The Neoteric poets', *Classical Q.*, XXVIII (1978), 167–87.
MACLEOD, C. W., 'Catullus 116', *Classical Q.*, XXIII (1973), 304–9.
—'Reason and necessity: Thucydides iii 9–14, 37–48', *J. of Hellenic Studies*, XCVIII (1978), 64–78.
MANSUELLI, G. A., 'La romanizzazione dell' Italia settentrionale', *Atti del Centro Studi e Documentazione sull' Italia romana*, III (1970–1), 23–32.

MARSHALL, A. J., 'Library resources and creative writing at Rome', *Phoenix*, XXX (1976), 252–64.

MOMIGLIANO, A., *Quarto contributo alla storia degli studi classici e del mondo antico* (Roma, 1969).

—*Alien Wisdom: the Limits of Hellenization* (1975).

—'The historians of the classical world and their audiences: Some suggestions', *Annali della Scuola normale di Pisa*, VIII (1978), 59–75.

MOMMSEN, TH., *Römische Forschungen*, vol. i, (Berlin, 1864).

—'Die Erzählung von Cn. Marcius Coriolanus', *Hermes*, VI (1870), 1–26.

—'Sp. Cassius, M. Manlius, Sp. Maelius, die drei Demagogen der älteren republikanischen Zeit', *Hermes*, V (1871), 228–71.

—*Römische Forschungen*, vol. ii (Berlin, 1879).

MORELLI, G., 'Sempronio Asellione e Cesellio Vindice in Carisio', in *Atti del convegno: gli storiografi latini tramandati in frammenti* (Studi Urbinati di storia, filosofia e letteratura, XLIX: Urbino, 1975), 81–94.

MUNRO, H. A. J., *Criticisms and Elucidations of Catullus* (1878).

MÜNZER, F., *De gente Valeria* (dissertatio inauguralis historica) (Oppoliae, 1891).

—and others, 'Claudius', *Paully-Wissowa Realencyclopädie fur Altertumswissenschaft*, III (1899), 2662–900.

—'P. Cornelius Scipio Nasica', *ibid.*, IV (1901), 1494–7.

—*Römische Adelsparteien und Adelsfamilien* (Stuttgart, 1920).

—'Valerius Messalla', *Paully-Wissowa*, VIIIA (1955), 125–6.

MURRAY, O., 'Philodemus on the Good King according to Homer', *J. of Roman Studies*, LV (1965), 161–82.

—'Herodotus and Hellenistic culture', *Classical Q.*, XXII (1972), 200–13.

MUSTI, D., *Tendenze nella storiografia romana e greca su Roma arcaica: studi su Livio e Dionigi d'Alicarnasso* (Roma, 1970) (Quaderni Urbinati di cultura classica vol. 10).

NASH, E., *Pictorial Dictionary of Ancient Rome* (2nd edn, 1968).

NÉMETH, B., 'How does Catullus' booklet begin?', *Acta Classica* (Debrecen), VIII (1972), 23–30.

NEUDLING, C. L., *A Prosopography to Catullus* (1955) (Iowa Studies in Classical Philology).

NISBET, R. G. M., 'Notes on Horace, *Epistles* I', *Classical Q.*, IX (1959), 73–6.

— and HUBBARD, M., *A Commentary on Horace Odes Book I* (1970).

NITSCH, K. W., *Die roemische Annalistik von ihren ersten Anfängen bis auf Valerius Antias* (Berlin, 1873).

OFFERMANN, H., 'Zu Catulls Gedichtcorpus', *Rheinisches Museum*, CXX (1977), 269–302.

OGILVIE, R. M., *A Commentary on Livy Books 1–5* (1965).

—*Early Rome and the Etruscans* (1976).

OTIS B., *Virgil: a Study in Civilised Poetry* (1963).

PAIS, E., *Ancient Legends of Roman History* (1906).

PALMER, A., 'Ellis's Catullus', *Hermathena*, III (1879), 293–363.

PALMER, R. E. A., 'The censors of 312 B.C. and the state religion', *Historia*, XIV (1965), 293–324.

—'The neighbourhood of Sullan Bellona at the Colline Gate', *Mél. école fr. Rome*, LXXXVII (1975), 653–65.

PASOLI, E., 'Catullo e la dedica a Cornelio Nepote', *Vita Veronese*, XI–XII (1959), 433–6.

PEARSON, L., *Early Ionian Historians* (1939).

—*The Local Historians of Attica* (Philadelphia, 1942) (American Philological Association Monographs, vol. 11).

—The pseudo-history of Messenia and its authors', *Historia*, XI (1962), 397–426.

—'Myth and archaeologia in Italy and Sicily – Timaeus and his predecessors', *Yale Classical Studies*, XXIV (1975), 171–95.

PETER, H., *Historicorum Romanorum Reliquiae*, vol. i (2nd edn, Stuttgart, 1914); vol. ii (Stuttgart, 1906).

PFEIFFER, R., *A History of Classical Scholarship: from the Beginnings to the End of the Hellenistic Age*, (1968).

PIERNAVIEJA, P., 'En torno al carmen I de Catulo', *Estudios clásicos*, LXXIII (1974), 411–17.

PIGGOTT, S., 'The sources of Geoffrey of Monmouth: I, the "pre-Roman" king-list', *Antiquity*, XV (1941), 269–86.

—*Ancient Europe* (1965).

PINSENT, J., 'Cincius, Fabius and the Otacilii', *Phoenix*, XVIII (1964), 18–29.

—review of Sordi, *Roma e i Sanniti*, *J. of Roman Studies*, LXI (1971), 271–2.

—*Military Tribunes and Plebeian Consuls: the Fasti from 444V to 342V* (Wiesbaden, 1975) (Historia, Einzelschrift 24).

—'Livy 6.3.1 (caput rei Romanae): some Ennian echoes in Livy', *Liverpool Classical Monthly*, II (1977), 13–18.

POUCET, J., 'Fabius Pictor et Denys d'Halicarnasse: "Les enfances de Romulus et de Rémus" ', *Historia*, XXV (1976), 201–16.

QUINN, K., review of Ross, *Style and Tradition in Catullus*, *Phoenix*, XXV (1971), 82–5.

—*Catullus, an Interpretation* (1972).

—'Trends in Catullan criticism', in H. Temporini (ed.), *Aufsteig und Niedergang der römischen Welt*, vol. i.3 (Berlin, 1973), 369–89.

RAWSON, E., 'Prodigy lists and the use of the Annales Maximi', *Classical Q.*, XXI (1972), 158–69.

—'Cicero the historian and Cicero the antiquarian', *J. of Roman Studies*, LXII (1972), 33–45.

—'The Eastern clientelae of Clodius and the Claudii', *Historia*, XXII (1973), 219–39.

—'The first Latin annalists', *Latomus*, XXXV (1976), 689–717.

—'More on the clientelae of the patrician Claudii', *Historia*, XXVI (1977), 350–7.

—'The identity problems of Q. Cornificius', *Classical Q.*, XXVIII (1978), 188–201.

RHODES, P. J., 'Athenaion Politeia 23–8', *Liverpool Classical Monthly*, I (1976), 147–54.

ROBERTSON, M., 'Geryoneis: Stesichorus and the vase painters', *Classical Q.*, XIX (1969), 207–21.

RONCONI, A., 'Note sulla poetica e critica letteraria in Catullo', *Studi Urbinati di storia, filosofia e letteratura*, XLI (1967), 1155–66.

ROSS, D. O.,jr., *Style and Tradition in Catullus* (Cambridge, Mass., 1969) (Loeb Classical Monographs).

SÄFLUND, G., *Le mura di Roma repubblicana: saggio di archeologia* (Lund, 1932) (Acta Instituti Romani Regni Sueciae vol. i).

SANDY, G., 'Catullus 63 and the theme of marriage', *American J. of Philology*, XCII (1971), 185–95.

SCHAEFER, E., *Das Verhältnis von Erlebnis und Kunstgestalt bei Catull* (Wiesbaden, 1966) (Hermes, Einzelschrift 18).

SCHMIDT, B., 'Die Lebenszeit Catulls und die Herausgabe seiner Gedichte', *Rheinisches Museum*, LXIX (1914), 207–83.

SCHMIDT, E., *Kultübertragungen* (Giessen, 1909) (Religionsgeschichtliche Versuche und Vorarbeiten viii.2).

SCHMIDT, E. A., 'Catulls Anordnung seiner Gedichte', *Philologus*, CXVII (1973), 215–42.

SCHULTEN, A., *Tartessos: Beitrag zur ältesten Geschichte des Westens* (Hamburg, 1922).

SHACKLETON BAILEY, D. R., 'Sex. Clodius – Sex. Cloelius', *Classical Q.*, LIV (1960), 41–2.

—*Cicero Epistulae ad Familiares* (1977) (Cambridge Classical Texts and Commentaries vols. 16 and 17).

SHATZMAN, I., 'The Egyptian question in Roman politics (59–54 B.C.)', *Latomus*, XXX (1971), 363–9.

SHERWIN-WHITE, A. N., 'Roman involvement in Anatolia, 167–88 B.C.', *J. of Roman Studies*, LXVII (1977), 62–75.

SINGLETON, D., 'A note on Catullus' first poem', *Classical Philology*, LXVII (1972), 192–6.

STADEN, H. VON, 'Experiment and experience in Hellenistic medicine', *Bull. of the Inst. of Classical Studies*, XXII (1975), 178–99.

STEWART, A. F., 'To entertain an emperor: Sperlonga, Laokoon and Tiberius at the dinner-table', *J. of Roman Studies*, LXVII (1977), 76–90.

STRASBURGER, H., *Homer und die Geschichtsschreibung* (Heidelberg, 1972) (Sitzungsberichte der Heidelberger Akad. der Wiss., phil.-hist. Klasse).

SUMNER, G. V., *The Orators in Cicero's Brutus: Prosopography and Chronology* (Toronto, 1973) (Phoenix Supplementary vol. 11).

—'A note on Julius Caesar's great-grandfather', *Classical Philology*, LXXI (1976), 341–4.

SYME, R., review of Gordon, *Potitus Valerius Messalla*, *J. of Roman Studies*, XLV (1955), 155–60.
—'The origin of the Veranii', *Classical Q.*, VII (1957), 123–5.
—*Sallust* (Berkeley, Cal., 1964) (Sather Classical Lectures vol. 33).
TAYLOR, L. R., 'New indications of Augustan editing in the Capitoline Fasti', *Classical Philology*, XLVI (1951), 73–80.
—*The Voting Districts of the Roman Republic* (Rome, 1960) (Papers and Monographs of the American Academy in Rome vol. 20).
THORPE, L., *Geoffrey of Monmouth: the History of the Kings of Britain* (Penguin Classics, 1966).
TRÄNKLE, H., 'Neoterische Kleinigkeiten', *Museum Helveticum*, XXIV (1967), 87–103.
TRAUB, H. W., 'Pliny's treatment of history in epistolary form', *Trans. of the American Philological Ass.*, LXXXVI (1955), 213–32.
TREGGIARI, S., *Roman Freedmen during the Late Republic* (1969).
TRENKNER, S., *The Greek Novella in the Classical Period* (1958).
TYRRELL, R. Y., *Latin Poetry* (1895).
VAHLEN, J. (ed.), M. Haupt, *Catulli Tibulli Properti carmina* (4th edn, Leipzig, 1879).
VON DER MÜHLL, P., 'Weitere pindarische Notizen', *Museum Helveticum*, XX (1963) 101–2; 197–204.
WALBANK, F., *A Historical Commentary on Polybius*, vol. i (1957).
—'History and tragedy', *Historia*, IX (1960), 216–34.
—'Political morality and the friends of Scipio', *J. of Roman Studies*, LV (1965), 1–16. [Cited as 1965a]
—*Speeches in Greek Historians* (n.d. [1965]) (3rd J. L. Myres Memorial Lecture). [Cited as 1965b]
—*A Historical Commentary on Polybius*, vol. ii (1967).
—*Polybius* (Berkeley, Cal., 1972) (Sather Classical Lectures vol. 42).
—'Polybius and the Sicilian straits', *Kokalos*, XX (1974), 5–17.
WALKER, B., *The Annals of Tacitus: a Study in the Writing of History* (1952).
WALSH, P. G., *Livy: his Historical Aims and Methods* (1961).
WARDE FOWLER, W., *Roman Essays and Interpretations* (1920).
WARDMAN, A. E., 'Myth in Greek historiography' *Historia*, IX (1960), 403–13.
—*Plutarch's Lives* (1974).
—*Rome's Debt to Greece* (1976).
WATSON, A., *Law Making in the Later Roman Republic* (1974).
WEINREICH, O., 'Catull, c.60', *Hermes*, LXXXVII (1959), 75–90.
—*Catull, Liebesgedichte* (Hamburg, 1960).
WEINSTOCK, S., *Divus Julius* (1971).
WERNER, R., 'Stellungnahme', *Gymnasium*, LXXV (1968), 509–19.
WHEELER, A. L., *Catullus and the Traditions of Ancient Poetry* (Berkeley, Cal., 1934) (Sather Classical Lectures vol. 9).
WILAMOWITZ-MOELLENDORFF, U. von, *Sappho und Simonides* (Berlin, 1913).

WILKINSON, L. P., 'Ancient and modern: Catullus li again', *Greece and Rome*, XXI (1974), 82–5.

WILLIAMS, G. W., *Tradition and Originality in Roman Poetry* (1968).

WINTERBOTTOM, M., *The Elder Seneca*, vol. i (Cambridge, Mass., and London, 1974) (Loeb Classical Library vol. 463).

WISEMAN, T. P., 'The ambitions of Quintus Cicero', *J. of Roman Studies*, LVI (1966), 108–15.

—*Catullan Questions* (1969). [Cited as 1969a]

—'The census in the first century B.C.', *J. of Roman Studies*, LIX (1969), 59–75. [Cited as 1969b]

—'Pulcher Claudius', *Harvard Studies in Classical Philology*, LXXIV (1970), 207–21. [Cited as 1970a]

—'Roman Republican road-building', *Papers of the British School at Rome*, XXXVIII (1970), 122–52. [Cited as 1970b]

—*Cinna the Poet and other Roman Essays* (1974). [Cited as 1974a]

—'Legendary genealogies in late-Republican Rome', *Greece and Rome*, XXI (1974), 153–64. [Cited as 1974b]

—'The Circus Flaminius', *Papers of the British School at Rome*, XLII (1974), 3–26. [Cited as 1974c]

—review of Coppel, *Das Alliusgedicht*, *Classical Review*, XXVI (1976), 270–1.

—'Catullus's Iacchus and Ariadne', *Liverpool Classical Monthly*, II (1977), 177–80.

—'Cicero, *de divinatione* i.55', *Classical Q.*, XXXIX (1979), 142–4. [Cited as 1979a]

—'Topography and rhetoric: the trial of Manlius', *Historia*, XXVIII (1979), 32–50. [Cited as 1979b]

WOODMAN, A. J., 'Questions of date, genre and style in Velleius: some literary answers', *Classical Q.*, XXV (1975), 272–306.

ZICÀRI, M., 'Sul primo carme di Catullo', *Maia*, XVII (1965), 232–40.

ZIMMERMANN, F., 'Parthenios' Brief an Gallus', *Hermes*, LXIX (1934), 179–89.

ZUCCHELLI, B., 'Un antiquario romano contro la "nobilitas": M. Giunio Congo Graccano', in *Atti del convegno: gli storiografi latini tramandati in frammenti* (Studi Urbinati di storia, filosofia e letteratura xlix: Urbino, 1975), 109–26.

INDEX